SONG OF ALBION

Rise of the West:

The Second Part

By:

Frank L. DeSilva

SONG OF ALBION

Rise of the West:

Second Volume

Being

The Second

Volume of the Culture,

History, Aspirations, and

Destiny of the People of the West,

To whom I dedicate this Work in the

Hope that through it, in some small Way,

Might provide the necessary impetus in which

They may, in turn, utilize for the Hope and future

Survival

Of our great and future People.

Dedicated to the Future of White Children

Acknowledgments

I wish to acknowledge a few individuals who inspired me in this endeavor:

To Randall Paul Evans (who has endured as much as anyone), Richard Girnt Butler, Robert E. Miles, David Lane, Revilo P. Oliver, William Pierce, Thomas Metzger, and all those unnamed individuals with whom I have had contact in both peace and war...especially you three; you know who you are.

To Sherryl, who lived a more Christlike life than most I have ever met, and gave pride to the name of Matriarch: and to Robert who, as a Father and Husband, stands taller than most; I will miss our conversations, Sis...sleep well.

And finally, to all those decent, sincere common-folk, who have shared conversations, coffee, their world-views, their hopes and dreams, their fears and silence, their love of family, god, and of their own children, who make all the sacrifices worthwhile.

And lastly, to that man against time...

To Bob

"Ten hearts, one beat…

One hundred hearts, one beat…

Ten thousand hearts, one beat"

Author's Foreword

The American Gulag, built to house those who, for one reason or another, subverted the law and intent of the existing order. Every Nation requires a place to house those who would subvert the law of the land, both in the present and, most importantly, in the future.

In the Summer of Nineteen Ninety, I was imprisoned at the Federal Penitentiary, Butner, North Carolina, my third in succession to this point. This housing was in direct consequence to the prison riot of Nineteen Eighty-nine, at the Federal Penitentiary in Arizona[1], due to prison staff's dereliction of duty in denying medical attention to one, John Chaffey, suffering from a brain aneurism, which was the cause of death.

---

[1] I wanted to add a small mention as to this particular place:

From the first 'drop-off' spot, after being delivered by plane to Lompoc, Ca., I was soon thereafter sent to Phoenix, Az., or simply *'phoenix'* to its many denizens, where I was to spend approximately four and a half years; the Warden there was one *Peter Carlson* who, I was to learn, kept a very 'clean ship', was an extremely fair man, intelligent, compassionate to both wives and children of his charges and, for me at least, represented an exemplary study in how 'civil servants' should be gauged.

The 'prison riot' which was simply a general 'reaction' to a tragic event, could not have been stopped, short of giving immediate aid to the individual who needed it, but a warden is subject to many intrigues, personal agendas by staff and the like, and was simply a party to an event which *transcended* any one individual. It is my understanding that Mr. Carlson was slotted to become the Bureau of Prisons Director within a few years but, sadly, was replaced by a Clintonian affirmative action placement, Janet Reno, which did nothing for 'morale' throughout the system, nor did it provide a better environment for 'staff' nation-wide.

Moreover, I suspect that Peter Carlson might well be embarrassed by his mention in this present work, however, it would be remiss of me to not mention a *worthy* and *professional* human character who, as one mucked through the dungeons of this nation, stood tall as a beacon of reason and professional discipline, as well as a moral compass (for many), that might have benefited his entire profession if allowed to achieve a higher status, based on *merit*, not on political cronyism. FLS

My stay at the american gulag, Butner, was done not so much to overtly punish me, but to 'keep me quiet' regarding the death of Mr. Chaffey. I was asked to sign a paper which, among other things, absolved prison staff of wrong doing; I refused to sign, and was willing to aid the Chaffey family in whatever venue they found themselves.

Butner, a true american gulag, housed John Hinckley, the attempted assassin of President Ronald Regan, the only sitting president I ever voted for. Butner, a prison where narcotics, of the psychotropic variety, were used liberally on prisoners/patients for any number of reasons; although, to my knowledge, none were ever used on my person.

It was a trying time, and the move from Arizona was stressful, not only because I was in an unfamiliar environment, but because it had placed me so far from my family. Nevertheless, that is how the modern american gulag system likes to operate; stress, and institutional perversity, does much in the way of destabilizing ones spirit. It can *conquer* you, or *you* can conquer it, there is no half way point.

Life, itself, is like this.

I was sentenced to Forty Years in the Federal gulag system for Harboring a Fugitive, and 'transportation of stolen money', under the RICO act, a system of 'law' designed to thwart the Italian Crime syndicates, a direct threat to Robert and John Kennedy who, like the Mafia, demanded control of their respective armies. One would use bullets, and the other words, to dismantle or defeat their opponents. Men, real men, fight their opponents based on conflict of interests, on territory, or faith; both sides know there are rules, parameters, and levels by which he is to conquer. RICO, as a tool, knows no boundaries or parameters when, using federal law, it seeks to conquer an opponent.

Such was my first and only run-in with the modern american gulag system.

I had met many diverse individuals, of every Race and Creed, up to this point, and it had been quite a learning experience. When faced with isolation from friends and family, and seeing ones life taken from them for periods longer than the human mind can translate into discernible fragments, individuals create independent resources and values which, with time, become their salvation – or their damnation. Within this context, each Racial group seeks its own *tribe* by which each individual, and as a group, may insulate itself from the dangers and threats it perceives will destroy him/them. This is Nature's Law. Not the 'law of the jungle', but Nature's divine plan for the extension of each particular specie. It seeks no absolution for its hardness; it seeks no redemption for its right to determine the destiny of its subjects. Nature can be a cruel Mistress, or she can be understood in the ways in which she, herself, is quantifiable; in which she serves the gods who made her. This american gulag, then, becomes the Crucible by which nature is compacted, formed, and presents the individual with truths and consequences, which are rarely addressed in 'civilized' life. Yet, all the elements and conditions, which the gulag presents is, as is natural, are present, also, in our *daily* living; it is present today, as you read this work.

I am a White Nationalist; a euphemism which will, hopefully, make its meaning clear as this present work progresses.

I did not evolve, or devolve into this dynamic in the gulags of this nation but, rather, entered the world at my *birth,* as a member of the Western race-culture; a *seed*, left as a legacy to Life. Like my Father and Mother before me, the elements of race and legacy were also present...and so, as before, and before that. This is the corporeal beginning of *unity*, both of purpose as well as function. It is the extension of both the family – which is the State – and the essence of 'who' that *family* is, and will ever be. What is that essence?

Aristotle, a man of Western stock declares[2]:

> He who thus considers things in their first growth and origin, whether a state or anything else, will obtain the clearest view of them. In the first place there must be a union of those who cannot exist without each other; namely,

---

[2] *Politics* - By Aristotle, Book I, Part I.

> of male and female, that the race may continue (*and this is*
> *a union which is formed, not of deliberate purpose, but*
> *because, in common with other animals and with plants,*
> *mankind have a natural desire to leave behind them an*
> *image of themselves*), and of natural ruler and subject, that
> both may be preserved. (emph mine)

Race, that element which we are *all* a part of. Race, that presence which defines us, molds us, and continues after we are gone. Race, that which separates us; marks us as unique, one to the other. Race, the element of *blood* and *soil*, that which binds us to *persons* and *places*, the *value* we place on spirit, on religious experience, government, and our 'will-to-express' that which we *are*, or wish *to be*. All this, bourne by a single seed, germinated and harvested; thus are *we* born.

The *crucible*, whatever the cause or condition – prison or war, hunger or riches – only brings out what *resides*, already, in the body politic. We are, *who* we are, long before we awake from that warm, comfortable and hospitable place which bore us, nurtured us, and protected us. Brought into this world, the rules are already set, the parameters already given us by nature's guiding hand; we do the best that we can, holding on to those things which seem right, those things which have harboured and sheltered many generations of life before us; this is the history of our past, a thousand generations of trial and error. This is, in its most primal and vital form, the *culture* in which each race, *specific* to its origin, is destined to live and die; to succeed or fail, a member of the greater tribe, in which he is but a single part. As another man of Western stock has said:[3]

"We are born to *die* and to *continue* the flow"

This is the natural, organic, state of Nature, which does not smile or frown upon us, each in turn but, rather, *embraces* whatever we bring as an *offering* to her. We strive, and in the striving, we realize, as often as not, that we are insignificant when alone; but as we look around, and realize as well, that each of us, you and I, belong to *each other* creating, as it were, a larger body of works, of strength and unity. We are connected. What affects one can, and

---

[3] Robert J. Mathews – Speech delivered at the National Alliance, 1984. [emph. mine]

does, affect the other, even if the ripples cannot always be seen in the here and now; throughout the ages, what is said and done now (or in the past) will be felt in the future. This is the law of *consequence*.

Law, that was the single reason why I, and several other co-defendants were given sentences ranging from 40 – 250 years. However, the law, as such, was and is seen differently by different people. First, there was the State, that edifice which we, as a Western people, including all the diverse people living with us, see as that unique motive force in our lives, arranging and rearranging our day-to-day environment. This is the truth of the matter – and religious thinkers and believers who would argue the point are duly noted – yet, as anyone can see, those persons, good hearted as they may be, however much they believe in goodness, justice, righteousness – in God – it is the modern state and its accompanying technics, which make us, or more rightly, condition us, to be. In the *image of the state we* are. Well, at any rate, most of us.

This work is not about, in any complete sense, the legal or historical machinations of the consequence which brought me and my fellows to this present day; rather, it is a work about the *cause*, those events and circumstances which, outside of destiny herself, were at work to bring me, indeed, the whole nation, to a boiling point. This work is a continuation of a previous work[4], which tried to present in my own humble way, the way-signs of the Western race-culture in a broad sense; and in a more microscopic way, the way-signs of our presence here, in America, or more rightly, North America, for we include Canada proper, as members of the West, in a racial sense, as well as the political technics which supply her with guidance and her form of function. My thoughts are split between just how to present this second work, whether to tell a story about the beginning of that nascent nationalism held within all the children of the West who have been raised in the shadow of our elders, of our forefathers and mothers which brought us to this point, or to strictly endeavor to present this work as a studious

---

[4] Rise of The West, 2003.

presentation for the academic proper. The distillation, I hope, will be satisfactory to those who have wanted to hear more about the *cause* of which prompted men and women, husbands and wives, sons and daughters, to take on a 'system' which, for all intents and purposes, was looking out for the best interests of their fellow citizens, their own racial Kinsmen.

In this respect, this work will be less academic than the first yet, as is my wont, and to the chagrin of many who know me, my prose may yet find a more serious tenor in such matters, which is my *style*. I do consider my role in life as being a serious one, for I have ever seen myself, and those to whom have mentored me, as participants, bringing those issues and beliefs as being of the utmost importance to my kinsmen, both in a racial and political sense, which would assure their survival and a fairer existence for them as well as their children. The characters present in this work, both historical and personal, are part of a great mosaic, a tapestry which, at present, has not been finished. Ripples, just as the accident which caused them, have consequences unforeseen, or expected, which only end when nature decrees it. This is the beauty of Life, for we can play the hand dealt us, we can figure we know exactly how it will end, but of ' the plans of mice and men' there is no knowing. Fate, destiny, pre-destination, whatever one calls it, or believes it to be, the great Author of all our doings is, ultimately, in charge. We can press on, all of us, duty bound to do the best that we can, and in the end, the only thing that matters is that we tried, each of us, to do what was 'right' for the betterment of our people – whatever that people - and to the *people* of the West, that people who *bore* us, for myself and my comrades, was that which was our *first* cause.

To be sure, some in this work will be seen as religious, pious, and extreme; others, as well, will be seen as short-sighted and politically naïve to others. Be that as it may, it is part of a real story, and a real history; both elements, to be sure, have not been heard by many, yet, millions have a sense of it, and hundreds of millions have, deep inside, felt the same passions and drives, the same desire for the understanding of *why* things are the way they are, and how they can make a difference in the lives of others; whether or not they strive on a daily basis to 'put bread on the table', as the first cause, it remains a constant, that what we feel deep inside is not being fulfilled in this modern age. What we are taught when young by our parents, our grandparents, our Church, our professors, our friends or the spirits of the books we read all, without exception, affect the way we see the world, but cannot overcome what we feel or are directed by, our natures, our blood.

Imprisonment is the last thing on someone's mind when they seek to do a thing that is above board, that which is duly understood by all, such as the churchman when he sees the error of someone close to him, and tries to correct what he sees as a stumbling block to the life of this individual. Patriotism is of the same stuff. It is a passion, a desire, a destiny predicated upon his life's 'world view', which was given him as a legacy by those who came before. Patriotism, is the stuff of Nationalism, for one's nation is himself, a hundred-million-fold; it is based, not on the concept of today's 'legal' interpretation of state and citizen, but on that organic strata, that very flesh and bone of race and its mystical apparatus which marks us as Human, oh! so human!!

Ecce homo, the elemental force of nature, our nature, that which belongs to us, specifically, as a Western People.

It is our nature to feel pride, revulsion, antipathy, sympathy and generosity to those things which seem as *natural* responses, and with time these senses and proclivities become a tradition which, in turn, is passed onto those whose *sub rosa* concerns benefit thereby, from the instruction of those who have experienced life in the truest sense; they have *lived* it. Those to whom we are indebted, in both a past and present construct are those specifically who have experienced life – they are the 'elders' of our tribe; it makes no difference if this tribe has 100 persons, or 100 million. This is a law, perhaps, which does not agree with nature, for nature cares not whether we, as a tribe or specie goes up or down, as long as she remains. But, we are *organic*, animal like in so many ways, and the uncivilized might forget their elders, allow their powers of reasoning to go unnoticed; civilized people, however, take care of their elders, and listen patiently to what they have to say and impart. This is only right.

Here, *we* come to our own crucible, relative to this work, insofar as we will now focus more attention upon the crux of the matter envisioned here.

Carl von Clauswitz[5], a man of Western stock, stated that "Politics is War by other means", and was speaking specifically in a Western sense he, being a tried and true warrior, setting the tactics and strategies of a western motif, War, and applying it to the practical applications of government. Therefore, it is safe to say that in our political inclinations, war is just as persistent as politics. As individuals, we are marked as either hot or cold when it come to war; the same is the same in politics. Those who are drawn to a 'thing', whether this involves politics/religion/war, become fixed, they are *known* for this particular passion. Zealots are made of these qualities, true believers, who work tirelessly to accommodate what they believe in, and would share with others. All civilization is bourne by these types of individuals. The mass, that centralized mechanism of persons who, for the most part, are cold and consistently make up the general herd will always follow the lead of those passionate individuals who are able to persuade them as to the right or wrong of a thing.

We all fit a plan; we are all designed to follow or lead. This is a 'classification' which is viewed suspiciously by the Modern[6], but serves the *truth* rather well. We, all of us, do fit this category; at one point in our lives we may be followers, and later, leaders. It is a rare case, indeed, to know and respond to both at the same time: This, the true Leader. This is the gem, which brings to bear the essence of what it means to be *noble*. To be sure, this leadership is seen in more than just the courage of the battlefield warrior; he can be seen in the form of your church deacon, your accountant, your spouse. Nobility is genetic, and is refined through the crucible of ritual and punishment: it is the long-term inculcation of *culture*, in

---

[5] On War – Carl von Clauswitz

[6] Readers of *Rise of The West* – will know this term; for those who have not read this work, here is the intended meaning: "Connotes a problematical example of 'today's' man; of the thinkers, philosophers, and government 'experts' which have, and are presently, leading us into a Dark Ages. Its overwhelming connotation is negative." FLS

its pure meaning, which is the *refinement* of social conditions which, among other things, demands a reciprocal response from those whom you share your life with. It is *more* than tradition, yet *belongs* to it. This is Community in the extended understanding.

Nobility, then, is the natural stratification, which exists, independently, yet is shared by those who have shared the same experiences and upbringing. The *higher-man,* that person of *both* nobility and culture who, at times, will show himself is, in the pure sense, the *absolute* Leader. He rules, without even recognizing this gift; he serves, he follows, yet the magnetism which flows from his veins is unique to him, and many who possess it are unaware, because they have learned to *expect* it in their peers, rather than themselves. Yes, these men do exist; they have lived and died in a world of our own inhabiting, some known, and others unknown to the rest of us.

We have, in this modern world, learned to *not* expect this *type* of man.

In the crucible of prison, *it* was there. In the dirty, noisy subway, *it* is there. In the train station, in the city park, in the civil service, in the local social club, in the local church or Kindred, all of them share a *spirit*, perhaps present in more than one single person who, without a doubt, is this *type* of man. No law can *create* this (this is the law of *meritocracy vs democracy*). It may, as either 'law' or 'institution', encourage this; it may reward it, but cannot *create* it. It is a value, which is indispensable to the future of any culture, for this *type* of man is, indeed, the *culture-bearer* of his people. It is this individual who, whether it is known to him, or *unconconscious* within his soul, who *represents* the whole. He is the best, this incalculable asset to the Race.

I have lived with men and women of this caliber; I have fought along side them. I have seen them die. I have seen them survive monumental obstacles. I have seen them watch as family and friends passed from them, the untold personal pain of loss, rejection or failure, and the long-term life-denying world of prison try to *poison* their Faith, their Hope, their Vision; but which have stood fast, anchored against the storm which life has allowed to batter and beat them. Some were *spiritual* men, concerned with their fellow man, and the travails which hammer into being their very existence, some Christian, some following the ways of Western man's ancestral gods, the God's of their fathers. Some were esoteric students, as were many of our Western antecedents before them.

Others, in retrospect, followed a more *simple* and *basic* calling: they believed in a vision which demanded a *response* to the ever increasing *denial* of their sovereignty, as *men*, to be both *provider*, and *protector*, of their wives and children; the *denial* of their rightful place in the marketplace of shared ideas, of debate and civic forums without being shouted down as being 'racists', homophobes, nativists, or simple rabble-rousers. They demanded the right to assemble in the worship places of their own choosing, with people of their own stock, and proud, without the 'consent' of the legal authorities who cannot grant these basic rights; these 'authorities' are able, only, to *deny* them.

By ethnic background, these were members of all the sub-racial groups of Europe: Keltische, Teutonic, Nordic, and Mediterranean and Slavic. There were Poles, Irish, Italian, Welsh, French, Scottish, Finnish, Latvian, Norwegian and Swedes, the *blood* of that ancient and honorable name of Aryan, or noble ones; this word, ancient and beautiful, having been dissected and forgotten by the Modern, is used here to denote the familiarity and interrelatedness of this connected People, this White Tribe, being used to describe the culture and people known as Western Man. This is used without fear or favor; this writer cares not one wit, jot, or tittle about what others, even of his own blood, have to say about the negative connotations, which have 'become' commonplace. This word is old, ancient, and has lived well with great men, and mean; it has bourne it's language, parent to many of our shared origins, and describes those 'long-heads of Europe', as Huxley wrote, and serves us now, today. Governments come and go, legislative bodies rise and fall, but Race, those markers which ever give us our identity, remain. These markers belonged to those persons who I was to share a small portion of my life's journey. I was, and will always be, proud to have known them, to serve with them, to learn from them, and to share that mystical apparition, Destiny.

I think, after all is said and done, that myself, all of us, are *destined* to enjoy the company of certain individuals for better or for worse; this, also, is Life in its fullest sense. There are no more, or less individuals, fated by the Wyrds with whom we shape our future. We are given a certain amount, and that is the end of it. This is not resignation, but the understanding of things, which are greater than the sum of each part. It is a living thing: Friendship.

This marks us as unique and temporary islands in the sea of *chance*.

So it was, that in the late seventies, on into the early eighties, that chance brought into my life specific individuals which made for those events and circumstances which, even now, bring happy memories to a life filled with both good and bad, highs and lows, life and death. I would not have wanted it any other way.

All in all, these lives, like yours, was worth something *greater* than the individual parts, which made up a Brotherhood, a family, and a nation. Lives, which are spent in the search and action of doing good for one's fellow man, are good lives; they have *nobility*.

ii

America. The home of the Free. The home of the Brave.

America, a place where dreams come true, or are dashed upon the cliffs and rocks of a distant shore; known but grown older, a paler shade of what was, a mirror of our inconsistencies and misplaced desires. America, a place we call Home, a *territory*, which houses our existence, nurtures our history and traditions, and which beckons us to breathe the air of our future. America, the place where our fathers and mothers were born and died; and their parents before them.

America, that *idea* which grew from the seeds of despotism, tyranny, and hubris, into that 'great experiment' by which *kindred* peoples could, for the first time in many, many years, start fresh. The hopes and dreams of a generation bourne from the abortion of a stagnant and tempestuous family relationship. Indeed, the new inhabitants of the 'colonies' were of the same root and stock. The *tree* from which they sprung was old, with branches outspreading, covering all with the shade of history and tradition known on both sides of the Atlantic.

Many years before the first 'pilgrim' set sail, those fair-skinned, ruddy faced Norsemen had landed and surveyed the fjords and islands of this far land using maps passed down or recovered from wayfarers, Portuguese sailors who valiantly protected their routes from competitors, and Irish monks, newly converted to the 'new' faith. Pilgrim's they were now, but this new earth had welcomed many before them of the same root and stock. Amorica, the new America.

The message was Freedom for the unsung children of her antecedents, those continental mothers and fathers who had forgotten the rush and exhilaration of conquest, travel, and the beauty of a 'strange new world'. To colonize, to harvest the fruits of one's labour, to see this happening in the 'now' was the *elixir* of a thousand generations before they became stagnant with civilization, before they made 'law' the overriding template of the human condition.

The consequence of all this was the nurturing of a generation of *brave* men and women.

It would take another dozen or so books to completely tell a tale, to be sure a wondrous tale, of those early days; this is no fanciful belief, there abounds many historical records of the courage, vision, and steadfast determination of *your* forebears, those men and women which modern history, that is to say, those *persons* who have denied you, all of us, that complete 'story', of who you are; who your parents were. There is so much more than the history of George Washington, great as he was, and Jefferson too, all great men; yet there are stories of individuals, women and men, boys and girls, that will make the hardest man wince in admiration of these amazing, proud, and simple persons. A strong Nation is made up of men and women of this calibre.

There is just so much more for all of us to sink our teeth into. For our generation, it is an epic, which was envisioned by the likes of J.R.R. Tolkien in the epic grandeur of its spectacle. This, once again, is no romantic wishful thinking; this is *your* History! Something to be proud of, something to warm the heart in the cold place of the 'hear and now'.

Through the years, these people lived and died. Most never made it into the books of renown; yet they *did* live, and helped to build one small village which, in turn, became a city, then a State until, finally, a Nation. No one will argue, if they are honest, that many things have transpired in Our name, which was not right or good in the eyes of the great Author of things. I for one am appalled at some of the dishonesty and absolute corrupt leaders who broke their word to various peoples, including their own. Better to not have given their word – and break it – than to have taken a thing by deception and betrayal. Be that as it may, and perhaps it could not have been any other, the West has been formed, once again, on the shores of this new land; the great Cities of this continent rising up, peopled with the fresh blood of immigrants bearing the same marks as the already vested. There were hard times, to be sure, between these peoples, these brothers, yet it was the thrashing process, and it hardened this people, made them conscious of who they were, what fathers like John Jay had proclaimed, "...that this land was given to one great, and connected people..." That there was a living *destiny* in which they were an active part; the people were getting restless.

Within this abundant people, there were elements, which sought ever for money and power. Human cargo was delivered to these, our shores, spearheaded by members of another race who, in turn, enjoyed the partnership of many members of the West, and promoted the age-old curse of greed, avarice, and power for powers' sake.

Soon the new nation was embroiled in various schemes to secure the natural rights and resources of the people; after all, this was the Kings *privilege*. Mustering armies to enforce his first cause of kingship, *taxes*, which would supply him with revenues, thereby ensuring that the populace remained in *servitude* to him. Restlessness then turned to rebellion, fraught with dissension, secret societies, brotherhoods, and assassinations. The new nation was rife with treason, sedition, and feelings of secession, each side looking to each other as having betrayed the trust and honour of the other.

Many elements comprised the core of these animosities. One, however, stood head and shoulders above the rest: Sovereignty.

Men could, for the first time, not be part of an aristocracy to own land. There were indentured servants and bonded men, but the opportunity was there, and had been tasted by a large majority of the populace. Once men had grown accustomed to being lord of their own house, the prospect of losing it was more than enough impetus to join in a grand resistance; taxation without *representation* was just the needed fuel for the revolutionary among them. So it was that little men and women, comprising an embryonic seed of new-found freedom, was germinated and began to grow.

Blood was spilt wantonly, and many who were both kith and kin were slaughtered; the propaganda machine was wound up, and declared any who fought for this treasonous idea of independence were 'enemies of the state', and would suffer the highest of punishments: Death. Mercenaries were hired for the sole intent of stopping this revolution; troops from the Continent, weighed and measured in the many battles of their ancient Fatherland. Troops, conditioned and trained, more like the modern armies of today, fighting the present generation of satellite tv, and fast food junkies, except that the men these mercenaries faced were Yeomen, farmers, artisans, clergy and merchants who had one difference than those of today: they *believed* in this notion of freedom and sovereignty.

iii.

Time to tell, it was a success for the fledgling nation. All the songs and poems of those days were sung and written by patriots, traitors to an old regime, but loyal to their shared desires and dreams. They had gained their freedom.

Soon after, documents, which we still hold dear, were drafted to include all of their *posterity* in the great experiment, which was America. These documents sought to protect man from himself; keeping a watchful eye upon that system of government which, while founded upon the people, was ever watchful of its own new-found power, not to mention the wealth of a new land. The merchant's early venture in capitalism, Slavery, was already eating away at the fabric of the new vision; *utopia* was fast fading into compromise and betrayal. For the first time since Caesar, racial weights and measures were being used to divide a people, a nation. Money, fought to a standstill by president Andrew Jackson, stood to gain enormous footholds in the new governmental bodies of a large portion of the population in the southern quadrant of the country, could be achieved; the more radical of these elements secured the aid of a country 'lawyer' who, either wittingly or unwittingly, became the most radical of them all, suspending the most cherished articles of these Western peoples: The *Writ of Habeas Corpus*. He also, declared War on his own kinsmen.

The attempts by some, now the majority, to control absolutely their fellow citizens in a federal commmwealth were successful; the sovereign rights of this great and connected people were now declared arbitrary, and shared with 'de facto' citizens who were not of their blood, ignorant children in a land far from their own, imitating at best, the ways of their masters. The children of the West who remained, earnestly trying to come to grips with the totality of the change which had befallen them, stood frozen, unable or unwilling to continue with a defeated proposition, namely, that since the new nation voluntarily had submitted to unification to form this Nation, then they could, in the same voluntary fashion, sunder it. Whether or not this would have proved a better history or not, is not at issue. However, the fact that force was used to *maintain* unification, where most of the issues of the day would have resolved themselves of their own accord, and slavery abolished in any event, since they took the jobs from the poor folk of Western stock, and wealthy landowners having already agreed to take a loss in the wages spent on the new working class, the action of *force* was all but useless. It only served those who *must* at all costs, maintain their hegemony in the fields of finance and personal power.

The age-old battles between the hot-blooded Kelts, and the Teutonic tribes were continued on this continent. This was prompted, however, by those age old enemies of the West, who financed both sides simultaneously, manufactured uniforms for both sides, and sold guns and ammunition to both sides. The merchants of money had succeeded. Blood and Soil had taken the back seat to wealth and compromise.

Through it all, the body of person's known as Western remained, fixed to the land, accepting the changes, both hot and cold, and continued to live and die. There remained as well, however, that *strain* of independence and visionaries who, to the chagrin of those in power, refused to surrender, neither their sovereignty after fifteen years of occupation, even when their own blood put above them, persons who had no idea of the processes by which these brothers of blood had shed their lives upon the altar of division and discord, for the right of the victor to rule justly, or unjustly, their brethren. The people remained, de facto citizens instead of *de jure*, hoping beyond hope, that someday a change would come, freeing them and their own from the despotism of the tyrant posing as democratic realism.

It never came.

Since those days of evolution, betrayal and change, the sons and daughters of this extended people, whether victorious or defeated, were fed the same broth of lies and deceit; that regardless of the colour of one's skin, we shared one common humanity, with one common destiny, and one common *soul*. One can, even now, hear the hiss of the serpent, trading immortality for the fleeting sound of one's own egotistical pandering to the god of mediocrity, the god of egalitarianism. The great reformation had been reborn; *reason* and *experience* now the stepchild of 'enlightenment'.

Soon, however, something began to stir within the breasts of these dedicated, loyal and long-suffering people. A soft breeze began to blow, and then a wind.

The intervening *epochs* brought a distillation, of sorts, to the fledgling western nation, by which the burgeoning diversity of *peoples* were sifted, strained, and finally brought together under the banner of international federalism; or, in another way, the Oligarchy of the *mass*. To the 'modern' American, that unique and disparate individual, that person of any number of antecedent proclivities, of unique faith, of gods and traditions, in short, that resident of Babel, the edifice of [western] man's attempt to push the limits of his humanity – or, more correctly, his Ego. His stupendous *stupidity*. His great, *first cause*, that of cowardice, money and power. For without this first cause, it would have been impossible to 'merchandise' both the civil and political organization, and the individual persons themselves. This, the legacy of the Modern.

The Song of Albion, as the title of this work implies, is a *new* song, that oft longed for *Western shore,* of dreams and hopes, and of new beginnings. It is a hope always felt, a belief known deep inside one's soul; it is the necessary *desire* of a people deprived of their inherent innocence, and their understanding of what passes for that 'unique place in the world,' in which they inhabit.

The descriptions and racial eschatology of this work are the author's, alone.

As in *Rise of the West*, few dates and lineal history will be necessarily presented; but, rather, an organic distillation of what this author has experienced, or learned, from individuals, happenstance, or life experiences as brought to him by the *Wyrd*. As Fate decrees, so we must yield, and do as we must to fulfill our destiny. Some of the names presented in this work will be recognizable; some will not. In most cases, it will be easy enough to search any library or encyclopedia for information regarding a particular person or place, for many of the others, it is the hope of this author to detail, as much is allowed in the format of this work, those individuals whom are not so easily distinguished by either reputation, written or spoken works, or historical veracity, as many of these 'lesser known' individuals have been 'weighed and measured,' not by their friends, acquaintances, or biographers but, rather, by their *enemies*, their *detractors*, their *prosecutors* and their small-minded brethren who digest, and conform too, the information given them by willing and practicing buffoons.

Any event or situation in which the author shared with persons known, or unknown, is true; the passage of time not dimming the memory of such friendships and actions. These characters will, of necessity, play a small part. The complete story has yet to be told.

So, as to not make this foreword any longer, I shall continue to present this work, specifically, to my People, my Folk, my Blood; those, in whom, the future of our children and culture are beholden, for without their active understanding and aggressive and pro-active stance, would deny all those previous assertions, hopes, aspirations, and survival of their fellow man.

The West *has* arisen.

Now, it us up to each of us, to aid and succor its burgeoning, and frail life. To feed and nurture its infancy, to fight those who would, even now, commit infanticide against its innocent existence and growth. I sincerely hope that you, dear reader, will not allow this to happen.

Frank L. DeSilva

Fallbrook, Ca.

January, 2008

Dedicated to a Brighter Future for All the members of The West

Chapter I

The origins of Life are consistent with the passage and evolution of its forms of Politics and Nation building; the first and foremost responsibility of each early individual was to his immediate family and, by extension, those nearest to him, this was his Folk-family, his Race. Any Nation, which was thereby considered and established by him, belonged to him in the only way possible:

By right of Birth.

It is said that we *all* are products of the Past. Everything we are, or can be, has been *gifted* to us by those who have gone before.

This is the *first cause* of all Nationalists. More precisely, this is the belief and knowledge of all Racial Nationalists who are called to stem the tide of suicide, murder, and retardation of their people who, as is known by all Nationalists, are their *nation*, entire, each *belonging*, by right of birth, that ever present gift, to that Once, and Future West.

I am a *White* Nationalist.

I was bourne, as we all are, into that great fraternity, that great Family of persons, known by various names and descriptions collectively, as Western Man, sent by forces unseen; a collective roll of the dice which marks every man and woman of this stock with a special responsibility to each one of its lesser or greater parts. No matter whom I was to come into contact with, whether black, yellow, brown all, each in turn, could not mistake me for anything else. My *mark*, that which housed me, is my uniform, my temple, and my honour. It is the recognition of my blood, my spirit, and my soul. It is the acceptance of Race, as part of the *natural* law of the universe; it is the *gift* given to me by the gods, by God.

As an individual, I am responsible to myself. As a member of a racial composite, I am subsumed and enveloped by the greater family of which I belong: The Race. So, also, is the family of man divided. This is *natural law*. This is *reality*.

To the inhabitants of the earth, collectively, these laws are not *unique* to one or the other race-cultures; the only difference is that of *form*. Not in function. All of us, each in turn owe that *first cause*, that first parent, the recognition due them, and the duty to our future progeny to survive in like fashion. This is *duty*.

Our political state, as such, is simply an extension of our smallest unit: the Family. Robert J. Mathews summed this up, thusly: *"We are born to die, and continue the flow..."*[7] This, and only this, is the continuum of our present reality; it is the reality of all the generations which have come before us, and it will be the reality of all future generations. Moreover, what will that future really be like? In addition, to *whom*, specifically, will this future be the *first cause* of a greater tomorrow? What will make them such? In addition, to *what* will they owe their allegiance and their duty? What *form* of government will our children, and their children's children, live with, and *recognize* as being a part of their 'flow'?

This work is about *race*, its construct, its duty, its obligations, and its role in the future of Western Culture; it is not, simply, about America, Canada, western, eastern and northern Europe, South Africa, Australia, parts of Russia, New Zealand, and beyond; it is about *all* of them. Moreover, as most thinking people realize, these far-flung colonies are part of the larger, organic, body of persons we consider as our own kinsmen, our blood. The archaic considerations of what the Modern calls, a 'past era' is,

---

[7] Robert J. Mathews – Speech delivered at the National Alliance convention of, 1984.

nevertheless, alive and well in the hearts and minds of millions of our fellows, and calls our attention, especially in these present days, to just what our role, as individuals, and as collective entities, really means in the 'modern' age of our evolution. Do we consign our every day lives into the bin of apathy and indoctrination, that passive 'patriotism' of the Modern which, if left to its own devices, like all 'faiths', will amount to nothing without 'works'? The *passivity* and downright ignorant *cowardice* of the modern western citizen is, without a doubt, the most troubling aspect of the future.

Who, then, *is* a Citizen?

This question, which has repeatedly cropped up in the debate of american sovereignty has, without exception since the american 'War Between the States', failed to be answered in any common understanding of the word. The average white american has blithely lived and died thinking that his tenure as *de jure* citizen was justified, solid, and sacrosanct. He, of course, has been lying to himself. The wheels of power, government, money, and direction have been, without exception, turning against those persons of Western Blood. Not that this great nation has not had its champions, its true believers who, as each case warranted, spoke up clearly and vociferously against those forces which sought *control*, rather than *rulership*, as their first cause.

Direction of purpose, that utilitarian understanding of '*just where one is going*', is ambiguous at best, and is rarely considered these days by the population-at-large. They are content to accept the spoon-fed rhetoric of those persons who rule, not lead, them in their daily lives; and could it be otherwise? A nation of three-hundred million persons is quite unwieldy, even if one could contrive and put to practical use a comprehensive form of government, which would educate, nurture, and direct a particular population. Utopia, as a dream, will never happen in anyone's lifetime, as this is a 'hope' and not a *reality*, and never will be. Individuals support and believe in governments which allow the majority to feel that, while they owe allegiance to a body of persons who rule them they, nevertheless, are comfortable in their daily lives, their routines fixed, and their neighbors consistent with their own view of the world, their nation, their spiritual constructs, that is, their *mores*, and their *understanding* of good and evil.

As we pursue this ethereal Albion, this state of mind, and literal creation, one will have to come to grips with, and form an understanding of, what it means to be a citizen of one's *own* nation: what boundaries are defined as, and what *prerequisites* are utilized to confine one to that particular nation; and finally, what *form* of government is best suited for that nation. Moreover, if anyone should anticipate and vocalize the sentiment of 'we have the best form of government' on the planet, let me say this: You have a life and a nation, you have a governmental institution called 'democracy', and you have certain day-to-day routines and habits. Nevertheless, are you happy? Do you feel familiar with your surroundings, with your neighbors? With the direction of your nation? Do you feel as though your thoughts and aspirations for yourself and your nation are the same as those who rule; are they the same as those who live in your city, your town, and your street? The answer is not hard to come to grips with, and most if not all of Western stock have answered more than one of the questions above, with a NO!

Does anyone care *how* you feel?

When I sit among strangers, of my own stock, and discussions of present day events filter through the remonstrations of alcohol, divorce, work stress, children, religion, politics, and race, many things become apparent which is not portrayed on the evening news. However, I am getting ahead of myself.

Firstly, let us examine, for those who are new to Nationalist conversation or nationalist sentiment in general. Specifically, what does it mean to be a *part* of a Nation? Does it make *any* difference that you are a nationalist compared too, let us say, a *democrat*, oligarch, libertarian, or dictator?

In today's commonplace society, the rationale of just 'what' or 'who' *comprises* a nation is tenuous, barely hanging on to the formula that nation is simply the *idea* of political symmetry; that it is the *part* or *whole* of the 'system of law' which encompasses a defined population: the People. All this presupposes the collective apparatus of the 'spectacle', the contorted 'mass' of persons *confined* within a controlled environment; not boundaries in the traditional sense, but an environment, which exists *solely* on the ledger sheet. The ledger, to coin a metaphor, is written on paper *only*.

In our present epoch, or phase of development, we constantly hear about, and discuss with our friends and neighbors, about the *changing* face of this nation, this America. In other quarters, this discussion persists, and has remained the focal point amongst individuals who require no *written* law to describe what they *see* of themselves and those to whom they call 'fellow citizens'. The same indicators, which require an immediate understanding between themselves, mark them: a similarity of origin. Of Race. This can include any *race,* in *any* part of the country. It defines the tribal unit, that embryo of all social dynamics and fledgling political structure: *cohesion.*

Every tribal unit, or familial structure, is a *community* of some kind; it is associated with kinship, both in a practical and personal context. Every community is established with an intention to do some good; for mankind, generally, always act in order to obtain that which they think good for themselves and those who make up their social order. But, if all communities aim at some good, it is the *state* or *political community*, which is the highest state of being of all, and that which embraces all the rest, aims at good or the most excellent, in a greater degree than any other, and strives always for the highest good. This is the *implied* contract between equals; that is, sharing equally the highs and lows of the human condition.

This is the *nascent* beginning of nationalism. There is no law; there is only commonality of interest, of survival, of that slow-paced growth which ever increases the stability of the tribal unit. It starts out small, it does not come about overnight, as it were, complete with science, technics, communications, or a sense of cohesion but, rather, all share an organic rhythm, a pace which encourages social interaction, of *friendships*, of confidence and betrayal; the pattern of daily routines, of a *fixed* relationship to the territory in which all call their own. All of this ineluctably creates the *essence* of nation, the *corporate* unit, as compared to the tribal.

Those who are willing to consider these *types* of things as their first elements of growth and origin, whether one calls this a state or nation, will acquire the clearest and most relevant view of both if they consider firstly, that it is in the *union* of both that brings to bear the fact that without one, the other may not continue. In a practical sense, it is the *sense* that one cannot exist without the other; in its simplest of forms, it is as if male and female are joined, for without this union of male and female, the race would cease to exist. This metaphor of male and female is, in the final analysis, a correct and logical description, for in common with the urges and instinct of nature and nature's law, not a 'prescribed set of laws', mankind has a natural desire and instinct to leave behind an image of themselves. This, then, becomes the corporate unit: the State.

The family, then, is the *association* established by nature for the supply of men's everyday wants; furthermore, it is the association which is the preamble to rulership, guidance, and authority, without which no cohesion may long remain; for the parts are individual by *inclination*, and will spin off without direction, if the head is not in control of the body. Family, as the term indicates, is of the same *corporeal* components, which multiplied a million fold, shares the same inclinations and proclivities which blood and territory have graced it. So it is, when several *families* are united, and the association or community seeks to attain something more than the simple supply of daily needs, the first *society* to be formed is the village.[*] In addition, the most natural form of the village appears to be that of a *colony,* or branch from the same family,

---

[*] Note: We have heard the ruminations of persons who attempt to create a sense of 'social cohesion' between the *disparate* elements of America, the different racial elements, religious, or social proclivities *into* a Village. What we speak of here *as* a village is the natural progression of a *single people*, its disparate elements comprising a single rudimentary source. A village cannot be considered a stepping stone to the larger national characteristic of stability and tradition unless it is in the only sense worthy of consideration, that of a People in a racial, and only a racial sense, for all value comes from a common source, and will die on the vine if it ceases to be rooted to that which gave it life. FLS

composed of the children and grandchildren, each in turn, who are said to be suckled with the *same* milk.

Thus it is, that when several villages are united in a single complete community, large enough to be self-sustaining, the *state*^{**} comes into existence, originating in the bare necessities of life, and continuing in existence for the sake of a *good life*. Therefore, if the earlier forms of society are natural, so is the state, for it is the *end* result of all good efforts on behalf of the persons who reside *within* the confines of that state, and will be judged good or evil by its very *nature*; and the nature of a thing is its *end*. This is what we call all things which are fully developed as to its nature; whether that nature is describing a man, animal, or family. It is the *legacy* from which all organisms derive their force, their vitality, and are *known* by it. Hence, it is evident that the state is a creation of nature. Therefore, man is by nature a *political* animal.

A social *instinct* is implanted in all men by nature. How much greater is the inception and creation of an organized environment created for the betterment of mankind; for when individuals come to know a sense of perfection, they are considered the highest of the animal forms, for animals follow instinct *only*, man it is hoped, follows law which is the handmaiden of justice, intelligence and virtue. Without virtue, in any case, individuals become savage and less than men; justice was the *sense* of those persons who formed the state for the betterment of all, its administration, and the development of the *determination* of what is just. This becomes the first cause of an *orderly* political society: *virtue combined with justice*.

Western men and women are *obligated* to their forebears by the *rite* of sacrifice and duty; there is no mistaking the continuity, which we all share with our antecedents. The structure, form, and sense of justice and virtue, which we as Americans, pride ourselves, has been hard won, steeped in self-sacrifice, life and death, so that we, their children, might enjoy the fruits of their labours. Yet, a gift, received too readily, or too often, can make for spoiled, rotten, lazy, and careless individuals; individuals who have squandered the gift, who have passed off the modern transient days of the present, as the righteous and rightful days of

---

^{**} In the ancient Hellenic construct of families and Kings. For there was one law and one lawgiver which, in turn, fell to members of the family.

yesteryear, careless as to the *value* of the gift nor, sadly, as to its rightful recipients. Instead of protecting the gifts of liberty, of freedom, and individual responsibility to the *whole*, the *children* of these once proud, indomitable and unconquerable people, have been taught to be *ashamed*, to shrink from the very concepts of courage, loyalty, duty, and affinity with, must I say it, to their own Kinsmen, *related* by blood and bone; related in spiritual abstractions, and spiritual manifestations. In short, instead of basking in, and accepting the similarities we, as a people should share, nevertheless, *deny* this affinity. What is worse, we deny this affinity with a purpose, locating and eradicating *any* vestige, no matter how small, of racial sympathy for our own western stock. We have even allowed our enemies to make these feelings a *crime*. Hate is the clarion call of the Modern.

Yes, the Modern *does* hate. He hates the natural demarcation of individuals but, only because he cannot control it within the confines of *his* state. He hates the division of the naturally divided empire; hence he seeks control he may call it the 'rule of law', or 'legal compromise', but it is still control, plain and simple. The Modern *hates* nationalists, for nationalism denotes that spectre of racial dynamics, and he has worked hard to destroy the natural inclinations of his own people, just as the revolutionist of the past – Russia saw this, as did France – the Modern was at work, even then. The Modern has brought to bear in the West, specifically the United States, a construct which, and with the *aid* of members of western stock, has demanded 'inclusiveness' at the point of a sword; this is no mere metaphor, for the Modern has impaled millions on the point of his *legal* fraternity, of *despotic* equality. We hear this all the time; we see it on every modern television show. We are inundated with the *spectacle* of inclusion. To each and sundry who envision the naturalistic environments of just a few years ago, they are marked as 'outsiders', 'troublemakers', 'haters' and breakers of the *peace*. They are marginalized, fired from the centers of learning – those centers which house, in many cases *our own children* – and are flung into prisons for 'questioning' events and *ideas*, which mark them as free Western men!

No longer are we, as Western men and women, considered *family, colony, village or racial state;* no, we are, and have been, *de facto* members of a legal empire, an empire of corrupted traditions, devalued virtues, and neglected sovereignty. In short, what the nationalist has warned of these past hundred years or so has, to be sure, come to pass; it has come to exist with a passion unrivaled since the last major epoch of empire and disintegration. The *dereliction* of these men of power which money has brought to bear upon their own stock, has *shattered* the once secure and vigorous imagination and self confidence of their fellows, and for what? So that those who claim power and rulership over their peers should *remain* in power? It appears this way.

My brothers and sisters, *wherever* you may live, in whatever country or province, remember this: When you were bourne living, kicking and screaming, awake to the call of a new life, you were given certain aspects held within your nature, your *spirit* and *soul*; this is your *gift,* which was given to you by your mother and father, and in turn, you will do the same for your children. It is a *gift,* which *implies* duty. It is a gift, which implies *obligation.* It is a gift, which implies *continuity* with your fellows. No legal manipulation can make it so, it was part of nature's law the second you took your first breath of free air. You owe no one for the *right* to feel the way you do. Moreover, no 'law' can take from you what is *ingrained* by right of natural law, that kind begets like kind, and laws, which deprive those persons of these gifts, are onerous and evil.

The subconscious does not control the waking state of the living; but it does remain fixed, just under the surface, and reminds us in those moments of doubt and uncertainty, no matter the quarter or country, of just who you are by right of birth:

Sons and Daughters of the West!!

Chapter II

Citizenship

The world-city means cosmopolitanism in place
of "home" . . . To the world-city belongs not a
folk but a mob. Its uncomprehending hostility
to all the traditions representative of the culture
(nobility, church, privileges, dynasties,
convention in art and limits of knowledge in
science), the keen and cold intelligence that
confounds the wisdom of the peasant, the new-
fashioned naturalism that in relation to all
matters of sex and society goes back far to
quite primitive instincts and conditions, the
reappearance of the panem et circenses in the
form of wage-disputes and sports stadia--all
these things betoken the definite closing down
of the Culture and the opening of a quite new
phase of human existence--anti-provincial, late,
futureless, but quite inevitable.

Oswald Spengler

i

A City is made up of individuals who, like cities, states, and
nations have a rhythmic cycle in which their lives and fortunes are
inextricably bound: Birth, Life, and senility, and in just this order.
Individuals, those basic building blocs which are the elementary
source and strength of any social dynamic, which envisions the
socialization of its unique tribal acquaintances, are, so called,
'fellow citizens'. Up until recent times, these tribal acquaintances

were, as the word 'tribal' implies, of the same racial stock, and was duly understood to mean that, *each* in turn, were part of an *extended* family, and basked in the sacred fraternity of *citizenship*, the gift which organized city-states inferred upon its fellows to mark them unique, and empowered with special *privileges* as compared to the dark and abysmal counterparts which, in ancient times, were considered *barbarians*. This marked a complicated and natural aversion to 'outsiders', and invoked the enmity of *opposites*.

It is said that opposites attract.

In this regard, as a simple matter which is axiomatic, the pull between light and dark, good and evil, small or large is a natural phenomenon which signifies either a lesser or greater degree of acceptance or rejection. In the first case, it is amity, friendship, and social intercourse which benefits the individual person or group; to *reject* a thing, person, or idea, as in the second case, is to utilize a proportionate sense of *discretion*, of *discrimination*. This is a person's, or people's *sense* of beauty, right or wrong; in short, their sense of what *belongs* to them by right of *affinity*, of personal desire. With time, and through the extension of biological groupings, this becomes the social *mores* of the social acceptance of what is *good* for the group, or what is *bad* for the group. This is the *true* meaning of discrimination.

To be a 'citizen', by definition, *is* to discriminate from persons who are *not* citizens. We, here in America, *are* citizens of villages, towns, States, and belong thereby, to a Nation. When we were first empowered with 'american' citizenship, it was through the right of conquest, the right of being empowered by military supremacy: Once the revolutionary dictum of *victory* imposed a new set of standards by which peers could demonstrate the fact that the English Monarchy no longer ruled and, hence, 'subjects' of the Crown were no more, a new set of standards became the law of the land. We were, after the departure of the English military occupation, citizens of a new *commonwealth*, a *new* sense of natural and legal definition of just *who* they had become. The term 'citizen' of the United States implied not only *legal* status, but *naturalized* status as well – being a part of a larger, connected people, a people connected by long-standing traditions, both in Law and 'common law' which allowed the disparate qualities of religion, ethnic sub-divisions, and familial interactions to merge, graft themselves, and finalize their aspirations into a voluntary assembly of persons in which the term Citizen became the nomenclature which described the *totality* of a People. Citizenship, not only by definition, but by inference as well, was a *racial* designation.

How far the Modern has taken us!

Citizenship has, since then, gone through quite an evolutionary *morphology*.

In this regard, Naturalization is the *acquisition* of citizenship and nationality by somebody who was not a citizen or national of that country when he or she was born, and has begun, once again, to make its rounds within the halls of government for many a convoluted agenda and social purpose. After all, in a democracy, the 'voting tallies' number the success or failure of both economic and social experiments in this new post-traditional America.

In general, basic requirements for naturalization are that the applicant hold a legal status as a full-time resident for a minimum period of time and that the applicant promise to obey and uphold that country's laws, to which an oath or pledge of allegiance is sometimes added. Some countries also require that a naturalized national must renounce any other citizenship that they currently hold, forbidding dual citizenship, but whether this renunciation actually causes loss of the person's original citizenship will again depend on the laws of the countries involved.

Nationality is, traditionally, based either on *jus soli* ("right of the territory") or on *jus sanguinis* ("right of blood"), although it now usually invokes both with the same meaning. Whatever the case, the massive increase in population flux due to globalization and the sharp increase in the numbers of refugees following World War I created an important class of non-citizens, sometimes called *denizens*. In some rare cases, procedures of mass naturalization were passed (Greece in 1922, Armenian refugees or, more recently, Argentine people escaping their own economic crisis). As naturalization laws were created to deal with the rare case of people separated from their nation state because they lived abroad (expatriates), western 'democracies' were not ready to naturalize the massive influx of stateless people which followed massive denationalizations and the expulsion of their minorities in the first part of the 20th century — the two greatest such minorities after World War I were the Jews, and the Armenians, but they also counted the (mostly aristocratic) Russians who had escaped the 1917 October Revolution and the war which ushered in the period known as *communism*, and quickly to follow were the Spanish refugees. As Hannah Arendt pointed out, internment camps became the "only nation" of such stateless people, since they were often considered "undesirable" and were stuck in an illegal situation (i.e., their country had expelled them or deprived them of their nationality, and were not then naturalized, thus living in a judicial no man's land).

After the Second war of Fratricide, the increase in international migrations created a new category of refugees, most of them economic refugees. For economic, political, humanitarian and pragmatic reasons, many states passed laws allowing a person to acquire their citizenship *after* birth (such as by marriage to a national – *jus matrimonii* – or by having *ancestors* who are nationals of that country), in order to reduce the scope of this category. However, in some countries this system still maintains a large part of the immigrated population in an illegal status, albeit some massive regularizations - in Spain by *José Luis Zapatero's* government and in Italy by *Berlusconi's* government.

There had always been a distinction in English law between the *subjects* of the monarch and *aliens*: the monarch's subjects owed the monarch allegiance, and included those born in his or her dominions (natural-born subjects) and those who later gave him or her their allegiance (naturalized subjects). Such as was the original intent of the *polity* of the founders of the United States.

Congress is given the power to prescribe a uniform rule of naturalization, which was administered by state courts. There was some confusion about which courts could naturalize; the final ruling was that it could be done by any "court of record having common-law jurisdiction and a clerk (prothonotary) and seal."

The Constitution also mentions "natural born citizen". The first naturalization Act (drafted by Thomas Jefferson) used the phrases "natural born" and "native born" interchangeably. Until 1952, the Naturalization Acts written by Congress still allowed only *white* persons to become naturalized as citizens - except for two years in the 1870s which the Supreme Court declared to be a mistake.

Moreover, naturalization is also mentioned in the Fourteenth Amendment. Before that Amendment, individual states set their own standards for citizenship. The Amendment states, "all persons born or naturalized in the

United States and subject to the jurisdiction thereof shall be citizens of the United States and of the State in which they reside."

Note also that the Amendment is ambiguous on the issue of singular or plural United States. In the early days, the phrase "United States" was used as a singular or a plural according to the meaning. After the Civil War, it was generally always a singular. The Amendment does not say "its jurisdiction" or "their jurisdiction" but "the jurisdiction thereof".

The Naturalization Act of 1795 set the initial parameters on naturalization: "free, White persons" who had been resident for five years or more. The Naturalization Act of 1798, part of the Alien and Sedition Acts, was passed by the Federalists and extended the residency requirement from five to fourteen years. It specifically targeted Irish and French immigrants who were involved in Democratic-Republican Party politics. It was repealed in 1802.

An 1862 law allowed honorably discharged Army veterans of any war to petition for naturalization without having filed a declaration of intent, after only one year of residence in the United States. An 1894 law extended the same privilege to honorably discharged 5-year veterans of the Navy or Marine Corps. Over 192,000 aliens were naturalized between May 9, 1918, and June 30, 1919, under an act of May 9, 1918. Laws enacted in 1919, 1926, 1940, and 1952 continued preferential treatment provisions for veterans.

Passage of the Fourteenth Amendment meant that, in theory, all persons born in the U.S. are citizens regardless of race. Citizenship by birth in the United States, however, was not initially granted to Asians until 1898, when the Supreme Court held that the Fourteenth Amendment did apply to Asians born in the United States in United States v. Wong Kim Ark.

The enabling legislation for the naturalization aspects of the Fourteenth Amendment was the Naturalization Act of 1870, which allowed naturalization of "aliens of African nativity and to persons of African descent", but is silent about other races.

The 1882 Chinese Exclusion Act banned Chinese workers and specifically barred them from naturalization. The Immigration Act of 1917, (Barred Zone Act) extended those restrictions to almost all Asians.

The 1922 Cable Act specified that women marrying aliens ineligible for naturalization lose their US citizenship. At the time, all Asians were ineligible for naturalization. The Immigration Act of 1924 barred entry of all those ineligible for naturalization, which again meant non-Filipino Asians.

Following the Spanish American War in 1898, Philippine residents were classified as US nationals. Moreover, the 1934 Tydings-McDuffie Act, or Philippine Independence Act, reclassified Filipinos as aliens, and set a quota of 50 immigrants per year, and otherwise applying the Immigration Act of 1924 to them. The quotas did not apply to Filipinos who served in the United States Navy, which actively recruited in the Philippines at that time.[8]

Asians were first permitted naturalization by the 1943 Magnuson Act, which repealed the Chinese Exclusion Act. India and the Philippines were allowed 100 *annual* immigrants under the 1946 Filipino Naturalization Act. The War Brides Act of 1945 permitted soldiers to bring back their *foreign* wives and established precedent in naturalization through marriage. This included quite a number of Asian wives.

The 1952 Immigration and Nationality Act (better known as the McCarran-Walter Act), *lifted* racial restrictions, but kept the *quotas* in place. The Immigration Act of 1965, following closely the internal reactions and social engineering foisted by many 'progressive' institutions, finally allowed Asians and all persons from all nations be given equal access to immigration and naturalization.

Moreover, illegal immigration has become a major issue in the US at both the end of the 20th century, and into the 21st. The Immigration Reform and

---

[8] This latter disposition has effects relative to the united states military of the present day, as the modern governmental technics of today, even as Caesar, seeks to extend the franchise to educated and itinerant immigrants alike, to bolster their lagging recruitment, showing the deracinated and short-sighted policies of expediency, at the expense and safety of the Western population. Civil wars, traditionally, presuppose dramatic changes in social constructs and evolution, as [racial] groups become independent and self-responsible for their own future will, of necessity, seek ever to protect and extend those privileges. FLS

Control Act of 1986, while tightening border controls, also provided the opportunity of naturalization for illegal aliens who had been in the country for at least four years. At present, the convolutions of political pandering and public postures, indicates a continuing of the same compromises, which have injured members of the West for more than a century and a half.

In this regard, the Child Citizenship Act of 2000 streamlined the naturalization process for children adopted *internationally*. A child under age 18 who is *adopted* by at least one U.S. citizen parent, and is in the custody of the citizen parent(s), is now *automatically* naturalized once admitted to the United States as an immigrant or when legally adopted in the United States, depending on the visa under which the child was admitted to the U.S., despite the lack of racial affinity with Western stock.

The following list is a short summary of the duration of legal residence before a national of a foreign state, without any cultural, historical, or marriage ties or connections to the state in question, can request citizenship under that state's naturalization laws:

- Argentina: 2 years continuous as a permanent resident immediately before the application (dual citizenship is allowed)

- Denmark: 9 years continuous as a permanent resident immediately before the application (dual citizenship is not allowed)

- Canada: 3 years continuous (1,095 days) as a permanent resident (dual citizenship is allowed)

- Netherlands: 5 years continuous (dual citizenship allowed under specific circumstances, such as acquiring a spouse's nationality, otherwise prohibited)

- New Zealand: 5 years continuous (reside in NZ for at least 240 days in each of those 5 years, 1,350 days in total) as a permanent resident immediately before the application (dual citizenship is allowed)

- Norway: 7 years out of the previous 10 (with out-of-realm vacations of up to 2 months per year) as a permanent resident immediately before the application (dual citizenship is permitted under certain conditions)

- Belgium: 3 years continuous (dual citizenship is allowed)

- Ireland: 5 years over the last 9 years, including at least 1 year before applying. Dual citizenship is allowed, however Irish citizenship can be revoked if a naturalized citizen obtains citizenship of another state (other than automatic citizenship by marriage) subsequent to naturalization or leaves the state for an extended period without periodically expressing their intention to return.

- France: 5 years continuous. (dual citizenship is allowed)

- Italy: 5 years continuous. (dual citizenship is allowed)

- Germany: 5 years continuous. (dual citizenship is allowed only for other EU nationals)

- A few rare massive naturalizations procedures have been implemented by nation states. In 1891, Brazil granted naturalization to all aliens living in the country. In 1922, Greece massively naturalized all the Greek refugees coming back from Turkey. The second massive naturalization procedure was in favor of Armenian refugees coming from Turkey, who went to Syria, Lebanon or other former Ottoman countries. Reciprocally, Turkey massively naturalized the refugees of Turkish descent or other ethnic backgrounds in Muslim 'faiths' from aforementioned countries during the redemption process.

Canada instituted a mass naturalization by Act of Parliament with the enactment of the Canadian Citizenship Act 1946.

After annexation of the territories east of the Curzon line by the Soviet Union in 1945, communists naturalized *en masse* all the inhabitants of those territories—including ethnic Poles, as well as its other citizens who had been deported into the Soviet Union, mainly to Kazakhstan. Those persons were *forcibly* naturalized as Soviet citizens. Later on, Germany granted to the *ethnic* German population in Russia and Kazakhstan full citizenship rights. Poland has a limited repatriation program in place.

The most recent massive naturalization case resulted from the Argentine economic crisis in the beginning of the 21st century. Existing or slightly updated Right of return laws in Spain and Italy allowed many of their diasporic descendants to obtain — in many cases to regain — naturalization in virtue of *jus sanguinis* [right of blood], as in the Greek case. Hence, many Argentineans and Latin Americans acquired European nationality.

Since the Fourteenth Amendment to the United States Constitution grants citizenship only to those "*born or naturalized in the United States, and subject to the jurisdiction thereof*", and the original United States Constitution only grants Congress the power of naturalization, it could be argued, and often is, that *all* acts of Congress that expand the right of citizenship are cases of 'massive naturalization'. This includes the acts that extended U.S. citizenship to citizens of Puerto Rico, the United States Virgin Islands, Guam, and the Northern Mariana Islands, as well as the Indian Citizenship Act of 1924 which made all Native Americans citizens (most of them were previously excluded under the "jurisdiction" clause of the 14th Amendment). The mass naturalization of native persons in occupied territories is illegal under the laws of war (Hague and Geneva Conventions). However, there have been many instances of such illegal mass naturalizations in the 20th century.

Denaturalization is the *reverse* of naturalization, when a state deprives one of its citizens of his or her citizenship. From the point of view of the individual, denaturalization means "revocation" or "loss" of citizenship. Denaturalization can be based, in part, on various legal justifications. The most severe form is the "stripping of citizenship" when denaturalization takes place as a *penalty* for actions considered criminal by the state, often only indirectly related to nationality, for instance, having served in a foreign military. In countries that enforce single citizenship, voluntary naturalization in another country will lead to an automatic loss of the original citizenship; the language of the law often refers to such cases as "giving up one's citizenship" or (implicit) renunciation of citizenship. Another case, affecting only foreign-born citizens, denaturalization can refer to the loss of citizenship by an annulment of naturalization, also known as "administrative denaturalization" where the original act of naturalization is found to be invalid, for instance due to an administrative error or if it had been based on fraud (including bribery). In the US, the *Bancroft Treaties* in the 19th century regulated legislation concerning denaturalization.

Loss of U.S. citizenship was a consequence of foreign military service based on Section 349(a)(3) of the Immigration and Nationality Act *until* its provisions were found unconstitutional by the Supreme Court in 1967. Following the 1923 *United States v. Bhagat Singh Thind* Supreme Court decision, which held Indian-origin immigrants could *not* claim to be of Western stock (race-culture), and thus be given the privilege of US citizenship, A. K. Mozumdar, who had been naturalized ten years before, lost his nationality.

Yaser Esam Hamdi was a U.S. 'citizen' captured in Afghanistan in 2001. The U.S. government claimed that he was fighting against U.S. and Afghan Northern Alliance forces with the Taliban. He was named by the Bush administration as an "illegal enemy combatant", and detained for almost three years without receiving any charges. On September 23, 2004, the United States Justice Department agreed to release Hamdi to Saudi Arabia on the condition that he gives up his U.S. citizenship, which was later revoked by the courts after his refusal to give it up.

Section 4 of the British Nationality, Immigration and Asylum Act 2002 gave power to the Home Secretary to 'deprive a person of a citizenship status if the Secretary of State is satisfied that the person has done anything seriously prejudicial to the vital interests' of the United Kingdom, except in the case where such might render the person stateless.

Before World War I, only a small number of countries had laws governing denaturalization that could be enforced against citizens guilty of "lacking patriotism". Such denaturalized citizens became stateless persons. During and after the war, most European countries passed amendments to revoke naturalization.

In Homo Sacer: *Sovereign Power or Bare Life* (1998), philosopher *Giorgio Agamben* mentioned a number of denaturalization laws that were passed after World War I by most European countries:

It is important to note that starting with the period of World War I, many European states began to introduce laws, which permitted their own citizens to be denaturalized and denationalized. The first was France, in 1915, with regard to naturalized citizens of "enemy" origins; in 1922 the example was followed by Belgium, which revoked the naturalization of citizens who had committed "anti-national" acts during the war; in 1926 the Fascist regime in Italy passed a similar law concerning citizens who had shown themselves to be "unworthy of Italian citizenship"; in 1933 it was Austria's turn, and so forth, until in 1935 the Nuremberg Laws divided German citizens into full citizens and citizens without political rights. These laws - and the mass statelessness that resulted - mark a decisive turning point in the life of the modern nation-state and its definitive emancipation from the naive notions of "people" and "citizen."

The 1915 French denaturalization law applied only to naturalized citizens with "enemy origins" who had kept their original nationality. Later under Raymond Poincaré's government, another law was passed in 1927, which entitled the government to denaturalize any *new* citizen who committed acts contrary to the national interest.

In 1916, Portugal passed a law, which automatically denaturalized all citizens born to a German father.

In 1922, Belgium enacted a law revoking the naturalization of persons accused of having committed "antinational acts" during the war; this was supplemented in 1934 by a new decree against people "in dereliction of their duties as Belgian citizens."

After 1926, in Italy, people who were deemed not to deserve the Italian citizenship or who were considered to represent a threat to the public order could lose their naturalization.

Egypt in 1926 and Turkey in 1928 enacted laws authorizing denaturalization of any person threatening the public order. Austria passed a similar law in 1933 by which it could denaturalize any citizen who participated in a hostile action against the state. Russia also passed several similar decrees after 1921.

In 1933, national socialist Germany passed a law authorizing it to denaturalize any person "living abroad" and began restricting the citizenship rights of naturalized citizens of Jewish origin, followed in 1935 by 'citizens by birth' on the basis and structure of the *Nuremberg* laws.

During Vichy France, 15,000 persons, mostly Jews, were denaturalized (between June 1940 and August 1944), following the setting up, in July 1940, of a Commission charged of revision of these naturalizations since the 1927 reform of the nations nationality law.

In the United States, the proposed, but never ratified, Titles of Nobility amendment of 1810 would revoke the American citizenship of anyone who would "accept, claim, receive or retain, any title of nobility" or who would receive any gifts or honors from a foreign power.

All nations, it seems, have a unique and fundamental appreciation of just *who* is, and has a right too, *citizenship*.

ii.

In the beginning of all *epilogues*, nature, as the instrument of 'accident', purpose, or destiny, has been present at the first cries of every life, at every instant, of this great Epic we call Life; each cry, resounding off fur, thatch, or walls of mason and steel has also been witnessed by its own, unique and natural corresponding kinsmen: A Mother, Father, family (by extension both immediate bonds of blood, as well as common acquaintances, held in common by racial affinity), and others known to the community-at-large. That first breath, inhaled involuntarily, a hot rushing wind into the organisms which, for eighty years or more, will function, unfailingly, to support the ongoing existence of this new, precious person: the newest *member* of the nation-at-large. The die is cast, a new Life, a new Citizen has been thrust upon, and interwoven with, the great tapestry of its own unique, and corporate destiny, which encompasses the entire movement and dynamics of the earth itself.

The picture created above is, or will be said by some, to be romantic; thus it is. To think of *life*, in its pure state, and not be romantic in all its considerations, is to say that the person who is that hardened by the modern technics of life today, is a lesser individual, and hence, *adds* to an already complex and disinterested population which has lost its way. Romance, by definition, adds to the *lusre* of human contact, making the dark places submit to the light; making the heart beat faster, and fonder; allowing the memories of first light, new horizons, to live more *vividly* within the recesses of our minds. All this, to the person who never asked (that he or she is aware of) that this spectacle be awarded them.

Romance, however, is soon lost in the ever quickening pace of one's environment and its various day-to-day habits and routines. It becomes the ever-present *compulsion*, which, in most cases, completely subsumes the individual and its innate personality. In the Modern's age, idealism, *real* idealism, is passed into the deep pit of *conformity*, and mediocrity. Each one of us, especially those of the West become, at an ever increasing rate, 'citizens of the world' as seen through the eyes and ears of those who have lost their way; who would submit you and I, all of us, to the daily vagaries of *mass* man, demanding only that we 'accept' the *status* of citizen in a brave new world, replete with technics unimagined by our Fathers and Mothers of yesteryear. Citizen, in name, and in fact, but citizen with no *raison d'être*; no passion, nor reason to live.

To what end are the great devices, machines, and technology to be used? The overabundance of non-utilitarian technologies by the average person seems, to many, superfluous. It all becomes, in fact, simply *production* without *direction*; a complete arbitrary distraction which benefits no one excepting, perhaps, the manufacturer, the capitalist, the banker. In fact, these latter are over extended, and have forced the *over-extension* of the Western world, and who knows where this will all lead? Not the common man or woman, this is a certainty. Those who seek to rule, and are ruling will, seek ever more and more power, and will usher in upheavals which none, not even those in power, can imagine. They are prepared, however, to suppress, control, or dissuade by means of finance, political pressure, or death, those who do not accommodate their plans. As said in *Rise of The West, all* organisms seek their own survival.

The disparate individuals who now reside, for better or ill, *with* us, and *within* us, demand the same recognition which we, those of the West, have declared ourselves, a unique and special people; they, too, *demand* citizenship in the *image* of their makers. This demand however, seems unlikely to take shape in any voluntary fashion; in fact, its *de facto* acceptance, is already obvious but, without the full import being realistically understood, except by few in academia, the common folk, and fewer still, those of a demonstrable Nationalist perspective. The Modern has done, and is doing everything imaginable to *force* this upon the citizens of this Western colony; future 'democratic' elections on all levels will, without doubt, *assure* this. However, for the sake of discussion, let us continue with the facts needed for this understanding of our near and present future.

iii.

Immigration and Citizenship

The *canard* of 'citizenship' will, if left alone, continue to mollify and confuse, to the detriment of all, the decisions necessary to *maintain* and *extend* ourselves as a distinct and viable *organism.*

We shall endeavor to cover, yet again, and there are truly magnificent studies which demand our attention yet, even these, erudite as they are, deny the passion, the need, the *demand* to have these issues heard; they are, for the most part, belonging to those *conservative* individuals who, in turn, allow their works to makes the conservative rounds, speaking at conservative gatherings, and aiding in turn, the same soft-spoken and dedicated individuals who will, as have all before, continue to wither and die on the political vine. Instead of dealing with Immigration, not alone, but with the corporate support of their very Folk, the common man and woman, in the venues of the street, for there is no other venue open to the People at this time, they often seem surprised when they are denied places to speak and are denied the very tenure necessary to earn a living. This is dawning on many of these sorts which, at this time, still command a certain degree of financial support, either through publishing or writing, being Corporate heads, or civil servants, with the common man and woman – most, however, continue to fleece or betray the common man or woman, just like they have for the past sixty years.

To develop a unique and abiding sovereignty, a corporate political state, is to assume a more aggressive and dominant role; this role may be organic, but it also assumes that political features known as political activism, political finance, and political revolutionaries will be supported, and this in turn, supports the active political designs of the nationalist corporate structure. Nationalism is the only conduit which is, or can be, revolutionary in scope, while gaining the greatest number of adherents, and consequently maintain any so-called *legitimacy* to the future programmes and institutional mechanisms necessary for the growth of any call whatever, for the protection and sustenance of the people; while also building the ability to *enforce* and *create* national policy regarding Immigration. To think otherwise, or encourage others to think in this fashion is racial treason, for it develops the old 'tried and true' wait-and-see mentality; a mentality which, as of today, has done little to reconcile the needs of Western stock, and the *special* needs of sovereignty. There is no middle ground, and there is no compromise. The jealousy's, which have always plagued the conservative 'movements' will, very shortly, be wiped away by the revolutionary tenets of the burgeoning white Nationalist. This new individual will, without fear or favor, replace the conservative, and all those who favor them, without mercy, and develop those resources, which the conservatives have squandered for so long.

The lack of 'support' for those nationalistic spokesmen, those who, from youth onward, have showed such promise, yet allowed to die, literally in some cases, will not be allowed to continue; the slow, yielding voices of the past, will not be allowed to suffer any more apathy and cowardice from their erstwhile supporters. We have no time to waste.

The conservative approach has brought some to their senses; but this has, also, died on the vine:

> The CCH FMLA-ADA Leave Advisor will walk you through the maze of federal leave law to help you navigate the process, make effective decisions, and know when to contact legal counsel. Learn More While the AFL-CIO leadership remains committed to what an immigration reform group calls "a massive illegal alien amnesty program," some rank and file workers and constituent locals are asserting that such a policy would do irreparable harm to American workers. The latest crack in the AFL-CIO's support for amnesty is Pittsburgh Plumbers Local No. 27, which approved a resolution October 10 demanding that their union dues not be used for activities that support undocumented immigrants.

The resolution sharply criticizes the AFL-CIO leadership's positions on dealing with illegal immigration. Local 27 "wants to express our outrage regarding the AFL-CIO's stance on supporting millions of illegal aliens." Illegal immigration is "harming our country," and specifically the interests of working Americans, it states.

> According to the Federation for American Immigration Reform (FAIR), the plumbers' resolution follows a similar position taken last month by the International Brotherhood of Electrical Workers, which represents some 750,000 building trades workers nationally. Earlier this summer, Teamster president James Hoffa expressed opposition to legalization for millions of illegal immigrants and called for an overhaul of U.S.

immigration policies that he believes are detrimental to the interests of American workers.

"Americans from all walks of life at the grassroots are mobilizing to stop a massive illegal alien guest worker amnesty program being promoted by a disengaged elite," said Dan Stein, president of FAIR. "Whether it is union members acting to protect their jobs and wages, or local governments acting to protect local residents from costs and crime associated with illegal immigration, Americans are making it clear that they will not sit quietly while their interests are being sold out."

Both the AFL-CIO and its rival federation, Change to Win, have embraced immigrant workers' rights. Recently the AFL-CIO announced a partnership with a national day laborers organization, which advocates for the rights of these workers, who are often undocumented immigrants.[9]

Resolutions like these, while well intended, have done nothing to reduce this threat. The majority of working-class men and women of Western stock continue to suffer as a consequence, having no one to demand that *their* 'citizenship' be enforced, without fear or favor, having been sold out by the very vested conservative elements which would have us 'wait just a little longer for reprieve', for the dissolution of hard-won workers rights.

As a White Nationalist, one must *never* submit to the compromise of corporate America; to do so, limits not only oneself, but that of your brothers and sisters which, on a daily basis, suffer the indignities of Institutions which have, long ago, left these individuals to fend for themselves. Nationalists, will *never* forget this betrayal. The monies which would have been realized by supporting the studious, the industrious, and fellow citizens of the West have, unfortunately, been discarded in favor of the promise of certain elites which, for a time, have bought and paid for the complicity of these paragons of finance and conservative principles. No more.

---

[9] Federation for American Immigration Reform (FAIR) - EMPLOYMENT LAW — (Immigration reform group: rank and file union members break with AFL-CIO over immigration) 10/23/06.

These same individuals have for far too long, avoided the coming apocalypse. All those of Western stock can see, clearly, the inevitable change and disastrous effects it is having on them, their children, and their nation.

iv.

The coming catastrophe is beginning to make itself known to all.

The betrayal of those who 'speak' for those of Western stock, those, who, for lucre's sake, have sided with the 'mob', with *canaille* speaks for itself; for to do less, in their mind, is the end of their power, their position, and their desires; the modern 'aristocrats' of the political machine, having made their compromise, their back-room deals have, at the expense of their fellows, embraced the ebony hue of *difference*, as the logical *end* of democracy, which they, themselves, ushered in, and bowed to the majesty of *numbers*, of that great leveling.

Citizenship, that particular and privileged gift, given away for the meaningless chatter of the voting booth, wherein those who cast their 'vote', 'vote only for their own special interests, which is normal, but which confounds and annuls the vote of each and every Western man and woman. With the weight of various misadventures, jealousies, power-grabs, and outright betrayal, the members of the West are confused, misdirected, and sensing, but not fully understanding, the source of their predicament, have also chosen to be swayed by slick tongues, and the cannon of *inevitability*, and have sold their birthright to any and sundry who promise them *security*, *protection*, and *compromise*. Such have all decadent rulers, be they 'systems', 'individuals', or technics of 'law', finalized their sway over the mass of men. Only one thing stands in their way: the Nationalist.

For many, many years, nationalists, specifically and independently, until very recently, were the only ones demanding an end, and extrication of foreign illegal immigrants; the call did not end there, and the demand for repatriation of a majority, if not all, immigration from non-Western nations. The abuse levied against these stalwart individuals and groups has been profound, and has continued unabated since just after WW II by the very 'victors' who held the world in their hands, for better or for ill: The *conservatives* of the day, leading the charge with purveyors of 'civil rights', and *progressive* leanings. These individuals *knew* the outcome of these policies, and hastened its inevitable consequences. The late, not so great, William F. Buckley is the perfect picture of such traitors as this.

Patrick Buchanan, cut from the same cloth, yet finding his way in more demonstrable ways, nevertheless *failed* to champion the cause of his own people, no matter the thousands of articles in which he describes the plight of Western peoples, as he ran a african-american female, to be his presidential running mate, courting the multicultural voting bloc. This effort, like so many non-racial nationalists, is the blatant earmark of the conservative political hack, that specie of american lethargy, and political suicide who, nevertheless, declares:

> Americans of European ancestry are also declining as a share of the U.S. population, down from near 90 percent into 1960 to 66 percent today. Anglos, as they are called now, are now minorities in our two largest states, Texas and California, and by 2040, will be a minority in the nation that people of British and European stock built.
>
> Last month, the Census Bureau projected the U.S. population would grow by 167 million by 2060, to 468 million.
>
> And immigrants and their children will constitute 105 million of that 167 million. That would be triple the 37.5 million legal and illegal immigrants here today, which is itself the largest cohort of foreigners any nation has ever taken in.
>
> With the 45 million Hispanics here to rise to 102 million by 2050, the Southwest is likely to look and sound more like Mexico than America. Indeed, culturally, linguistically and ethnically, it will be a part of Mexico.[10]

---

[10] Patrick J. Buchanan-Official Website - http://buchanan.org/blog – The Decline of The Anglos, September18,2007.

This message has, dutifully, been preached to a certain conservative readership, yet the political action in real terms, has fallen much too short of the mark; the passive tendency to meekly submit what millions already know, and continue to 'hope for the best' has been the main impetus – for all enemies, foreign and domestic – seek ever to push their opponent to the limit, seeking the level by which will prove their advantage.

I, personally, am persuaded that Mr. Buchanan is a refined, cultured, and honorable man; the point here is, that he, truly, is no Nationalist, and his reticence regarding Race, knowing full well the imperative nature of this dynamic for at least the past 40 years, if not longer, and yet not even one time coming out in support of men like David Duke, or Tom Metzger, in support of the [white] nationalist positions held by these men, and this latter having created a stir in the Buchananite camp at the nations border, in California, and was rebuffed by Mr. Buchanan. It would seem that conservatives are ashamed of their racial-nationalist brethren. On the part of the Nationalist, regarding any who treat us this way, we have our own feelings: Disgust.

Yet, there is hope, as a new song has been written, it's harmony and melody becoming all the more audible; the open Sea, awash in powerful tides and currents calling, as in ages past, those children of yesterday, those innocents of today, with the song of Albion.

Chapter III

Man is not by any means of fixed and enduring form (this, in spite of suspicions to the contrary on the part of their wise men, was the ideal of the ancients). He is much more an experiment and a transition. He is nothing else than the narrow and perilous bride between nature and spirit. His innermost destiny drives him on to the spirit and God. His innermost longing draws him back to nature, the mother. Between the two forces his life hangs tremulous and irresolute. What is commonly meant by the word 'man' is never anything more than a transient agreement, a bourgeois compromise. Certain of the more naked instincts are excluded and penalized by this concordat; a degree of human consciousness and culture are won from the beast; and a small modicum of spirit is not only permitted but even encouraged. The man of this concordat, like every other bourgeois ideal, is a compromise, a timed and artlessly sly experiment, with the aim of cheating both the angry primal Mother Nature and the troublesome Father Spirit of their pressing claims, and of living in a temperate zone between the two of them. This is why the average person tolerates what he calls 'personality', but, at the same time, surrenders the personality to the Moloch 'State' and constantly plays off one against the other. For this reason the bourgeois today burns as heretics and hangs as criminals those to whom he erects monuments tomorrow.

Hermann Hesse - Steppenwolf[*]

The Territorial Imperative

Man continues through stages, both physically and mentally.

The Rise of The West continues to manifest itself throughout this evolutionary change and, perforce, shapes its own destiny. The shaping, thereby, being led by those who are drawn, compelled,

---

[*] *Steppenwolf* – Hermann Hesse, Copyright 1963, Random House (The Modern Library).

and necessary for the epoch chosen for them strive, each in their own way, to envision, form, and build what suits their interests, and the interests of their children, in the most desirable, functional, and intelligent ways possible.

In facilitation of this prospect, many realities and spiritual nuances remain fixed.

In the first *prime symbol*, we see Land, a Territory in which the West may, after a fashion, begin afresh; and the *reintroduction* of those elements necessary for a healthy building bloc, a host, virgin in design as well as political organism. This concept, known and accepted by many will, to be sure, be unknown by many more.

The purpose of this chapter will be to acquaint the reader with the knowledge of impending change; change which will aid all who desire it, a change, a *chance* at being free; free to live with those who, like themselves, seek to secure a future for themselves and their children in a world hostile to those elements of growth and inspiration which have led inexorably to what we define as the western culture of our ancient past, including our early american experiment.

Territorial Imperative.

Just *what* is this grandiose sounding term? Moreover, just *why* do you, the reader, need to be acquainted with it? Why, for instance, in a world which is ever frustrating the individual and personal imperatives, which demands ever and anon the compulsion to ever smaller and meaner minds, greater national and personal debt, the continuing and bleaker race relations which is seen daily in personal and political life, the rampant violations of the liberties of man by erstwhile 'democratic' leaders, and the replacement of long-standing Traditions by those of Western stock, with traditions, formulae and practices which assault our very *inner spirit* and personal inclinations, should anyone bother about a new term, a new and arbitrary addition to our complex and, seemingly, confused state of reasoning?

To answer this, we can begin by reacquainting the People of the West with the most common thread known to man: *Life*.

All Life requires *space* to live; this is axiomatic.

As humans, we share the rhythm and vitality of this *gift* called life, and what we choose to do with it is not, strictly speaking, a choice *limited* by intellect; it is, on the other hand, fixed in its performance, a character study which is bound by the *external stimuli* which surrounds a given people. What surrounds us, as it were, is *geography*: The Mountains, Plains, Rivers and each specific undulating movement of the physical landscape itself; the indigenous plant-life, evergreen or deciduous, desert or ocean which, in its own subtle and unique ways, *marks* those living within it, unique from those who live on the plains or mountains. Thus, a People create and live within a grand mosaic of diversity, encompassing the People *entire*. The colour and beauty brought to bear upon people's by their locations is manifest the world over. Race-culture, as a construct is genetic, bent through the prism of location – through its Territory. The West is no different, nor its People.

In the modern history of the West we have, most of us, grown up in a more or less homogeneous environment; the political mechanisms having been *derived* and propounded by the *decendents* of the original stock which had conceived, fought, and unified these concepts proposed by their own antecedents who, in turn, received these mechanisms from *their* ancestors – all this stemming from a unique European landscape – transplanted and grafted into the burgeoning american experiment. All this, seen through the prism of *location*.

In America, our territory was *unlimited*.

It has often given me pleasure to observe that independent America was not composed of detached and distant territories, but that one connected, fertile, wide spreading country was the portion of our western sons of liberty. Providence has in a particular manner blessed it with a variety of soils and productions, and watered it with innumerable streams, for the delight and accommodation of its inhabitants. A succession of navigable waters forms a kind of chain round its borders, as if to bind it together; while the most noble rivers in the world, running at convenient distances, present them with highways for the easy communication of friendly aids, and the mutual transportation and exchange of their various commodities.

With equal pleasure I have as often taken notice that Providence has been pleased to give this one connected country to one united people - *a people descended from the same ancestors, speaking the same language, professing the same religion, attached to the same principles of government, very similar in their manners and customs, and who, by their joint counsels, arms, and efforts, fighting side by side throughout a long and bloody war, have nobly established general liberty and independence.*[11] (emph. added)

John Jay, the man who penned these words chose to present *location* first, then the People. This is only common sense.

Territory, the *land* made usable by Man was a *gift* of Providence. It has also *bred* and *developed* a People who, for the last 300 years, have remained relatively free, produced some the of earths most profound discoveries and innovations by *individual genius* which the children of the West may be proud of without fear or favor. All this, to be sure, was not handed to this people; certain it is that many a man or woman faced tremendous natural odds, faced severe inclemental environs, lacked 'traditional' education, and faced starvation and brutal city conditions to, nevertheless, overcome all this and more, and proceed to continue to develop untold legacies for their children.

The 'states' of their European antecedents were small compared to this new, virgin territory; the opportunities unlimited without established 'houses' demanding hereditary rights and duties. The children of those continental parents unfettered and determined to mark their own passing with that which destiny had ordained. So, first, the ingredients of location, territory, and environment – the alchemy necessary to produce the cauldron of emerging creation.

---

[11] Federalist Papers – John Jay

The People, themselves, as stated in *Rise of The West*, and reiterated by John Jay above, was one great *connected* People – the new fledgling 'american' race-culture; each (i.e. Territory and Race) must have the other to contribute to the elixir of Life, of that struggle and conquest necessary for a people to grow into their own. Through the War of Independence, to the War Between the States, this struggle has become one of *contest*, rather than conquest. Many powerful influences, not the least of which has been the control of Finance, have been used since that intrepid time of discovery, conquest, and freedom to make, designer-like, a cookie-cutter american who has no *sense* of what it meant, indeed, what it imbues in a man or woman, that feeling of unlimited freedom – of conquest, of the *making* of a thing; of the ability to *conceive* and *achieve*. Until now.

To the second *prime symbol*, then, we have a *People*.

As a distinct *organism* we, men and women of the West, remain a viable, living, breathing group; the various sub-groups only make the beauty and vibrant soul that much more distinct. It is to this colourful and unique specie that the imperative of Territory has called again and again. It calls us even now.

i.

The Ethno-State[*]

The Ethnic State, as comprised in this work, will be specific to those members of that far-flung family of man known as Western. Specifically, and regardless that this process is practiced and patterned after aeons of experimentation, warfare, disease, and long-lasting or short-lived attempts at structuring some device or mechanism by which this or that people would remain fixed to a

---

[*] Ethno-State – a term brought to bear by *Wilmot Robertson*, and utilized to denote a *specific* racial characterization, delineated by territory, political apparatus, military and commercial endeavors. This is a broad view, as Nationalism will, most assuredly, play a part, but will be used to introduce a 'thought process' which, sadly, has been slowly eroded from the mental process of many Americans of Western stock. Those that have not forgotten this 'mental process' are becoming fewer and fewer as the generations pass away. The once ancient tribal conceptions of Kin, blood, and soil discarded in favor of failed attempts of some One World vision. FLS

territory, *live* and *die*, extend those values most necessary to the sustenance of that progeny created by their original progenitors, to those of Western Stock who inhabit this Northern Continent – what we call America.

Yes, the America of today, even of *our* time-period now, today, exists only and specifically, as an *ethnic* State – the concept, and its familial, albeit sparsely acknowledged, racial origins, being relegated to obtuse distractions and attacks by politicians, clergy, and academia, nevertheless, cannot eradicate the simple *truism* that we are what we are, because of what went *before*. Traditions, economics, philosophy, Art, science, all these, or at least the remnants, remain fixed in the *values* and *perceptions* we all share according to our specific 'world view' as relates to what we see as America. The Modern, as always, seeks another path, for *his* value is not that of the West; his 'will to power' of another source. And so it is, as we delve into the affairs of state, of ethnicity, of imperatives and personal/tribal *will to power* we also, of necessity, delve into the spiritual and mind altering perceptions of 'self', and the manifestations of self multiplied a hundred-million fold. This, the *idea* of Nation.

The idea of Nation is a construct both felt and understood; the articulation of these manifest thoughts and ideas are held closely by relatively few persons who have seen 'beyond' the rest, beyond the mundane and superficial to the heights unencumbered by small and petty needs or wants. The mass, not as *race-culture*, but as *mob*, is incapable of this type of studious contemplation; if they were, the crass mediocrity we see today would not have become the festering sore, that cancerous disease which has taken the dreams of our Fathers and Mothers of yesteryear and spit on their very reason and existence. No, the mass ever seeks the lower path, the easier road – the road paved with *good intentions* – to Hell. The ethnic-state, that imperative of territory, spirit, and consolidation as a unique and beautiful entity, must be formed and presented in a more understandable and definitive way for the 'majority' of Western stock to participate and understand its evolution and future undertakings.

On this same principle, seeing that all our philosophies and moralities have been traditionally directed at a *mass* and at a *mob*, we find that their elevation must, of necessity, be decided by the broadest account of our people, the common man or woman. In today's world, *mediocrity* has brought about a *baseness* in individuals, a smaller and meaner perception of Life in general. Hence, all passions are banned, because *base* men do not know how to enlist the common man into their service; even if this service were to a higher calling. Men who are masters of themselves and of others, men who understand the management and *privilege* of passion, become the most despised of creatures in such systems of thought, because they are *confounded* and *confused* with the vicious and licentious common cause of the mob; the speed of mankind's awareness and spiritual elevation then, gets to be determined by humanity's slowest vessels. The Modern is such a 'ship of state'.

This analysis of the world's collective values and, more importantly, to the *new* value of the rising West, their ascription to a certain "will to power" may now seem to many, both skilled and unskilled, erudite or common, as but an *exhaustive* attempt at a new system of nomenclature, and little else. In fact, it is very much more than this. By means of this nomenclature, this new perception of values and its necessary and incumbent will to power, is designed to show mankind, and specifically those of Western stock, how much has lain, and how much still lies, in man s *sense* of power. In short, that he *has* Power, in and of himself, without asking for permission. By laying one's pronouncement on everything and declaring to Western man that it was *human* will that created it, so also, do we wish to give man the *courage* of this *will*, and a clean conscience in exercising it. For it was precisely this very will to power which has been most hated and most maligned by the Modern and those who serve him.

The Ethnic State then, is a specific *value*, a perception, which marks each culture and race with its distinct mark; it is a natural outcome of specie and specie survival.

The Beginning of Ethnic Evolution...

Identity

The great *epilogues* of all great cultural attempts are followed closely by confusion, fear, uncertainty, and hope in a better tomorrow. This experience is not limited to persons of the West, and may be charted with certainty by historians and demographers alike. The majority of this continuing discussion will center on America, and her Western people; not its historicity of *mechanism*, this is only the superficial 'history' of its past. What we are to discuss is the Future. The future of a people tossed in a tempest of changing mores, political agendas and wayward spiritual values; a course charted by 'circumstance' and the loss of *memory* – the loss of *Identity*.

While the mass has, indeed, lost their way, seemingly *careless* of breed, of distinction and worth, of integrity and honour, of courage and direction; there remains, as always, a small few who have studiously worked to inform, direct, and empower their fellows. There have been many, but this work will cover only certain of them; let the reader know that many have sacrificed their fortunes, lives and peace of mind, and have committed to never rest until their kinsmen, those men and women related by blood, are secure in a future which will be their *own*, owing none for the right excepting, perhaps, those few who remained fixed on this goal, working tirelessly for them all.

ii.

In the early eighties, a transformation started to congeal, brought about, in part, by the divisive and tumultuous change in America, by *racial* and *spiritual* conflicts. The West, as a race-culture, also was affected throughout the world. In response to this world-view, this 'new order' of things, individuals and groups who had maintained a wall, a defensive wall, against this changing view, congealed as well, their disparate theologies, political aspirations, and particular mechanisms which sought essentially the same thing: a *new* homeland for their People, men and women of the

West, a *place* which would house, maintain, and sustain those members of the West who, for many reasons, sought shelter from the forces who were, ineluctably, *depriving* them of their past, their *right* to be who their parents were; in short, killing the very *kernel* of spiritual identity which made them unique, viable, and beautifully *distinct* organism.

Although unknown by the majority of white americans, men like *Richard Girnt Butler*, *Robert E. Miles*, and certain Christian sects of the day fostered an unfettered imperative of independence for the race-culture of the West – theirs was *spiritual* in nature, although both men utilized, and were aware of the necessity of physical participation in efforts to secure this spirituality – and were often allied with others inclined to the more utilitarian nature of politics and its assorted mechanisms, and levels of achievement. The overriding imperatives of both the spiritual and secular devotees were the *actualization* and *implementation* of a physical territory, a *ethnically* racial State, by which to promote the values inherent to the sons and daughters of the West. This concept was, and is, one of secession; the existing governmental technics, owned and operated by the Modern, had ceased to be of, and for, the people of the West, as seen by millions, articulated by those mentioned above, as well as many others.

The term 'white nationalist' was created about this time, at least it was made manifest for the first time, articulated by many a fledgling fighter for the dream of a unification of purpose. The political climate was rife with dissension, disillusionment. At the same time in which White Nationalists were working for their goals, the *Nation of Islam* (NOI) and *The American Indian* (AIM) movement were in parallel agreement, if not tacitly feeding off each other. The overriding agreement between all these disparate groups was one of fundamental race-cultural need: Identity.

The american public, unaware for the most part, of this transcendendent philosophy of Race, blithely went about their business of working for wages, bent over long and unhealthy work conditions in factories, laboring in the construction fields, fending off, as each saw it, other races vying for a limited amount of convenient local employment, and being deprived of new technological fields because of the departure of those selfsame corporate structures to overseas commercial compromise – and this, being most necessary, for the long-term articulation of infrastructure, dependent on generational work *ethics*.

In the case of White Nationalists, the concept of the 'Rocky Mountain Republic', as envisioned by Robert Miles, or the 'Aryan Nations' as envisioned in a distinctly quasi religious/political identity by Richard G. Butler, was not unique at the time. It was, however, articulated in a uniquely Western sentiment, using the framework of freedom, freedom to *associate* with members of the Western race-culture as was the wont of our ancestors; yet, the American Indian Movement (AIM) and the Nation of Islam (NOI) and, to a lesser degree at the time, the mestizo movement of the Nation of Aztlan were simultaneously working for their own version of a 'territorial imperative' for their own unique imperatives. The aspirations of each, however, were to take on differing manifestations. The voices of the 'free', it seems, were to command differing levels of political *acceptance*. The concept, however, of a 'homeland', a 'territory', and 'political independence' were to morph into varying degrees of vitality and political evolution.

The concept, if not the construct, of a *homeland* was taken to heart by many. Today, in our present political apparatus, the idea of secession and realignment are spoken of from the far corners of the 'american' experiment; from individuals and States, to the common man and woman – the idea of separation has been *modified*, but it has taken more and more of the magic of 'actualization' than was witnessed in the early years of an embryonic separatist movement. The early members and leaders of this separation, as is always the case, were to fight for their lives, and the vision, which made them what they were: *visionaries*.

Like all visionaries, present within their souls, their spirit, was a *fire*, a burning desire and hope that, for them and their children, indeed, all who were, by extension, *part* of them, nurtured and maintained by that same *blood and bone* which tied all together for a common future; a People who shared the same *fate* and *destiny*. It was, seemingly, an easy direction, for individuals of this vision felt this was necessary, an instinctual *duty* which asked no permission nor offered apologies for this dream.

The Modern, however, ever ready to deprive individuals of their deeper essence, the threat to their power and control too abrupt, severe, and long-lasting, to be allowed to continue would do what was necessary to preserve their status quo. Thus, it became a matter of will-to-power between these opposing elements. Religion, utilized by all and sundry who would promote an interest, as seen by each and every distinct group or body, was also utilized by the fledgling White Nationalist separatist movement; the 'theology' of Race, as inspired many years before by such [american] men as, Dr. Wesley Swift, Bertrand Comparet, Richard Butler, Robert Miles, even Herbert W. Armstrong (e.g. Anglo-Israelism) and others, made up the 'eschatology' of the evolving separatist movement.

In the early Eighties, several events were to propel this fledgling movement into the national spotlight. It is not possible to cover all these points of contact with these individuals and their impact, that is for another time; two names, however, stand out: Gordon Kahl and Robert J. Mathews. Each of these individuals were, for all intents and purposes, the first-blood, the first *martyrs*, to this ideal of separation and freedom, of Independence.

In Gordon Kahl's case, he was a member of a constitutionally bound activity, the *Posse Comitatus*[12], or 'Power of the County',

---

[12]THE POSSE COMITATUS ACT: A PRINCIPLE IN NEED OF RENEWAL, Washington University Law Quarterly, Vol. 75, 1997. Cite As 75 Wash. U. L.Q. 953 I. INTRODUCTION: In response to the military presence in the Southern States during the Reconstruction Era, Congress passed the Posse Comitatus Act [1] ("PCA" or the "Act") to prohibit the use of the Army in civilian law enforcement. The Act embodies the traditional American principle of separating civilian and military authority and currently forbids the use of the Army and Air Force to enforce civilian laws. In the last fifteen years, Congress has deliberately eroded this principle by involving the military in drug interdiction at our borders. This erosion will continue unless Congress renews the PCA's principle to preserve the necessary and traditional separation of civilian and military authority.

The growing haste and ease with which the military is considered a panacea for domestic problems will quickly undermine the PCA if it remains unchecked. Minor exceptions to the PCA can quickly expand to become major exceptions. For example in 1981, Congress created an exception to the PCA to allow military involvement in drug interdiction at our borders.

Then in 1989, Congress designated the Department of Defense as the "single lead agency" in drug interdiction efforts.

which were seen by many, both for and against, as the 'ground level' constitutional power of any community made up of citizens of this country, and empowered to keep the 'peace', protect each other during inclemental emergencies, and any *other*[13] threat to the commonwealth, no matter the quarter; men were subordinate to the 'sheriff' of a particular county, and were expected to serve in that local 'posse' should the need ever arise. Gordon Kahl, as well, was a Tax Resister and Christian adherent, both of which, Mr. Kahl believed in deeply.

In the footsteps of his own, unique destiny, Gordon Wendel Kahl would die a fiery death at the hands of government, a government which Gordon Kahl had served with distinction during the last 'great war'. Upon returning, as were many men in his position, he was somewhat dissolutioned by what he saw upon his return to his native homeland. The rousing suspicion that what he had 'fought' for, what he was willing to 'die' for, was changed in no uncertain terms. His resentment began to grow, as would any man who knew of betrayal, and cowardice. As a Christian, not of today's milk toast and puffy variety, Gordon was a *true* believer, and also maintained his sense of blood and bone, recognizing that he was a member of the West, a white European who, as was his right, demanded to be treated as a Free man; and he would not pay taxes to those who would deny him, his family, and his countrymen the right to live and associate with those he chose, rather than those he was *forced* to accept. Gordon Kahl was killed in a massive assault on the Ginter farmhouse in Lawrence County, Arkansas, on June 4,

---

The PCA criminalizes, effectively prohibiting, the use of the Army or the Air Force as a posse comitatus [11] to execute the laws of the United States. It reads:

"Whoever, except in cases and under circumstances expressly authorized by the Constitution or Act of Congress, willfully uses any part of the Army or Air Force as a posse comitatus or otherwise to execute the laws shall be fined under this title or imprisoned not more than two years, or both."

Though a criminal law, the PCA has a more important role as a statement of policy that embodies "the traditional Anglo-American principle of separation of military and civilian spheres of authority, one of the fundamental precepts of our form of government."

[13] *U.S. Constitution*: Amendment X - *Powers of the States and People*. Ratified 12/15/1791 - The powers not delegated to the United States by the Constitution, nor prohibited by it to the States, are reserved to the States respectively, or to the people.

1983. [14]

In this same year, was also an occurrence, and the interdiction of a singular man, and the events which were to compel the fledgling White Nationalist movement into a chain of events which were, to this present day, to reshape the dynamics, purpose, and long-term tactics utilized to finalize the concept of a Territorial Imperative; this man, was *Robert J. Mathews*:

Robert Mathews, was born in Marfa, Texas, 16 January 1953, the last of three boys born to Johnny and Una Mathews. His father, of Scottish descent, was mayor of the town and president of the Chamber of Commerce, and a businessman and leader in the local Methodist church. His mother was the town's den mother.

His family moved to Phoenix, Arizona when he was five years old. An average student in grade school, he was interested in history and politics. At age eleven, he joined the John Birch Society. While still in high school, he was baptized into the Mormon faith.

He formed the *Sons of Liberty*, an anti-communist militia whose members were primarily Mormons and survivalists. At its peak, it had approximately thirty members. After filling out his employer's W-4 Form claiming ten dependents (reportedly as an act of tax resistance), he was arrested for tax fraud, tried and placed on probation for six months. After a falling out between the Mormon and non-Mormon members, the Sons of Liberty became moribund and Mathews withdrew from the association he had created.

After probation ended in 1974, he decided to relocate to Metaline Falls, Washington. Mathews and his father purchased 60 wooded acres, which became their new home.

Two years later, Mathews married *Debbie McGarrity*. He began to raise Scottish Galloway cattle in part, to *extend* his Scottish heritage. Soon after, 'bob and debbie' adopted a son, Clint, in 1981. In time, Robert Mathews was also to Father a daughter, and a son[15], whom the federal government

---

[14] See Appendices for full draft of Mr. Kahl's Open Letter.

[15] Not known but by close associates, is the fact that Robert 'bobby' Mathews did, in fact, sire a son, albeit by artificial insemination. Robert J. Mathews located, through a Service, a 'mate' which met his criteria for a healthy offspring, paid his fee, and the deal was struck. It is known, that prior to his death, government agents, upon learning of this development, made themselves known to the chosen 'mother', convincing her that, in the best 'interests' of all concerned, it would be wiser, and 'safer' for her, to abort the child. This healthy,

murdered.

The years past with his wife, Debbie, and son, Clint, the national political scene continued to change; Bob (as he was called by his friends) saw the change as harmful to his way of life, the life of his family but, more importantly, he drew a large net over what he considered his *true* 'family', that is, his *racial* family. Bob worked in the local Mine and, by all accounts, was a studious, energetic, and loyal employee. The days continued to pass, and by this time was a irregular attendant of Richard Butler's Aryan Nations/Church of Jesus Christ Christian, its political arm, The Aryan Nations (AN) was devoutly dedicated to the interests and extension of the white European Peoples of the United States, and all colonies established by them – this being the national States, or *ethno-states* which, for the most part, were founded and peopled by that larger European commonwealth of persons known as the West (hence, the 'aryan-nations').

Bob's loyalty had always been to those who, like himself, emanated from the same source, had the same upbringing, for the most part, and saw liberty and freedom in the same american point of view; yes, like *Xenophon*, that champion of the Greeks, Bob saw the danger of disparate races and race-cultures having at once seen the possibilities of political power, demanding more and more, were bound to *escalate* their demands, and invoke the 'democratic' process for 'equality' and the largess they felt which was theirs by right of citizenship.

At first, Bob did not readily see the *totality* of his feelings as being part of a *system* of Natural Law – but Bob was a voracious reader, and one work, in particular, affected him deeply. *Which Way Western Man?*[16] a tome, assembled together over a 60 year period of Living. *William Galey Simpson*, the author of this work, succinctly had put the issues facing the men and women of the

---

beautiful Western woman, her background and personal psychology unknown to this author, did what was common to her generation: the Abortion happened without delay in the spring of 1985. FLS

[16] Simpson, William Galey – *Which Way Western Man?* – Yeoman Press, National Alliance, 1978.

West that, heretofore, had not been so eloquent, poetic, and so deeply spiritual, and coming from a man who had participated in the great american dream; he helped to *found* the ACLU, worked in the Ford factory, was a Franciscan priest, and a deep, and forthright thinker in the ways of the West; he was a *philosopher* in the ancient sense, and loved his People as he saw them. The facts and information in this tome are wide and broad, taken from the great minds of the past, and utilized the present leading minds [of his time] in the various fields of Science, Art, racial biology, eugenics, and the racial politics of the day. Yes, Bob was impressed, as are all who have been exposed to this man's mind; it was essentially the motive force behind everything which had come before in Bob's upbringing – the fire of his passion became a furnace.

A thought which had struck Bob many years before, had blossomed along with the exposure to the thoughts and ideas of Robert Miles and Richard Butler who, independently and together, promoted the concept of a White Homeland for those Americans who felt that the present system had deserted or betrayed the *original*[17] intent and inception of the american Republic. Bob's answer: *The White American Bastion.*

This was, in its purest and simplest terms, a 'territorial imperative' which Bob Mathews saw, nestled in the greenery of the American Northwest, was perfect to offer a safe haven to the millions of disenfranchised fellow americans with whom he now felt a growing sense of familiarity, kinship, and destiny directed by those oft times fickle and determined Fates; the great Wyrds of the ancient continent. I, personally, do not feel that Bob knew the width and breadth of this desire on the part of his, our, Folk; but he felt as do these persons, separated by distance, religion, and political accords, the same calling for harmony, peace, and *community*. The same dream which had led our ancestors over the seas to establish this republic, to embrace this Manifest Destiny which ever called this People, and ever drove it onwards and upwards, if left to its own devices, was the same gut-felt feelings

---

[17] See the Preamble to the Constitution: "We the People of the United States, in Order to form a more perfect Union, establish Justice, insure domestic Tranquility, provide for the common defense, promote the general Welfare, and secure the Blessings of Liberty to *ourselves and our Posterity*, do ordain and establish this Constitution for the United States of America." U.S. Constitution. [Italics added] FLS

which stirred within Bob's soul.

Bob set out to enhance his property in Metaline Falls, and continued to see his herd of Galloway cattle increase; he built a small 'out building' which would house workers, friends, or those wishing to move from the city, into the naked forest of this pristine northwest. It all became a *living* thing to Bob, and it nurtured his soul; he saw, on a daily basis, the embryonic growth of his own family, the living breathing land which he possessed, and benefiting thereby, wished to share all he had striven so diligently for with his fellows.

Bob was a quiet man, but he met, in the course of events, his hunger for knowledge and truth being fed accordingly by personal contacts and burgeoning friendships; several men who stood out from the rest were Gary Lee Yarbrough, Bruce Carrol Pierce, Randy Evans, Randy Duey, Richard Kemp, David Lane, Richard Scutari, Andrew Barnhill, and David Tate; this author, with time, would meet and be befriended by this man as well; setting off a lifelong relationship with this devout, simple, and honest man which was shared by all the above, and more. Truly those who knew and loved this man will never forget him; those that became, or were by circumstance his enemies, those of his own stock would, as well, remember him always. To those who ultimately murdered this man, a curse, and a lifelong antipathy remains.

The dream of a homeland continued to burn within this man and, with time, he formed a unified group of stout and diverse men into a cadre, a Brotherhood of common ideals and intentions for the best interests of those included in the racial family of Western peoples, dedicated to the *realization* and *promise* to, as David Lane was to immortalized years later: We must secure the existence of our People and a Future for white children. This, the Fourteen Words, canonized upon this man's death within the confines of the american gulag; a dedicated prophet, poet, and visionary of all White Nationalists the world over. His friendship remains, even now, with all that knew him.

Such is the width and breadth of fellows of such temperament, dedication, loyalty and devotion to a cause greater than themselves – lovers, not haters, as their enemies imagine, propound and are ever seeking to belittle such great men of passion and even greater vision because they, as individuals and groups, lack *every* basic emotion and character trait as those listed above; the ever smaller and meaner; the ever jealous and intellectually dwarfed – the ever led, rather than the leader. These, the *minions* of the Modern and his demand for adherence to his view of the world, a world devoid of [racial] commonality, of tribe, of blood. His spectacle, that of Babel; his minions, those who, for lucre's sake, would betray themselves, as well as those greater than themselves; and not once asking why...just to do or die – a fitting motto for the unthinking, un-heroic agents of destruction and jealously.

The Dream of a homeland, however, does not stand or fall with one man, or ten; it stands or falls with the desire, sense of sacrifice, and need inherent in its adherents. If the future of a people's *children* is not the prime cause of a people then, surely, this people is dead already; nature will not shed a tear; and those who have fought for them already have shed too many tears for them to shed any more. Now, as always, those who would be free *must* fight for it of their own accord. This, the eternal cycle of *young* and *old*.

The Territorial Imperative is for the young; it is the Future in which this *idea* will be manifest. As this idea becomes reality, with time, a once and Future People will emerge. This, is that to which the Rise of The West will become. To this end, have many given freely of their Lives, their Fortunes, and their sacred Honour.

Sacrifice, if given freely, and without reservation will, in the end, continue to grow in the hearts of others, and will see its fruition manifested in another experiment, another chance at harmony, peace, and nationhood. To this end, we do swear.

iii.

The *nature* of this idea, that which commands its adherents to mobilize, sacrifice their lives, and continue come what may, defines itself by the very natural elements which surround us; all *must* declare a home, a spot in which to grow up, grow old, and be given to the *earth*, comforted by the fact that what was given to them in life would, ultimately, be given, also, to their children, and their children's children, *unbroken* and *continuous*. This, the wish of all peoples. Western man and woman are no different.

With the somewhat sparse and indirect mention of individuals who, unlike many today, actually *fought* a war, undeclared, yet *actively* pursued by those in established power, the instruments of the Modern, nevertheless were not alone; the zealous and intimate feelings felt by all who call themselves Nationalists are strong, especially today. In the coming elections, one sees over the horizon the blood-red rosy-cheeked sunrise of change; the ministers of propaganda are minion. We have, as well, the first non-Western political figure who, put in front of the non-western elements see, for the first time, a messiah, a leader worthy of their support; his opponent, declares himself ready, a veteran of foreign wars, from a family of long-standing military service; as members of the USS Liberty will attest. Members of the West, however, unused to the 'tribe' mentality, having been conditioned to refrain from this underhanded feeling of worth, this trough of guilt, so ineluctably a part of their common pursuits – that of money, comfort, and decadence, that many of them, in fact, the majority, remain captivated by the simplicity of it all: they are *patriotic*. Not Patriots of yesteryear, but patriots of the *lazy*, the *ignorant*, and the *naïve*'.

The non-western, it seems, has a more *vibrant* and *healthy* vision of their tomorrow.

As the rise of the west anticipates, the question of racial politics surfaces into the discussion of the future of 'man', and all its social constructs and important legacies for the future of all men, everywhere.

As before, this study will not delve into the overly numerous and professional studies – the baggage of too many statistics, however well it is presented, serves only to *overly* intellectualize the discussion at hand; each side of this discussion can 'prove' some point, some position which, ultimately, rests upon the converted. This belongs to the age-old 'nature vs. nurture' crowd. Each crowd, I might add, has developed the most succinct and elaborate expositions to prove their doctrine; some would say, as they did fifty years ago, with the same effect – the intellectual masturbation continues unabated, and the people, especially those of the West, suffer the greatest.

In passing, however, let us look to one who has proved his scientific analysis, and erudite disciplines of the Western branch of 'scientific discovery through experimentation'. *J. Philippe Rushton*, Department of Psychology, University of Western Ontario, London, Ontario, Canada is seen by many to be of outstanding character and impeccable professional standing; he does, as well, have his detractors.

In his study on 'genetic similarity' he states:

> Of all the decisions people make that affect their environment, choosing friends and spouses are among the most important. Genetic Similarity Theory was first applied to assortative mating, which kin-selection theory sensu stricto does not readily explain since individuals seldom mate with 'kin'. Yet, the evidence for assortative mating is pervasive in other animals as well as in humans. For humans, both spouses and best friends are most similar on socio-demographic variables such as age, ethnicity and educational level (r 50.60), next most on opinions and attitudes (r 50.50), then on cognitive ability (r 50.40), and least, but still significantly, on personality (r 50.20) and physical traits (r 50.20).

And more:

> Several studies have shown that people prefer genetic similarity in social partners, and assort on the more heritable components of traits, rather than on the most intuitively obvious ones, just as Hamilton (1971) predicted they would if genetic mechanisms were involved. This occurs because more heritable components better reflect the underlying genotype. These studies have used homogeneous sets of anthropometric, cognitive, personality and attitudinal traits measured within the same ethnic group. Examples of varying heritabilities are: for physical attributes, eighty per cent for middle-finger length vs. fifty per cent for upper-arm circumference; for intelligence, eighty per cent for the general factor vs. less than fifty per cent for specific abilities; for personality items, seventy-six per cent for 'enjoying meeting people' vs. twenty per cent for 'enjoying being unattached'; and for social attitudes, fifty-one per cent for

agreement with the 'death penalty' vs. twenty-five per cent for agreement with 'Bible truth'.[18]

We will return to this material at a latter time.

In the meantime, the relationship between 'likes' continues to make itself apparent excepting, perhaps, the dullest, the most inured with social conditioned and religious discontent and maligned orthodoxy of the present mass-religious sheep who, unlike their forebears, have attained true bliss, the bliss of the led, of the unquestioning herd. This, specifically, is the lot of the modern western man and woman. The non-Western is under no similar illusion and, like the impending Presidential election, see nothing but what is valuable to them, and their interests; the above quoted remarks are, in any event, present in social constructs which are non-western, as well as our own constructs. The power, then is, once again, with those who *understand* tribe, community of interests, in short, what a 'imperative' really means, Once this dynamic sinks in, *territory* will follow. Territory, in this case, the known boundaries of the United States of America.

This relationship, that of democratic and demographic shifts, have been encouraged by apathy, and the misdirected intentions of the classic symptomatic characteristics of altruism for ones own kind, transferred, to others dissimilar to themselves, to the absolute dissolution of the one, and the empowerment of the aggregate of the others.

In 1964, evolutionary biologist William Hamilton finally provided a generally accepted solution to the problem of altruism based on the concept of inclusive fitness, not just individual fitness. It is the genes that survive and are passed on. Some of the individual's most distinctive genes will be found in siblings, nephews, cousins and grandchildren as well as in offspring. Siblings share fifty per cent, nephews and nieces twenty-five per cent, and cousins about twelve and a half per cent of their distinctive genes. So when an altruist sacrifices its life for its kin, it

---

[18] Nations and Nationalism 11 (4), 2005, 489–507. r ASEN 2005, pgs. 7-8.

ensures the survival of these common genes. The vehicle has been sacrificed to preserve copies of its precious cargo. From an evolutionary point of view, an individual organism is only a vehicle, part of an elaborate device, which ensures the survival and reproduction of genes with the least possible biochemical alteration.[19]

Self-evident to some.

To those others, whether well intended or not, it becomes a matter of distinction and position; of power and status. The common man or woman knows this instinctively; but who listens to them?

This altruism, however, is under greater and greater strain.

Members of the West are receiving smaller and smaller portions of the great pie, the milk from which *Romulus* and *Remus* drank from, so long ago, has dried up; no longer is the nourishment of *community*, political power, of racial *similarity*, present from which to draw that particular *esprit de corps* inherent in homogeneous societies. Moreover, the *denial* of a place to live (and this absolutely means alone, with at least a significant 'majority' of Western stock) has, without a doubt, left the majority of those of Western stock the *weaker* for it. Land, if it must be said a thousand times, is necessary to create that unique sense of identity inherent in any peoples long-term sense of self, and long-term health.

The long-term health and extension of any people must, of necessity, be inextricably bound with ownership, *outright* ownership, of the land in which they inhabit. There can be absolutely no diminishing of this fact. In fact, on its face, the farce of annually paying for the 'privilege' of renting (so-called *ownership*), for long or short durations, *denies* the legacy of true ownership. In fact, all landholders in America, are simple serfs, share-croppers, and simply buttress the *capitalization* of a long-lost freedom, which, for a time, was endemic to the American way. This, however, has changed.

While the fight for true ownership continues, the demand for land, in the ancient sense, that of farming, is being re ignited. Since the

---

[19] Ibid, pg. 5.

eighties, the Western Farmer has lost a significant amount of individual power and usefulness. The background to the Kahl incident was, primarily, over the *loss* of American Farms, and the displacement and disregard of that legacy left to the sons and daughters of the West. In any event, in our present day, the search for a return to the farming/agricultural way of life is steadily growing; there are many movements afoot to bring back this legacy.

Not a day passes that West Virginia doesn't forfeit another 4 acres that once was devoted to the agriculture industry. And it's not a trend unique to the state. A century ago, half of America was rural and 30 percent earned a living off the land. Today, about 2 percent of the country's population is engaged in commercial farming. When World War II ended, getting 100 bushels of corn from 2 acres required 14 work hours. Less than three hours were required by 1987 to get the same amount from just over 1 acre. Six years ago, a farmer could produce those 100 bushels from less than an acre. Mike Teets, the Republican nominee for agriculture commissioner is seeking office with a fresh outlook, one that calls, among other things, for a new initiative to encourage small tracts of land lying fallow for years to be tilled and planted with crops. As an incentive, the Hardy County farmer says the state should guarantee the purchase of cash crops for resale at farmers markets. "A lot of these places are just growing up in multi-flora rose and weeds," he told The Register-Herald last week. "If somebody has, say, 5 acres of land they're not using and the state could contract with them, say to raise potatoes or cabbage or some other produce, and we have significant amount of cold storages over the state, we could contract for that crop and put it in cold storage. " That way, we could keep that produce fresh throughout the year for our farmers markets." If deer are a problem, and many is the farmer and small gardener who can attest to this, Teets says the state could come up with a fencing design to keep the animals from foraging through crops. "We would actually pay them for that produce and then sell it," he says. "It wouldn't be a subsidy. It wouldn't cost the taxpayers anything because that money would come back in when it was sold through the farmers markets."[20]

Yes, the taking back of fallow land, encouraged by the large and overbearing state-run administrations, some say a virtual copy of the Communistic programmes of the revolutionary Communist Party of post Czarist Russia, are being challenged by the small rural farmer, and rural communities which have long-standing relationships, and familial connections with this life-style and the Land which created and molded it. It, in fact, reached a pinnacle of emotions in the same region of the Nation:

> Congressional candidate Jack Davis, in a speech earlier this year, warned that increasing immigration from Mexico could lead to a new civil war between northern states and Mexican-influenced Southern states that may want to secede from the United States. "In the latter part of this century or the next, Mexicans will be a majority in many of the states and could therefore take control of the state government using the democratic process," Davis said in the speech. "They could then secede from the United States, and then we might have another civil war."[21]

The battle for land is, indeed, *eternal*.

The *need* for land is felt by *all* race-cultures; there is *no* exception. A Territorial Imperative is necessary for all organisms to survive; the racial factor, as listed above, only enumerates the imperative nature, and potentially provocative battles, which will be fought over it. This is Natures *eternal* Law.

Yes, this imperative is instinctual. Those millions of Western stock which, over the years, have forgotten this imperative, makes no difference in the life and death struggle of our co-existence with the natural laws in which we must *obey*, or die. The morphing of our own stock, not withstanding, we shall, to be sure, be *replaced*, if we are too weak to demand and fight for it. The impulse, deep within a majority of our people, although articulated by few, needs only the fuel, the confidence, and the desire to accomplish this.

---

[20] [article]"Ag candidate seeks more small farms" – by Mannix Porterfield, Register-Herald (reporter) August 23, 2008.

[21] [article] The Buffalo News – "Davis warns of a new civil war with Southern states", by Jerry Zremski, 08/25/08.

iii.

The region of the Northwest[22], the so-called 'Rocky Mountain Republic' by certain nationalist groups and their respective leaders, whatever it may be called, exists in both a *metaphysical* state, as well as a *driving* physical imperative, a rallying cry, for those who would not only secede from this voluntary union, but rely on their own impetus and drive, to *secure* an existence for the people of the West, and provide for the future of Western white children. This imperative, however, is problematic.[23]

The dissolution of these bonds will, of necessity, provoke reaction by those held within the thrall of the Modern; every organism seeks its own survival. Moreover, the contest of cultures will both

---

[22] This would include, but is not limited too, Oregon, Washington State, Idaho, Montana, the Dakotas, Utah, Minnesota and Arizona. This does not exclude Alaska, which, over the years, has also defied the federal government seeking, as it were, a political ship-of-state, by which the People of Alaska could follow their unique image of themselves, Alaska is in the final analysis, a vast territory and the acceptance of statehood is only the outward manifestations of statehood, and belies the fact that the federal government claims inclusive territorial control of the of this 'territory'. It is a State of our 'united states', but it is so much more. FLS

[23] The denizens of the northwest, including Oregon, Washington, Idaho, Montana, Utah and northern California have, without exception, been turned into something other than a 'white homeland', as they have suffered firstly, from heavy government investment and subsidized immigration from mexico, the pacific rim and, most recently, african sources. Being altruistic by nature, these hard-working and industrious people, originally immigrants from our Western common source, Scandinavia, Germany, and parts of the Mediterranean, had become ripe for the integration of ideas and persons who were, in no other terms, so alien in outlook and physical manifestations that it is more than shocking that the general populous, specifically in the large metropolitan centers, so willingly entered into this failed-experiment. Washington, for instance, had a negligible amount of african decendents, yet were up to the duty of creating a MLK highway, just to prove how 'liberal' they really were. No one likes to mention, however, the increase in brutal crime precipitated by these empowered africans – many of whom had 'escaped' the large cities of the western coast, now also including the many areas of the east.
A cursory review of the local press say, in Seattle, would see an exponential increase in these statistics, since the year 1985, and the federal governments involvement in the dismemberment of the various embryonic 'white' movements. Of course, this was for the best – simply ask the denizens of that city – I'm sure that members of the 'social and cultural institutions' would have an explanation...I wonder what that could be? FLS

seek to claim the highest spot, the right to rule themselves, and others, and will be accepted only through the demonstrable *shift* in demographics to these regions – both in a true democratic process, and on the field of battle. The Modern has, in any event, already seen to it that this region of the country be flooded with non-Western elements, ensuring in their own minds, that this *nascent* nationalism be stifled, murdered within the cradle, before it ever gains a life of its own. This was seen, specifically, soon after the failed attempt by the first *military* arm of the new White Nationalism – The *Bruder Schweigen* – (Silent Brothers) - or Silent Brotherhood of Robert J. Mathews.

Truly Military in scope, this group of men, this band of brothers had, in many cases, the active or passive support of many military officers, both retired and active duty, which saw the need, the *pressing* need, to make a claim to a future which was more cognizant of the 'traditional america' which, in their case, they had *sworn* to uphold; their varying views held that the 'civilian' government had recused themselves from actively protecting and supporting the very institutions and specific people, who founded, built, bled, and died to establish and maintain, Western people, all. The Modern, to pacify the populace, and to inculcate the meaning of 'defeat', 'servitude', and the like, made a grand spectacle of the trials [sic] in which the Modern demanded, and received, the maximum sentences for many of these stalwart men. The public, not fully understanding the implications of these actions, as usual, either held little attention, or with small yet grateful hearts, rejoiced that such 'haters' were to receive their just deserts.

The prosecutors in the above case were varied.

As government agents, firstly, they were sworn to uphold the law. At first, not knowing exactly what this case was about, for who had ever heard of a group of Men who want a 'homeland' for their people? It was surreal. Soon, there were men aplenty. whom had been culled by the Modern. to facilitate the components necessary to extinguish the fire and spirit of a new sort of revolution, a revolution dedicated, not to institutions, but to those ideals which were, even so, held by these selfsame prosecutors; for these emotions, long-suppressed in their own hearts, were both understanding and sympathetic, to a point.

One prosecutor[24], for example, was a hunter, outdoorsman and, by all accounts, was a fighter for truth and justice; it was this man, however, who held the greatest of resentments against these idealistic soldiers, these simple men, loving fathers and brothers all, who he manifestly and vigorously attacked. Another prosecutor was, as well, to head the prosecutorial team against Randy Weaver, a man whose own wife, mother of his own children, and his only Son, were to be murdered by those who shared the same hatred of these men, At that time, this prosecutor faced Gerry Spence, a rogue in his own right, who defended Randy Weaver, and received a victory for himself, and Mr. Weaver. This particular prosecutor however, on the other hand, was to see his health deteriorate rapidly, experiencing guilt, no doubt, as to the part he played in the shooting death of Vicki Weaver.

Gene Wilson[25], the lead AG in the first case, was more reasoned; if

---

[24] At this present time, I cannot ascertain, with certainty, the 'actual' name to fit the face; the two that come to mind are Ron Moen, and Mr. Mueller. I apologize for the lack of veracity in this case, but it has been a long, long time. FLS.
[25] A 1966 graduate of the School of Law, University of South Carolina, he served on active duty as an officer in the Army Judge Advocate General corps, trying court-martial cases in Germany and arguing appeals before the United States Court of Military Corps in Washington, D.C.

He retired from the Army Reserve as a Colonel, having completed his military service as a Military Judge. He is listed in Who's Who in America. It is apparent that this man, in particular, understood the relationship and implications of the intent and implications of a 'war time' atmosphere, as he had adjudicated many cases which involved 'military' nomenclature and structure; this points to the observation by many, that the trial of these burgeoning 'white nationalists' should be served within the confines of a 'military court', as it had been made clear that the 'rules of engagement', as well as the Geneva War conventions had been observed in the field.

In fact, excepting but a few isolated incidents, the active rule of 'combatants' had been respected; only the most base of government employees had broken the first rule: No Women, No children. For whatever it is worth, it is this man's opinion, that Mr. 'gene' Wilson, would fall into the later category if left to his own devices, as he showed restraint in several instances relating to this case excepting, perhaps, not more subtly ruthless; he knew, for instance, the *relative* roles, of each of the defendants (Bruder Schweigen), yet actively pursued, at the behest of a Mr. Kowalski[26] from Washington, D.C. (yes, just like in soviet Russia, the Modern has his own 'commissars' which sit, and judge, how the government agents present their cases) all the defendants under the RICO Statutes, *bypassing* the 'state charges' of the 'Hobbs Act', in lieu of lesser charges being attached to the defendants. This was, perhaps, to serve a two-fold mission: State Prison would have given this band of brothers a more *militant* and 'street savvy' crowd with which to work; and by keeping the charges 'federal', would assure a more *direct* role of government controllers, and their ever-changing 'rule of law'. In fact, by charging some of the individuals , along side of 'public' political leaders, with the charge of 'Sedition', was to also ensure the Modern's attempt, a *pre*-Patriot Act, to *finalize* the perception of the populace as to what, and who, were to be considered 'patriotic' or 'terrorist'. This was to fail, for a time, for the moment of their final *seizure* of public control was not to come for another sixteen years.

Irony, in this case, might not be the right word; but all those who participated in this particular Passion Play were, in varying degrees, to be affected for the rest of their lives. The eternal quest for territory and the right to rule one's own destiny, was to run against itself, its own nemesis, in the 'corporate' persons of the prosecutors – who, if they had been honest with themselves, would have *seen* the tragic future which was in store for their families, their neighbors, and their very People, by stifling the embryonic attempt at racial self-expression, and the whispering voice of

---

when trying to negotiate with myself and, after offering me a ten year sentence (the equivalent of the 'two charges' predicate in RICO), with the condition of 'testifying' being discounted, then proceeded to prosecute me for the full term of 40 years. Who better, in fact, then a 'system' man for his entire adult life, to recognize a 'player' and 'non-player' to succeed in the world of politics'; men of true ideological persuasion, of true belief in traditional american mores was, apparently, above his pay-grade.

He now serves as a ninth-circuit court appellate judge.

[26] Mr. Kowalski would, at a later date, prosecute David Lane in a Colorado courtroom, proving to the world that 'double jeopardy' is alive and well in the 'courts' of America. FLS

survival. They chose the route of cowards and mercenaries; worried more for their careers, than for *their* people for, like all the minions of the Modern, their *selfish* ends predominate.

So it is, with most of the citizens of this northern continent.

The understanding of this *longing*, this dream, is felt by fewer and fewer of the those of Western stock these days, having been taken in by the day-to-day glitz, the catch-words of equality (as if the average person really believes this) and what it means to be considered 'normal', words not coined or fashioned by themselves, but articulated by the herd, by canaille; the Life and Future, of their *own* children, they leave to the 'educators' of the 'state', those servants who care nothing of the nobility of their *own* traditions, the value placed on them by their own parents – given over to those *not* of their blood – sharing neither traditions nor outlook for a propitious future in the vein as those who, before them, had given their very *lives* (a coward then, by any other name, is still a *coward*). At home, these 'sheep' revel in the fact that they are 'free', yet will crumple into meek nay sayers, at the first sign of opposition by 'accepted' civil servants. Free they are – free to run in circles within the confines of their pen. Tragically, as is the custom for cowards, it is not themselves which suffer the most, but the precious gift of life which they bestowed on their offspring; the *life* of these children, then, *dying* on the vine before they have a real chance to *live*.

We must secure an existence for our People and a Future for white children.

These fourteen words, this clarion call, was created many years ago; they have been idealized by many who seek to confront the elements of resistance who consciously seek to deprive them of their identity; but those who follow the Fourteen Words will *demand* to be heard, for they know exactly *who* they are and *why* they fight. In their simplistic implications, these words are vilified continuously by those who ever seek to destroy, those who ever seek to level the mass, as they see it, for *their* own good. This is not happen chance, for it has been used in various forms throughout history; the *antithesis* of organic Life, it discloses, as before, the *jealousy* with which individuals, used to power and control, are not now *willing* to release.

The vision of a 'homeland', not the homeland of diversity, of multi-culturalism, of the eternal egalitarian compromise, but the Homeland of *affinity*, of *relatedness*, of Race becomes, then, a matter of *priorities*.

The millions of persons inhabiting this continent up to about fifty years ago were in agreement – the issues of *patriotism, servitude* (in a nationalistic view – One People, One Nation) and *obligation* were accepted by the majority of persons claiming one thing in common, Race. It was not uncommon to view the *entirety* of our nation as *belonging* to one another; this was taught in our Schools at that time: in our History, our Political Science, and our economics. In short, our social propaganda was *distinct, specific,* and *directed* at the youth of our people; this was only right and proper, and continued the extension of just *who* we were, had *become*, and would *remain*. The discussions, not direct, but broad in scope, allowed for our youth, including this writer, to have a more than adequate understanding of foreign countries, also of the West, and within acceptable boundaries, those of the non-western world as well.

In today's world of overreaching *denial* of Western race-culture, the almost *demonic* zeal with which our young are denied their own history, in favor of the non-western, is more than dismal – it is an *evil* thing, a thing which, by most accounts, has changed the very actualizations of the children of the West, for their *heroes* are not of their stock, their perceptions of beauty, *counterfeits* of the real expression of their future mates, the roles of masculinity and nobility being given to superficial, banal, and sociologically different *types* of men and women. This is more than dangerous, and will, in all likelihood, be discounted by many, but it is always a good thing to prove a postulation: So, I urge you, the reader – no, I *dare* you, to look to your own children, compare them with yourself, and then to your father or grandfather, and see just how far they, and you, have strayed. I dare *you*.

iv.

Let us, then, dig deeper, and broaden our basis for the concepts of Land, and the need to claim our own unique, and lasting *place to live*.

Each race-culture has its own new, unique, and potential possibilities for self-expression, which arise, live their own life, and fall away into distraction and ultimate death, never to return in the original *form* in which they were first created. There is no single painting, no single work in stone, no single formulae encompassing all mathematics, no one science of physics, of metaphysics, but *many*, each in its singular and expressive *essence*, limited in duration and self-contained, just as each specie of plant has its peculiar smell or fruit, its unique and singular *type* of birth and passing. These independent cultures, these sublime life-*essences*, grow with the same superb arbitrary nature as the flowers and organic life, of the wild, un-inhabited veld. They belong, like the plants and the animals, to the living *nature* of the poet, of Goethe; not to the *lineal* nature of Science. I see the *organism* of the West as an ongoing mosaic of *endless* formations and re-formations, of the rising and setting of organic forms. The 'professional' historian, to be sure, sees this process as a sort of 'mythical' metaphysics, adding little to the process of 'reason', one epilogue after another, but counting only duration and numerical certainty helps very little when dealing with *real* life, with *transformation*.

The passing of the 'true' Classical civilization of Greece, to the comprehensive Roman civilization was such a transformation. One being bourne by poetics, and one by science; by a purely mental, arbitrary, and rootless experiment. Like our own Republic, we started out pursuing the 'classical' *reasoning* of our ancestors; later, however, after the great 'civil' War, we slowly passed into the realm theoretics, arbitrary, and devoid of Western roots.

There is no 'mythos', no Saga, no Songs[27] of what we once were; only the ever present *need* to belong to the mechanism, the machine of 'law', and to those ends which law produces – *Institution*. In the classical world, laws were arbitrary too, and based on the pantheon of gods, and their own needs; secular laws, then, being based on the *perception* of 'aspects of the god-heads'. This, of course, a distillation of both the 'greek' race-soul, and the 'roman' cold-fast intellect, and this antithesis describes, precisely, the unique difference between what white nationalists call the *race-culture* and that of *civilization*. It is this difference, this *type*, which is compared with the intellectual and metaphysical man, or Age if you will. This contest is always found at the very *epilogue* of each recurring nexus, or birthing of a new culture, at the expense of 'civilization. Such are the great epochs of Sargon, Menes, Ming, Alexander, and Caesar.

In these late periods of the classical world, just as today, do we also see the new 'faiths' of the 'stoics', and of Socialism, and 'magianism' of foreign Levantine thought, cabbalism, and Moorish imperialism (casting aside the metaphysics of Zarathustra and Eckardt for these alien forms). All these, 'faiths', which are induced into the Western mind, just as it has become a moribund creature, ripe for such transformation into a new type of being. The old, tired *logos*, being torn down, and remolded *into* a 'civilization' different from what had gone before. The *people*, as well, of course, of a new character. The Old, making way for the New.

Why the *zeal*, then, of those of Western stock, who *demand* that this transformation occur at all? After all, is not the wealth, the distinction, the rightness of the past, in all its technics, not enough to hold each to the other? Apparently not. Greater and greater

---

[27] This is doubly important to consider, as many of us remember well, the church gatherings, pot-lucks, youth activities, such as summer camps and the like, which included Music from the Western past, both *secular* and *religious*; the active participation by dozens or hundreds was a great social technic, bonding the 'group' and individual to something greater than themselves. I am not being trite when I say that 'sesame street' does not come close – it certainly imbues its audience with 'group' indoctrination, but this is anti-western in nature – yet is acclaimed by 'white mothers' who, in many cases, are simply too lazy or impoverished of racial identity to seek out others who, like themselves, *want* to impart these beliefs. It is easier, do doubt, to 'go along' with the crowd, than to show courage in the face of mob reaction, than to fight like the men above, those who would deny them this identity. FLS

demands are made upon the 'state', by those who once stood on their own; like their ancestors, those who stood proud on their own territory, each *holding* a part of the organism entire; this was a *shared* duty amongst those who partook of *this* existence, and were proud to emulate those who came before. Not now – now is the time of the great *breaking*, the *forging* of new directives, of new *priorities* and new *expressions* of freedom. Or so we are told.

The Freedom to move, to search the farthest horizon, has always been the higher goal of Western man; it is, as always, the *Faustian* spirit – that which seeks to go *beyond* itself. Rome, for instance, was not necessarily the 'imperial rome' many would have us believe; they settled only conquered territory; they simply protected 'possessions' attained by them. Our 'republic', on the other hand, has become, as represented by our own unique *hubris*, begun that long, tedious, and dysfunctional path, of *true* imperialism – the Nationalist wants none of this reckoning – he only wants enough to consider his needs, and the needs of his own kind. This, in the final analysis, is the Territorial Imperative.

However, there is more.

The *search* for Land is over – for there is none left; with the exception of Alaska (and this only in a relative sense, as we have, in fact, laid *claim* to it) and parts of Canada. The insertion of the existing ideas of a *Pax Americanum*, the broadest of ideals, which would include all of South America is, to only of the few élite, a non-issue; but Land, usable and healthy, remains in abundance in the existing confines of the 'american' dream.

The move into the Northwest region of this continental habitation, or any such 'territory' is still a vigorous idea within the hearts and minds of millions of Western stock. To be sure, there are detractors, even within nationalist circles, but these will yield as the momentum of the Presidential elections of the Year 2008 come into clear relief (no matter *who* is elected); soon, the driving force behind all the intellectual primers abounding on this issue will be pushed to the background in favor of getting on a ship, any ship but the coming 'ship-of-state' – it makes no matter who is elected -

as the decision to *finally*, disenfranchise those sons and daughters of the West, is a *certainty*. Those who care for our People will, when the time comes, take up the mantle hesitantly, but *will* take it up.

A 'territorial imperative' is the only *real* security by which Western peoples, *your* People, may remain free; it is the only Homeland, which, truly, can be your *home* and *land*. The United States, the hearth and home of many sons and daughters of the West, and an *integral* part of the Race Culture, is also traveling through a revival, a renaissance which will surprise many. America is unavoidably being drawn into the same awareness, as is the European commonwealth. How we, as a People and 'political technic' deal with this eventuality is what will determine our future – it is the *presence* of our Tomorrow. As always, any race-cultural revival is purely *cultural*, that is, *spiritual*, almost intangible, and is seen only with the 'eyes that see'. Many have seen the trends; many have experienced the Modern's vision of the future. Those that share this reality are already demanding separatism at once. Those, which advocate complete 'separation' are small, numbering only a few million (many who feel this way, and lack any real *substantive* ability to show this feeling are, nevertheless, manifest; the 'common man' has no real way to share with his fellows in the present climate of political control – dissent *appears* not to exist). However small, one may use these numbers as an *indicator* of a reality, rather than an existing, functioning, reality. In any event, if any so-called 'rainbow' coalition becomes dominant in the future, with or without the aid of the present government, it is a foregone conclusion that opposing Western technics of the same caliber will be manifest.

The Modern cannot *conceive* of any separate nation on this continent, yet he is *coercing*, *intimidating*, and *fomenting* this exact phenomenon in Europe and the Middle East at this very date. He calls it the great coming of 'democracy' in once totalitarian systems, while *he*, at the same time, *practices* the same totalitarian dictatorship here at home. The Modern is a *hypocrite*. His hypocrisy stems from the original idea of *universalism* – of all beings being brothers in the sense of 'community'. His idea, or more rightly, the 'idea' of Montesquieu, was the crystal clear rationalism of separation of powers, a separate but equal *idea* which has been discounted by the Modern in every other sphere of political dialogue in this century, to accommodate a smooth transition into the realm of a *living* world. Like all rationalistic thinkers, however, his reality of life-process is muddied by a *natural* reality. That reality, as always, is the continuing *un-*equality of man.

To some, the future 'ethnic/political' relations are horrifying. To others, it is welcomed as natural, inevitable, and sound practical race-culture politics. To those moderns which are fearful of this trend, they mask themselves with self-righteous condemnation of all those who seek a different path. They point to the 'democratization' of Eastern Europe. But that should not deter us long, if at all, since it is precisely because eastern Europe was breaking apart along racial lines that any change in the political environment was necessitated. The role of *money* was secondary. Race was primary. The once great Soviet Empire, like her mirrored sister, America, has finally realized that ethnic 'groups' (i.e. Biological nations) must determine their own future and political realizations – based on their organic needs and will-to-express. The Modern knew this, does know this, and is precisely why he has kept the West confused; continually fighting himself over who is going to be the *greatest* democracy; who is going to bend over backwards in helping all others but that of his own kind. To those in America, the Modern would have us believe that Europe will be weakened by the apparent separation of its individual collective states – nothing could be further from the truth! In reality, the Western race-culture of 'old' Europe will become stronger than it has ever been. The casting aside of years of forced assimilation has, or will produce, a *nation* of truly epic proportions. The Modern shudders at the thought.

Isolation tends to mark the race-culture with *will, strength, and a will-to-power* that will, with time, create a positive destiny. In this light, must America, also, decide its own destiny. But only if America, truly, remains a higher-culture. If she is not, then the coming isolation from her sister, Europe, will dim her epoch making flame to that of a dead ember.

The Balkanization of the contiguous 'states' within the boundaries of these United States is unacceptable to most, if not all those that carry the flame of the Modern. To all and sundry, the cry is heard: 'to all *one* god', 'to all *one* people', 'to all *one* government'. This is, and has become, the rallying wail of the Modern; this is their *imperative*. They must, their power depends upon it. Yet, the ancient drive to realize, to actualize a particular race-culture with the necessary developments required to succeed in a vast world of competition is the kind of struggle the Modern will, at any cost, keep Western man from attaining. The Modern, however, is wearing thin; he fears the technics of *organism*. The Cosmopolis, that crowning achievement of the Modern, has been split between the *visible* lines of racial demarcation from their very inception, and the visible realities of equality and diversity in the coming Babel of the 21st Century.

In the past, this presented little problem – he [the Modern] controlled his environment – now, however, it is controlled by those 'individual' racial units who, with political power have, *ipso facto*, created a balkanization effect with no thought whatsoever of their future excepting the single imperative of breaking up the political state of the Western. The Modern, of course, supports and aids in its implementation. In the 'cities', they already have *control*. Their very numbers demand this control – *the mob now in control*. Democracy, once again, serves the Modern, yes, and even the Western who created it, and allows his technics to pass from him to the *mob* of the Modern. The Western [man] cannot complain. Nay! He must welcome this passing – it is, after all, the 'people's choice'! Freedom of choice, however, cuts both ways, but not always in those ways predicted. The Nationalist as well, has made *his* choice.

It is now true, unlike any time in our history, that large segments of the Western race-culture of America has realized the loss of political power as a 'race-cultural unit'. Let us be more specific: members of white European stock have not only decreased numerically through abortion, self-denial, and intellectual decisions to 'decrease' family size, and fundamental encouragement of non-European immigration over that of European immigration has, most assuredly, put the 'white race' at an untenable crossroad: his extinction as a 'voting majority' is already here; and extinction of his racial sovereignty follows close behind. Let the Modern say what he will, let him denounce this position until he is blue in the face; the fact remains, that Western man has neither the power to change a thing on the National level, nor the power to claim any sovereignty other than what his 'status' as a de facto citizen of the republic allows him – with rights and privileges granted by those who hold power over him – even by those who neither know his past nor have any inclination or knowledge of how his future must be formed and shaped to guarantee his future. Western man, those white Europeans of America, is facing a future directed by *others*. The Western fecund rate, the ability to create and raise children, is ever decreasing, and now forces one to contemplate the reality of a non-western increase in *real* numbers, which equate into a *real* increase of voting power of the non-western – this simply is the way of nature. The collective 'units' of the various diverse race-cultures *feel* the present presence of their *own* power; the resultant spin-off leads, of necessity, towards separation. So, also the Western. Where will this trend lead us? It is the question of a new century; of a new future – Destiny awaits *in vitro*.

The birthing of a new order, of a new destiny is apparent in all we do and see. It must be addressed now, for if this continent is to be sustained as a Western race-cultural unit, as well as a 'safe haven' for the other existing units, it must be determined to just what *extent* this trend is manifested, indeed, as to just how far along we already are. More importantly, in the long run, is the understanding of what this fulfillment of separation and diverse individual unity will bring to *our* culture and race, that is, the Western Culture and Race.

Broad predictions can be made. Anything other than predictions is highly unlikely. As was stated in the first part of this work, however, we can learn, if we have eyes to see, the lessons of the past for the organization of our future. The great *cause*, the seemingly insignificant apparatus which turned the first gear in the machinery of the race and culture can be identified by the very application of causes – the practical *result*. Its technics are never to be isolated in the context of 'this' or 'that' was the *cause*, but rather in the overall outlook of the entire personality of the particular presence being analyzed. The Future, likewise, may be seen in the light of the past and its *continuous presence in manifesting itself in Industry, Political technics, and its Military endeavors*. The disposition of the past is the manifest spirit of any age – as change evolves slowly, the recognition is, therefore, also slow and, consequently, may take several centuries to be analyzed effectively. Only during the siege of revolution may one ascertain, on a daily basis, the future of this or that particular culture. Therefore, as in this case, generalized predictions may be made in the expectation of a 'high certainty' as to the eventual outcome of this present discussion. The long-range prediction, of course, is symptomatic of a lesser degree of certainty. Deviations always occur – this is the *great cause* – the working prime lever of the machine of change in the period of, say, a hundred years or so which may, or may not, fix any one or numerous predictions to a set course. The trends we speak of now is based solely on those experienced here, in the United States of America, as well as based upon her international conduct. These predictions, as well, are predicated upon a 'liberal' policy of immigration towards non-western elements; any tightening of this policy will slow, but not stop, these predictions. Predictions are *not* prophecies. This is, rather, a safe series of probabilities and possibilities as seen in the present presence. Here, then, listed below, are such predictions as are warranted in this work:[28]

1.   ETHNIC   TENSION   **WILL**   INCREASE   **RATHER THAN** DECREASE:

> This simply recognizes that Whites will begin to show less and less sympathy for **nonwhites**. Their feelings of *charity* and *aid* to these groups will be limited to the altruistic, and philanthropic **principles**. Ethnic factors and values will be ever more prevalent in the political arena; the deadlock realized from this positioning will create ever more conflict, and prolong the process of governmental stagnation. Separatist movements will increase.

2.   AMERICAN FOREIGN POLICY WILL CONTINUE TO DETERIORATE:

> Internal conflict will rise above the level of any party to handle; this will raise the International specter of instability, and indecisive political technics. In the International view, the American political and cultural outlook will be more and more of a 'third-world' manifestation. These manifestations will conclude with the 'international' outlook of military/political imperatives which, at this date, would be 'anti-american' if put into practice. How the American people respond to this remains to be seen; apathy will be consonant with cowardice and

---

[28] These 'predictions' first appeared in Rise of The West, amended, pg. 151-156. FLS

betrayal, and action to deny this [internationalism] will be condemned as betrayal to the principles of the Modern and his minions.

3.   ETHNIC 'MOVEMENTS' WILL CONTINUE TO GROW IN SIZE AND POWER:

The path and direction laid out by 'black power' movements will continue to gain increased dominance in the realm of minority reality. *Hispanics [mestizo] will gain the most impetus from this manifestation of power* by 'asserting' those desires in *maintaining* the same space as their hosts; this *desire*, having some 'historical' validity, will only encourage and promote more separatism.

4.   COMPETING 'MINORITY' GROUPS WILL FIGHT FOR SUPREMACY **IN THE POLITICAL** REALM:

The dissimilar values and attitudes expressed by these minority groups, as well as a predisposed animus toward the Western race-culture will, undoubtedly, cause in direct proportion to the level of conflict an animosity unparalleled in a modern democracy – since, in this environment, all contending parties will be able to have 'their' voices heard. Unification of these 'groups' will, however, find the value of cooperation with each other, against those of Western Stock. The expression of this cooperation will take on more strident and 'defensive' racism [as seen and promoted by these groups] against those of Western stock.

5. AFRO-AMERICAN REACTION TO PERCEIVED
    DILUTION OF POWER BASE BY MESTIZO-
    AMERICANS AND OTHER NON-AFRO ELEMENTS:

In the Future, Afro-Americans will realize their limited
position in relation to Hispanic [mestizo] political acumen,
which, after being in the shadow of European cultural
technics have gained superiority in technical understandings
of Western political innuendo. Problems of just *who* is the
'oldest minority' and, consequently, who will garner the
greatest favors of the Western political leaders – [this is
perceived as being a 'social contract' between the 'whites',
and the blacks for their rather close association between
the Western, as seen by afro-americans]. It is not
coincidental, that 'black' criminal activity has surfaced in
areas, which promote such interactions between Mestizo
and Asians in numbers, neither familiar nor experienced by
African-Americans. This will continue to escalate.

6. WESTERN AMERICAN [white] CULTURE WILL
    SHOW A SURPRISING AMOUNT OF RESISTANCE
    IN VARIOUS FORMS:

Once passive, whites will become combatants in continuing
ethnic violence. Not being politically astute in the areas of
'specialization' areas such as immigration, housing, and the
like, the average white-worker will, inevitably, become
more estranged and enraged by the amounts of money
spent on 'social reform', and 'grants' of housing and other
commodities, as those of Western stock start to feel the
loss of what they had come to expect of their 'way of
life'; while they, the white American, are seemingly doing
without, paying exorbitant taxes, and seeing little in any
real return which affects them, personally, they will soon

react. Whites will soon shed the 'image' of black, or any other 'minority' *as* victim – this will allow his [white] true feelings to come to the surface. Anger and resentment in the 'work-place' will continue to grow at an enormous rate. Frustration will turn to anger – for all parties involved – and one or more groups will elicit various responses including, but not limited too, violence against persons and property; political challenges such as 'education', 'jobs' [i.e. once *granted*, never given up], 'citizenship', and **nationalist** sentiments, on all sides, as to their idea of racial, and political hegemony on a local and national level will continue to increase. The modern Tea Party movement is simply one of many such movements to be seen in the future political scene representing the *rage* of white people.

7. EDUCATIONAL AND CAMPUS HOSTILITIES WILL INCREASE IN DIRECT PROPORTION TO LEVEL OF 'MINORITY' INVOLVEMENT AS COMPARED TO WHITE ENROLLMENT:

Conflict of twenty years ago between black and white used to take on the picture of 'small' rising against the 'big'. Now, it takes on the picture of 'inter-group' against 'inter-group'. The lines of political demarcation are diminished. Racial antagonisms are increased based on perceptions of the level of achievements between 'groups' and 'sub-groups'. Black students, as with other minorities, receive 'preferential treatment', be it real or perceived, and then fail to 'make the grade'. This further disenfranchises whites. The 'right' to address these issues by White Student Unions, papers, and staff will create issues of 'freedom of speech' and the real ability to use the 'forum' of the Campus for their attempts at recognition as a racial unit. The policy of 'selection' in regards to enrollment of 'special' groups will further alienate the white student. He will sense the shift in traditional norms in every field of education. European studies will decrease – those who wish to follow this traditional 'western' path will be termed racist, and insensitive. All this will sow the seeds of racial discord and anger, and see a loss in actual Western alumnae.

8,   WHITE 'Political' RESPONSE TO **GROWING COALITION** OF NON-WHITE POLITICAL BASE:

The political *outcome*, of minority political power, will be predicated upon *which* group holds the coalition together, and what 'alliances' are made, and with which 'sub-group'. In response to this, will be the emergence of a new Nationalist/Racialist Party – or some racially conscious PAC embolden by a central figure – either an individual or an [existing] institution which has a more radical approach to the issues of the day. *This will be a racial alliance first and foremost.*

Religionists will be drawn to one another, or be forced to split that party or institution, which is now representing them. Hispanic 'Catholicism' may prove to be a decisive factor amongst Irish, Italians, or others traditionally of the catholic experience. The 'Poles' as well, would be drawn to their co-religionists – but the racial distinctiveness between themselves and other non-Western stock will force any realignment necessary. The Irish, and Italians will be valuable assets in any coalition; should the Irish prove to be inclined, as have their fathers, then whichever they decide, their religion will be first and foremost, as their sense of 'race' has been contravened by their religious history, to follow their deity. Italians will, as is their nature, follow their passions, wherever this takes them, but are inclined to follow their sense of 'western imperialism' and will be split here in America as to how, properly, to address this issue. All in all, those of the West will, ultimately, choose to participate in a 'working' relationship with each other, no matter the small dissenting minority 'within' Western culture, and support the growing sense of Western *identity*.

Continuing 'legislative' dominance by minority pressure groups will force the growth of this 'white coalition' and will receive the support of the military over those 'interest' groups, which have facilitated the breakdown and massive social experimentation of the armed forces. This would be needed, of course, to qualify the largest amount of 'public' perception as to the legitimacy of political change. The trappings of military 'order' will draw the white-mass for good or ill. The extent to which the military and civilian forces, both political and personal, will accommodate one another will be gauged by both the 'internal' and 'external' stimulus exerted on either one individually, or collectively. A militarization of the populace will occur spontaneously regardless, as a matter of course.

9.   BIOLOGICAL 'Affirmative Action' WILL FORCE POLITICAL CHANGE:

The continuing understanding of just 'who' one is will, in ever increasing amounts, force a realignment of historical realities: for White, Black, Asian, and Mestizo. This understanding, of one's root and stock, will cause continued imbalance in the day to day working relationship of any one or all-existing racial groups. Of course, this 'type' of polarization is natural and must be fostered by each individual 'type' – assimilation by the weaker group, or group that refuses to acknowledge his past will occur, inevitably. The Western race-culture will be the most powerful since, as has been shown before, he is capable of solidifying his power base more quickly when threatened from the outside. His past is marked by more marital conflict, and his diplomacy is usually relegated to violence of the most extreme nature. The expression of 'racial' memory will take on greater and larger meanings as time goes on.

10.   WHITE 'Ethnic' REVIVAL:

As Western whites, increasingly, see themselves as a *distinct ethnic group,* threatened by invading cultural aliens, coupled with the submergence of their own racial stock to that of other diverse groups, *their* particular 'reactions' will imitate, in large degree, that of *traditional* 'ethnic groups'. They will *react* violently to racial slurs, job discrimination, inter-racial couplings, and will therefore assume a more demonstrable kinship with 'their own kind' as has been accepted in the past with non-Western 'minorities'. Ethnic 'revival' will be largely Cultural, and will not take on political shades until they have first made their cultural needs manifest – more likely than not, in the 'streets' or in the traditional 'institutions' of the country. From this reaction will come the *political manifestation* of Separatism, seen as the only method of survival.

11. MESTIZO 'Ethnic' REVIVAL:

The greatest possibility of a 'first' separatist movement is seen in the Mestizo population. The hotbed of contention is in, and over, the Southwestern portion of America. New

Azatlan is already a part of the 'cultural' mind of the southwest Mestizo – it is, after all, the ancient historical homelands of his ancestors – the Aztec Indians, who controlled a Mexican Empire prior to Cortez. Religious leaders (such as Father Florecio M. Rigoni), looks at the mass immigration of Mexicans across the American borders as 'a peaceful conquest' of territorial lands. Some may think this fanciful thinking by an aspiring culture who, those of the West, have had little feelings for one way or another, as their religion boasts of 'the love of mankind', and thereby rationalizes this transformation. The Mestizo, on the other hand, believes strongly in this possible realization. There are two main reasons why the chance of success is high for this race-culture:

a. There is some justification of their ownership rooted in relatively recent times. They, at one time, controlled the Southwest as a People and Culture.

b. There is simple evidence that Mestizos will be a numerical majority in all or large **parts** of the Southwest in a relatively short period. If the latter happens, and there is an almost certain possibility that it will, then Separatist sentiment will certainly thrive. The French in Quebec is just another example of the way this contest is about to play itself out.[€]

[€] Note: The fact, that the present American government has approved the 'fast track' to Mexico, as of this writing, should make all those of Western stock raise their heads in anger

12.   BALKANIZATION   OF   THE   WESTERN
        CONTINENT INEVITABLE:

The 'break' of even one traditional race-culture from the
norms of the United States will create a domino effect that
will not subside unless tremendous force is utilized in its
suppression. This is not, however, the worst-case scenario.
A more dramatic, if not less popular, would be a
continuing 'state of war' carried out by guerilla's in a
small scale civil war. Terrorism would be the watchword
of the day. The examples of Lebanon, Sri Lanka, India,
and Northern Ireland will suffice to make this point. Even
in forms not as concrete as total separatism, the probability
that the various groups maintain a more than rigid
conglomerate in the large cities of the United States is
highly likely. This will be *de facto* separatism.

13.   OPEN   U.S.   BORDERS   WILL   ENSURE   THE

---

and demand an explanation. With the close proximity that Mexican mestizos and American-
Chicanos have in both culture and geography, it is certain that any 'extra' positioning of
these groups by the government will lead to the rapid deployment of these kindred people's
between Mexico proper, and those American 'centers' which house the greatest numbers of
Mexican mestizo immigrants and Chicanos. This will reinvigorate the 'old' contacts
between agitators and leaders of every persuasion – marking, even more so, the difference
between the opposing groups. This may well facilitate a situation much more militant than
that of Quebec. Mexican mestizos *will* fight when the time is right. At the very least – in the
case of a positive Separatist movement – the southwestern mestizo will demand autonomy
on levels not seen since Pancho Villa. The Modern, it would seem, is trying to placate these
elements by their fast-track proposals. For those that think this possibility of annexation, of
separatism, as illogical, let it be remembered that our own revolutionary leaders and people,
were certainly not logical to take on the entire British Empire for something as esoteric as
'freedom'. Whether we, those of Western stock, accept the aspirations of the immigrant
Mexican mestizo, or other non-Westerns, it is, nevertheless, part of a racial imperative,
which will, and does seek, release. FLS

DISSOLUTION OF TRADITIONAL AMERICAN IDEAS OF 'Federalism':

This is over and above any real 'nationalism'. America will be truly International in scope. The 'open border' concept will bring a two-way traffic, which will usher in the new [American] and will usher out the old [American]. This 'may' create the largest white flight in the history of the Western race-culture, or they may stay and fight for sovereignty like has not been seen since the first wave of Aryan invaders crossed the eastern steppes. The consequent loss of scientific and educational levels in America by the latter situation would completely rearrange the face of this continent.

14 THE RISE OF A 'New' WEST:

This manifestation will be regarded as 'revolutionary' by the powers that be. It is, however, a necessary prerequisite to the continuation of the Western race-culture, either as a distinct 'ethnic' group, isolated, and sharing a possible 'portion' of this Western Continent, or as a racially dominant legislative bloc – this latter, however, will not be necessitated if the present trends continue. The new conscious Western man and woman will, most assuredly, demand their part of the pie – what is left of it. He will face growing opposition from the established order, which, after the levels of determination will convince those of Western stock of their betrayal. Military and civilian contacts will continue to facilitate joint ventures and, when that 'personality' becomes known, will voluntarily commit to each other's cause; the presence of 'money' will manifest itself in, and from those American interests which have succumbed to ventures of International Finance by forcing their economic interest to go abroad, thereby denying their own people work and sustenance. Militarism, coupled with money, will bring about the venues certain to establish Culture over that of the mechanism, of civilization, and will eventually be   overcome by Culture created, formed, and lived by those of the West.

These predictions, as said before, are broad in scope. To face the facts as we see them is to be honest with ourselves, as well as to the future of our [white] children. To drive all the foregoing home however, let us add this: The *fact* that non-Westerns are numerically growing is evident; the *fact* that political power is based solely on the *majority of the voters*, regardless of their race, is supported by the ideal of 'democracy' – a Western concept – and will, eventually prove the maxim of 'one man, one vote' is the essence of modern democracy – and the *end* of the Western Culture on this continent as we know it, as well. Forcing these various 'groups' inhabiting this continent to be *like* the Western race-culture will only add fuel to the already burning fire of Nationalism and Separatism.

The feelings of Nationalism and Separatism are felt by *all* groups, regardless of its racial makeup. The present system only artificially suppresses these feelings. In America, the 'traditional' minorities such as Blacks and Mestizos will continue to localize their political *unity* and increase their demands for a larger and larger role in their political destiny – this is only natural and expected. The eventual coalition [between black and mestizo], while not very palatable to either party will, nevertheless, be realized – if only to take a shot at political mastery. To *not* take this gamble, for it would truly be a gamble, would show that their ability to match the Western is of an inferior nature. However, between the two separate ethnic groups, the Mestizo-Hispanic is the more technically advanced; hence, it will be the dominant *culture*.

The tendency of ethnic 'units' in demanding 'equal' time politically, economically, *and* culturally will increase in proportion to each individual units size and social needs. What the Western [man] cannot, or will not give up will, most assuredly, *force the needed cooperation spoken of above.* In the present evolution of [Western] democracy, the right of every voice to be heard will be protected – imagine the million voices, the million needs, spread out, demanding attention to their individual concerns that will, and presently is, sucking the life-blood from the entire apparatus of the present system. The majority 'rules', no matter what majority [coalition] this represents. African Americans, on the other hand, will rightly feel betrayed by any upsurge in the mestizo-Hispanic power base. Any 'historical' consideration that has benefited the black race in the past will be of no account to the newly powerful mestizo-Hispanic voting bloc. Independent and powerful, the mestizo-Hispanic American will take them to task for inferring preference by *another minority*. This perceived loss of respect and lack of political acumen will force them to conclude, and with some veracity, that it is the Western, that must bear responsibility for this state of affairs; this will only exacerbate the existing ethnic turmoil even further.

We will see, here in America, an *increase* in scholastic prejudice against racial nationalists and spokesmen on campus, a direct violation of 'freedom of speech', and collegiate investigation into the social and political bodies which make up the national mosaic – even at the height of racial tensions during the 'civil rights' movement in the latter half of the twentieth century, debates between George Lincoln Rockwell and Stokely Carmichael received better academic sponsorship than today's academic arena. This latter, however, may be seen in the light of honest 'white' liberalism, rather than minority achievement, and since this white 'majority' has been lessened to the point of replacement, one can only observe that the 'civility' present in the past, has long since passed from the national spirit.

The rules of civility have changed, not only for academia, but for the body politic on a national level; the backlash of Western thought, however, is becoming assertive once again. Teachers Unions have, with time, changed into a body of 'oversight' PC committees, working hand-in-glove with government propaganda, and I foresee major unrest from the student bodies wishing to voice their opinions in spite of the pervasive control which the modern teachers 'collective' have built in this country.

Moreover, on the topic of 'unions', it is rarely talked about much by white nationalist leaders, yet there is ample evidence that 'unions' will, and have played, a pivotal role in maintaining and extending the rights of workers, especially white workers; the present union leadership does not, strictly speaking, stand for the right of white men and women to work, as they have, over the past generation, *consistently* promoted hispanic labor in a majority of 'construction' fields, over that of needs of whites. Certainly, gone are the days of the IWW. This, I predict, will change in coming years.

With economic unrest looming over the horizon, the needs of many will face uncertain futures. In work, as well as scholastic enterprises, the obvious imbalance in foreign immigrants within both areas will, with certainty, force major restructuring or face vocal, if not violent, reaction from the common people on the state and national levels.

White Nationalists have seen and spoken of this for years, and it does not necessarily make one feel better that "...we told you so...". It is incumbent, then, that all of us continue to promote the truth as we see, to our fellows throughout the coming years, and continue to support those that have given their lives to this struggle with largess, and public support, no matter who is in opposition.

Chapter IV

Into the Abyss

I pursued the living; I walked the widest and the narrowest paths that I might know its nature. With a hundred-fold mirror, I still caught its glance when its mouth was closed, so that its eyes might speak to me. And its eyes spoke to me. But wherever I found the living, there I heard also the speech on obedience. Whatever lives, obeys.

And this is the second point:

He who cannot obey himself is commanded. That is the nature of the living.

Thus Spoke Zarathustra

The path less traveled makes for beautiful prose; but it does not fully describe the path *created*, and *chosen*, by those of a once, and future West.

It is to the 'third point' of Zarathustra's discourse which, when applied to our discussion, ferrets out the inner most workings of the technics of the West's new direction: *Command*.

To all directions conceived or mobilized, there are those special persons inclined or, perforce, destined to command – to *lead*. To this *class* of men (and to some extent, our women) comes the burden of command; for it does, indeed, requires vast amounts of personal *obligese'*, of obligation to their fellows – those who follow. In the human experience, many will falter, come to ruin, or simply be crushed by this exertion. Indeed, to command, one must, firstly, *command himself.* One must, of necessity, pay for this decision; one must accept Charon's toll, and pay for it wholly. There is no personal exception to this rule. To command, truly, one must become judge, avenger, victim and creator of his own law – that is, law of his kind, that natural law, which has only one purpose: the survival and extension of its kind – its children.

In other works associated with this author, the entire concept of a rising, fledgling, and independent people, *presupposes* a natural and independent Political State. Without a *state*, there can be no real *affirmation* of either independence, nor freedom. As such, the dream of many of those Western men and women must, at all costs, come to grips with the reality of both a *natural* and *geographical* State. To this end, to be sure, have been many and varied attempts to *distill*, and explain to the various adherents and visionaries which encompass the racial/nationalist struggle for a homeland dedicated, and created for members of the West – just as had their forefathers and mothers realized, of yesteryear.

The rise of a *new* West is predicated on this.

In today's world, a world in which the *common* man and woman are simple statistics to the modern culture destroyer, his minions, and his world-vision, the common thread, as stated in previous works, is that *nationalism* is, and has become increasingly, the way-sign of the future; this is, of course, just the opposite of what the Modern has preached, and has woven his *lies* around. That a *'one world order'* should rule, literally, is the *imperative* of control and organized chaos, which so illuminates the culture-destroyers view of the world. However, in our present presence (2008), the lie has been found out; to the smallest of *ethnic* enclaves have come the sounds of *independence*, of *freedom.*

It has come with a price: *War.*

To name just a few, the list will include *Kosovo, Croatia, Serbia, Georgia, Ossetia, Albania, Kurdistan.* All these exist, and have existed, in varying states throughout history; it is only in the modern age (primarily since the Great War, *part dux*), that the *reinsertion* of the will of each of these ethnic states have, partly on their own, and partly indirectly because of intervention of America[n] interests; *interests* which do not, speak for the interests of the denizens of the West, here, in America.

For the past eight years, under the Presidency of an *army* of what, today, is called 'neo-con', the *new* conservatives, a monumental undertaking has taken place: american armies are now far-flung, our men and women inhabiting, killing, torturing, and accommodating a presence which, as we are often told, is making us safe with the advent of democracy in the farthest reaches of the planet. War, is a natural thing, developed to protect our large and varied interests around the world. It is to *maintain* democracy.

A microscopic look at these political factors can now be witnessed in any major American [or European] city, which shares this *disparate* population. An already existing racial hodge-podge presently exists in the *southwestern* United States trying, it would seem, to function in the 'democratic sense' of a new world order. This study, into '*new politics* ', can be seen in the ascendancy of 'brown'; however much this is a political fact, the Western now emerges from his *stupor* of the sixties. The Western man of today is tired; he cares not for the minority, for the *victim*. He sees *himself* as a true victim– a victim of betrayal, a victim of a Modern who is no longer a *part* of his West.

The Western perception, real or imagined, that *affirmative action* has now canceled out his productivity, will *force* his hand. He will, and is seeing, the *life-value* of his family passing into *oblivion*. He will, with some help from the nationalist , project himself as a *new* political force. If this new found power, however *embryonic*, will not help him in any way recognizable to him on a daily basis, he will force the modern *culture-destroyer*, to play the final hand: war in the streets. The Modern will seek, at all costs, to avoid *urban* warfare. He already has a plan – a plan, which has been in effect for over a hundred years – that of the destruction of the Western, or any 'nationalist ' prone groups or individuals who have gained any credible political favor, through the process of assimilation; the *degradation* of the racial-stock, which founded this American West. The Modern must, at every opportunity, revamp this idea of *obfuscation, misdirection and destruction* since, it being unnatural, will always show itself to those with the eyes to see, and must do this before the Western realizes just what is taking place in the arena of politics – politics that will affect the Western in the most direct and influential ways. The Modern realizes that if he does not *merge* the various ethnic units he will face his own *annihilation* at the hands of his creation. Faced with the various decisions he must make, marked with the obvious race-cultural contradictions that are present, he will be shown for the *hypocrite* his is. His power will fade into oblivion.

To 'unify' this prodigious amalgamation, the Modern, typically, has tried the band-aid method of Language. This theory, oddly enough, has been proposed by a stalwartly proponent of ethnic isolation in a cultural sense; himself a child of Asian ancestry, and a proficient spokesman for the 'conservative' cause. This *theory* runs thus: An *amalgamation* of diverse ethnic groups will be forced to *submit* to a national leveling based on the commonality of language. The [Western] English language in this case. This will, in theory, provide a 'common' ground – on a cultural level! – hence, the prosperity and peace of the entire nation will follow. No lack of skills , no lack of opportunity– such is the *utopian* dream of the modern culture-destroyers.

 In its great diversity, the various ethnic units will, ultimately, rely on the coalition political party. This so called 'coalition', to use a present term, will undoubtedly play a larger and larger part in the political 'cat and mouse' games of the democratic process. At best, however, this conglomerated rainbow coalition would be an uneasy one. In its growing political power, the destabilizing effect would be manifest. Everything would depend on 'compromise' and 'smoothing' the way for these disparate groups. Put to the test however, say, in the cases of a 'national emergency' or war, this system of 'coalition; would be stifled from the outset; it would be besieged with atrophy such as Poland was during the interim period between world wars.

Western response to the above coalition will be a heated one. The response, already in the making, will be, also, a cultural one – call it a *Pan-European* expression if you will – and it will include all those of European descent as a voting bloc. This, as with all that has been stated before, is a natural one; it will be as natural to the West as it is natural to the non-western to form with his own. The tribal mechanism of Western history is replete with the opposite occurring; but as time goes on, the various democracies will come to grips with the methodology requisite to *maintain* our Culture– as the culture distorters have in past derailed this imperative we, all those of Western stock, must remain vigilant and never let this imperative recede to the background.

The two largest and most predictable groups in any Western alliance in this *potential* coalition would be the great *Celtic* and *Nordic* elements – combined with *German* (the single largest ethnic white group in America). The potential problem regarding religion, that is, the *technics* of Catholicism, Lutheranism, etc., specifically the interests of the *Irish* and mestizo-Hispanic element is worth some consideration but, in the end, will *opt* for its racial affinity with its own kind – and put religion to the side, when the case warrants. The Pope, as an 'institution', however, could very well prove to be a dangerous 'wildcard' if any real religious threat presented itself on behalf of the Roman *Pontiff*. If the West has learned (?) anything, it should be that *religious wars* are fought for political power – the Race, sad to say, matters *least* in these types of war.

Religious Wars must be avoided between those of Western stock at all costs!

Economic considerations will precipitate the final breakdown of the diverse ethnic units here, in America. As the *competition* increases for jobs, and their related skills *diminish*, the need for 'outcome', not 'income', will increase. Production in traditional fields will expire, the necessary 'high-tech' areas will lack the competitive edge needed to stay afloat in a world of high demand for *high quality* material; we will all be expected to accept everything which is *mediocre*. The *welfare* rolls, already pushed to the limit, feeding on those vast amounts of *'prepared'* savings , the greater of these savings by our *elderly*, and using them to keep the indigent and homeless fed on a daily basis. Even those of the Western race-culture will and is being forced to *accept* this handout. Income will be offered by the 'state', and outcome as well. No production– just a *cycle* of burden to the entire nation. The tremendous amount of litigation, which we will experience in this area alone [e.g. those who are on 'welfare', and those 'intending to enroll'] is massive, and is only really known by those that are already on this system. The monstrous, 'bigger is better' *Pax Romana*, is yet another *lie* of the Modern; that debilitating *hubris* that has been uncovered.

All this, however, has its rising star. The rise of a *new* West is predicated upon it. Between the bashing , political or otherwise, along with the obvious fiscal realities facing the race-culture of the West, and the continued growing *dominance* of the non-Western race-culture to become an 'identifiable' and genuine ethnic group – this will provide them with the legitimate technic of political *determinism* – which, in turn, will provide them with a sense of community, and into a breeding ground for political, and racial thought. The realization that race and culture actually exists and has viable power will bring those of the *biological* nation together; once the significant understanding of 'racial ancestry' is taken to heart, the People of the West, *world wide*, will consider their political decisions as being an integral part of their daily lives. This will breed *true* and *healthy* nationalism . The feelings of a great white tribe will grow increasingly as the political events of the United States and the Western world deteriorate.

The time involved in this ethnic *tension* , and its eventual culmination is uncertain. But it *will* take place. The *revival* of the West, as well, is seen to have started [by the Nationalist] about seventy-five years ago. Its contemporary zenith is to be seen in the numerous events in Europe, especially in German (i.e. European) reunification, as well as the smaller states like *Serbia, Albania, Yugoslavia, and the entire Balkan Region*. The reaction of these states, once being freed from the 'occupational' powers of the West, was to dramatically show the world that Freedom, Sovereignty, and a *reaffirmation* of nationhood is the wave of the *future* – this, of course, is contrary to the new world order– hence it will, undoubtedly, cause future tension and possible *war* between those elements of the West still under alien domination and political persuasion. All this, and more, is the organic result of the technics of race-culture. Economics plays a secondary, if not also a *supportive* role; money is necessary for all great revivals.

The United States, the *hearth* and *home* of many sons and daughters of the West, and an *integral* part of the Race Culture, is also traveling through a revival, a *renaissance* which will surprise many. America is *unavoidably* being drawn into the same awareness, as is the European *commonwealth*. How *we*, as a People and 'political technic' deal with this eventuality is what will determine our future– it is the presence of our Tomorrow. The Presidential Election will bring all this into relief.

The discussions occurring just before the present election are, daily, trying to 'avoid' the *presence* of race, a fanciful and dubious claim, as the 'candidate' of the Year is African, dispelling the notion that 'race' has no place in the present day political struggle. Tell that to the almost forty-million black voters in the U.S.! Win or lose, the African *race* is tasting the sweet smell of success and change – a change only created with the legions of *deracinated* white americans who blithely enter into the new America of 'sharing the land' for the betterment of all, welcoming the *suicide* of their own independence and freedom and security; the *fate* of their children a dim and ever present *denial* of reality.

The reality, if one is allowed to digress, is the example of South Africa.

Digression, however, will not detain us long, and one only has to travel back in time a few years; for what has transpired since the fall of 'white rule', although not a perfect analogy to what the West faces in America, will add to the *spectre* of what type of Future faces *all* those of Western stock, if the present trends continue.

ii.

The Military Option

Every White Nationalist knows that history *repeats* itself.

The *birth*, *life* and *passing* of all cultures and races repeats itself, endlessly.

Many individuals have dissected this process; many have missed the mark. Moreover, who really knows *whom* the gods favor, and what *path* they require for *sustained* victory?

During the past 3500 years one can, with a degree of *clarity*, see the necessary ingredients for a successful change in political and social standings; *democracy*, being that *ubiquitous* sign of degeneration, having tasted the droppings of power and authority, seeks ever to distill the *best* from the *worst*, thereby, regardless of the principled men and women who inhabit and work endlessly to promote equal representation, and the continuation of the people, as a ruling construct, at least the shadow of this desire remain, forever. outside the shadow of reality.

Power *comes* and *goes* in the halls of justice.

What *remains* is the constrained, and ofttimes *rogue* elements of real power: The Power of The Gun.

Standing Armies have always been the *vanguard* of entrenched ruling classes ; whether for ill or good, men underarms exist. The *Brotherhood of War* is a long established fraternity, with implications far out-weighing the intransigent politician who, for lucre's sake, peddles his wares.

Ultimately, men of War are necessary, be this *Fyrdung*, or Army of the Folk, or traditional 'professional' armies, *limited* by land and tribal necessities, to protect common relations, and citizens in the larger sense.

Democracy, as we see its fulfillment today, is no different than Caesar's precursors or of Napoleon; the difference, today, is only one of *timing* and *perseverance*, with a little help from our friends in the Military.

Those of us who come from a background of military or law-enforcement services, can not be defined, as was the case a generation ago, as *protecting* a class of persons akin to the rest, patrolling streets where we knew most of the residents; or in the Field, fighting for causes which were *ingrained* with patriotic zeal, ideological affirmation, that *traditional* basis for mass mobilization.

American Military Officers, in the main, went through *traditional*, mostly Southern War Colleges, and thereby passed on to future generations of Western stock, the accumulated knowledge of sacrifices and intrepid courage, necessary to survive war, at whatever level, so that the *host* might survive and extend its hard-won achievements.

The Loyalty of the Officer Corps in European history is a *storied* one, but *reaffirms* the need and necessity of this class; Soldiers, as a rule, *exist* for the tactical and logistical support of an Officer class who, in turn, are *maintained* by a worthy State-craft. As we all know, this 'civilian' counterpart, as in our present time, has *betrayed* the yeoman-folk who maintain the legacy of our fathers and mothers; the Officer corps, straining at the bit, have followed the orders and strategies of a dozen presidential offices which, by any account, have allowed an international and domestic degeneration to grow and continue unabated.

Wars breed warriors. This is *axiomatic*.

Democracy, as a construct, maintains the will of the people, and armed *cohorts* remain their weapon of first choice. What, then, do warriors *do* in a democracy? As the civilian government maintains hegemony, the warriors are scuttled back into their barracks, to play at more war, waiting for orders. Officers, as well, study, and are paid very well by their masters to 'stay out of the way'. This works in general, but the *tension* between the two is millennial .

So, *how* to get the Military on our side? Money.

Knowing, and having much personal relationships with the Officer Corps, as well as knowing the historical nuances of this discussion, it has become apparent that the integrity and moral fiber has, once again , gone to *those* who make or break a people, for the highest bid. Like medieval Europe, the creation of 'mercenary armies' have become the *mainstay* of our modern State.

American corporate interests, as a rule, support the infrastructure of the government, and by *tacit* complicity, bankroll the military, as the functioning arm of both their *protection*, and their *expansion*. As long as the money and power flow, there is a *symbiotic* relationship. Once this becomes estranged, a vacuum becomes apparent and must, of necessity, be filled; this requires, in many instances, a new and friendly government, as well as a *trusted* military component. Moreover, this follows an atmosphere of change, of revolution and becomes the watch-word of the day. This has always been *inevitable*.

The military, such as we see generally as being a part of the necessary regimen of Western life, is beholden *not* too ideology, such as the Nationalist sees, but *lucre*. General Smedley Butler said as much; Caesar as well, and Napoleon. Nationalism, a racial grass-roots phenomenon is, by definition, *folk*-based, yet these elements of power are *transient*, as seen by those in power, and *remains* in the shadow of fear and mistrust.

Gaining the support of the Military proper is, without doubt, a *dubious* one, at least on a large scale. How, then, do nationalists gain the support and respect of our traditional 'brothers-at-arms'?

Firstly, entrenched fraternities are *self-absorbed, myopic*, and fraught with the idea that *might makes right*, as *prima facie* evidence of their superiority; this has much historical *validity*. To support, or ally themselves with a 'new' power, whether retrograde or forward-looking is relative to the *exchange* of currencies - such as public acclaim, wealth, social position - in short, the necessity of transformation or alliance is based not on the right of a thing, but on the *expediency* of the end-game.

Secondly, cut the military out of this equation, and the Corporate privateers become those slippery, mobile bishops in this game; the ability to 'make money', if jeopardized, becomes the necessary countermove to overt Taxation, outright confiscation of material production, or enterprise which, cumulatively, make up an entire class of people. When threatened, regardless of the dire straits of the People, money becomes the pivotal mark of their survival. Hence, the Military.

The common 'grunt' in the military is another matter.

Getting support from a White Marine is relatively easy, especially relative to the recent 'wars' on foreign soil. They are angry, scared and disgusted. The present regime is rightly concerned about sections of their 'armed guard'. As White men and Women, they are already converted against those who sent them to be killed, but lack that specific ingredient for group change: *Permission* .

Nationalism *gives* that permission, because it speaks to the heart and soul of our kind, yet lacks the acceptance of the established military order. *This is changing.*

The opposing debate from certain quarters of the 'brotherhood of war' that, service related members share more than a uniform, that race does not matter, is proved *false* if one visits any military base, or war-field experience. The *duty* or *treason* of our military is seen in stark relief, when the training, expertise and largess are spent on *multicultural* cohorts who, then, *pass* this training onto others of their kind who, when the tough times come, will pass that training on to others of their own kind, at the expense of their masters, such as Caesar experienced. We are no different.

There will have to be a cleansing, and this will be problematic for Nationalists for, at first, the Nationalist will be attacked from both sides; the lines have already been drawn. He will have to brave the elements, pass through the system, and *convert* both the social class as well as the military. This will, once again , depend upon the *fear* and *anxiety* of the Corporate class . It is moving in this direction, how fast is another matter.

Do we need the Military, yes.

Do we pursue military contacts for the sake of offensive strategy? This remains to be seen. Do we wait for their support, in lieu of addressing the issues most dear to our people, and ourselves, no. In every field of endeavor, the military have *proved* themselves worthy of distinction, as professional men, intent upon *defining* and *refining* their profession. Nationalists must do the same for mutual respect to be gained. The days of *Ludendorff* may be in the making, once again; or maybe not. Nevertheless, the *overtures* of that time have their merit today, and we should not hesitate to make our positions known, on a case by case basis, to those who are sympathetic.

14 Words

Chapter IV

The Promise of a New Land:

The belief in Territory

Diverse populations, that is, in a racial sense, no matter the cosmopolis of its language, has never realized a higher culture in the real sense, at least not for long. The many attempts, including the great "experiment" of the United States, have failed. The antagonisms are many. The brutalization of the many inhabitants by each opposing "group" is natural, albeit dysfunctional, and cannot support the integrity of any given organized culture. The platitudes given the populace by its erstwhile leaders are political posturing, plain and simple. They elect to sympathize with "special interest groups" in order to gain an advantage in a "numerical" democracy; this does not promote the real interests of the "host-race" on which mores, spirit, and *destiny-will* the Nation/Culture was founded. This exacerbates this entire dysfunctional process. Anyone who questions this process is considered a radical by the existing order.[◊]

In *ROTW*, the entire concept of a rising, fledgling, and independent people, presupposes a natural and independent Political State. Without a state, there can be no *real* affirmation of either independence, nor freedom. As such, the dream of many of those Western men and women must, at all costs, come to grips with the *reality* of both a *natural* and *geographical* and State. To this end, to be sure, have been many and varied attempts to distill, and explain to the various adherents and visionaries which encompass the racial/nationalist struggle for a homeland dedicated, and created for members of the West – just as had their forefathers and mothers realized, of yesteryear.

[◊] National Pan-Aryanist Party – Position Paper, 1989, NPAP Press.

The Rise of a New West is predicated on it.

I have often said that "…*the search for Land is over…*", and so it is.

As this discussion has been in the forefront of many personal, as well as public discussions and debates, and seeing the smallest of movements, once again, in the reemergence of this basic, and pivotal role of White Nationalist *policy*, as it relates to the future growth of a national direction.

Moreover, I feel it is opportune to bring this discussion to the fore again, although in a more oblique, and revised version.

Rather than quote all the 'usual suspects', erudite and world-worn though they are, and most certainly deserve our attention, such as Hobbes, Locke, Rousseau, Kant, Plato, Aristotle, Jefferson, Adams, Jay, and even Franklin, I will try and encapsulate (even offer a few quotes…a mean feat, but remembering also, to assuage those who thrive off this obligatory bulwark of *fact and faith*) the construct, although not the methodology, of my antecedents, our forefathers; those who made us, who gave us this elusive and mercurial process of 'thinking for ourselves', and thereby creating, that environ most suitable for us and our children.

It is well and good that we, White Nationalists, proceed and direct our ideas and common-sense applications of form, as it were, to our fellows, those rudimentary and common-folk who, in actuality, are our neighbors, our wives and sisters, our work-place brethren and, most importantly, to ourselves. To inculcate ideas and forms of methodology are fine, in the main, and what other recourse can we count on? The innumerable words and phrases are, of course, a necessity, until that time that necessity, itself, requires more of us.

In my mind, the penultimate Idea, or as the converse may be attributed, is that Land, or in the abstract, *ownership* of land, is the absolute cornerstone of White Nationalist philosophy. Moreover, the realization that *soil*, unlike blood, is continuous, even when changed, superficially, by erosion or man-made enterprises; blood, on the other hand, may be changed, diluted and made more malleable by indifference and lack of responsible attention.

Therefore, it is Land, in its permanent and decidedly unique inference of human habitation, that our discussion relates to a more mundane, yet not so distant interaction with ourselves and our posterity. Land, in a Western ideation, is sacrosanct, a veritable 'holy grail' to those independent and sovereign souls who, among the larger body of the earths populace, see the harnessing of a 'natural' thing, to be a duty, a responsibility of a dutiful husband man, who would till the land, thereby bringing forth the substance of life, guaranteeing him and his family, the necessities of life and, by extension, those that come after.

Yes, and what comes *after*?

Those who have made the study of Natural Law a life-long pursuit have, almost to the man, decidedly come to the conclusion that it is *longevity*, by its very nature, is that which precludes the loss of sustained serfdom. Slavery is, by all accounts, a state of un-natural affairs, although is understood by such as Ragnar Redbeard and Darwin, as a state of nature, however unsavory it might be. Nevertheless, it is to longevity that we address ourselves, namely: *Perpetuity*.

To 'hold land' at the behest of a State, or any authority is, without reservation, opposed by White Nationalists. The revitalization of a racial state is predicated upon this simple realization.

Moreover, to secure Land, proper, is the basis for action of a free people:

> the inhabitants of any country who are descended and derive a title to their estates from those who are subdued and had a government forced upon them against their free consents retain a right to the possession of their ancestors...for the first conqueror never having had a title to the land of that country, the people who are the descendants of, or claim under, those who were forced to submit to the yoke of a government by constraint have always a right to shake it off and free themselves from the usurpation or tyranny which the sword has brought in upon them...' [§192]. 'Their persons are free by a native right, and their properties, be they more or less, are their own and at their own disposal, and not at his' [§194].

This, of course, leads the stouthearted to conclusions, ironic though it might appear to some of us, that:

> No damage therefore, that men in the state of nature (as all princes and governments are in reference to one another) suffer from one another, can give a conqueror power to dispossess the posterity of the vanquished, and turn them out of that inheritance, which ought to be the possession of them and their descendants to all generations....¶184 Once again: *Their persons are free*

by a native right, and their properties, be they more or less, are
their own and at their own disposal, and not at his. ¶194[29]

The insistence of tried and true methods, however, seem to have been
passed by in the frenetic attempt to 'convince' our brethren of the
'rightness' of our cause; instead, we should, all of us, attempt to reaffirm
the basis, yes the basic realizations of the primacy of our attempt to
become a People, once again, by fostering, and inculcating every waking
day, the realization that without that personal interdiction of our basic and
most intrinsic need for a viable estate, firstly, of personal property, as well
as the necessity to *maintain* this property, in perpetuity, is of the most
permanent and *incendiary* qualities of White Nationalism.

I believe that most of us agree to two things:

1. That a 'place', physical and identifiable, be a prerequisite to a
future homeland/ethno-state'

2. That a 'physical' and identifiable People populate, as the sole
representatives of that people this 'particular place, so indicated.

This may be an inversion, to some, of 'blood and soil', but I feel it
places the chicken before the egg; this does not, however, decrease
the ideation of 'blood and soul', but only reinforces it.

White Nationalists know, or should know, that it was Law, both of the
legal variety, as seen conditionally by our English forebears, as well as
seen by those considering the natural variety, as the above quotes
emphasize. Even *Njal*, in the *Icelandic Saga's*, saw this clearly as "*Me
lögum skall land byggja og ólögum eya*[30]," which recognizes both a
'discipline' as well as a causual effect upon the relationship between the
two elements.

One must, firstly, *possess* property, before one can lay claim legally to it.

This brings us to today's effort to reclaim, as well as establish, a real
territory, an ethno-state, in which we might begin, again, the long process
of revitalizing our status as free and sovereign people; to accumulate

---

[29] John Locke, *Second Treatise of Government* (1690)

[30] "By law is the land built; by lawlessness (unlaw) destroyed"

wealth as our skills support, and begin the long and perilous route of establishing a viable Industrial America, that productive state in which we can, honestly, compete with ourselves, as well as others, to build a nation consonant with our advances in technology and our innate desires.

Once we have convinced our people of the 'natural rights' of possessing, in a generational setting, the environment in which we live, we may better and more forcibly, remain *fixed* to our 'place', thereby inculcating and making real, our duty and obligation to our Nation.

Such is the *hope* of White Nationalism for all our people.

****

With equal pleasure I have as often taken notice that Providence has been pleased to give this one connected country to one united people--a people descended from the same ancestors, speaking the same language, professing the same religion, attached to the same principles of government, very similar in their manners and customs, and who, by their joint counsels, arms, and efforts, fighting side by side throughout a long and bloody war, have nobly established general liberty and independence.

John Jay ~ First Justice of the United States

Funny, how History repeats itself.

The body of works enjoined by John Jay, *The Federalist Papers* seems, at first glance, to be opposed to the whole discussion of White Nationalism, separation, and secession from something that, to most of us, is sacrosanct, traditional, and a model which has, and will, work for our lifetimes and that of our children. Moreover, throughout, and in spite of their combined efforts, John Jay and his contemporaries, were nationalists, creating something where there had been only allegiance, and superficial interaction with Authority which, by historical experience, was not enough to temper the ideals and spirit of men who had seen a greater vision, a vision which emboldened and made clearer the choices which would mold their lives and the lives of all of us, their children.

The irony, which many observers may assign to inexperience, that men like John Jay and James Madison were federalists, in a modern sense, would have been opposed to a modern day schism, or absolute separation from the present system is, of course, a matter of conjecture on the part of these same said observers. In any event, the characteristics and political implications, as seen by the present day White Nationalist exactly parallel the experiences of the above writers.

The experiences of today, in fact, far surpass the original founders in both form and function. At least on this Continent.

The belief, by many, that the time is long past, in which the grievances of this generation may be addressed by political maneuverings, and cultural modification is over. Moreover, gone are the dreams and hopes of a generation, in line with tradition and white ethno-based historical imperatives with which they were raised.

The irony at first blush is apparent.

We are a country which houses Fifty States, each unique, both by its own landscape and by its political evolution; joined in a 'federation', this uniqueness is subsumed, as Mr. Jay and others hoped, for in the bonding, in the unity, was the only hope for a fledgling nation. Ironic then, indeed, is the conversation of dissolution when looked at through the eyes of others.

Yet, not so different.

White Nationalists are looking for another unification, a unification based on the same elements of race-culture and similarity, just as Mr. Jay saw when he penned the lines above; the interconnected relationship is racial, no matter the slings and arrows of the Modern and his various allies; the interconnected land mass, the network of water-ways, and the natural pathways to collective responsibility – in short, the need for a re-unification of those body of persons related, by blood, to those very authors of the federalist papers.

More and more material is being penned each and every year regarding the premise of a new Republic:

> I've since learned that those calling themselves "white nationalists" are not necessarily nationalists in the sense of wanting

to secede from the United States in order to form an independent ethnostate. Most, I think it's fair to say, are racially conscious conservatives who want to work through the existing institutions to regain control of the country their ancestors made — in order, ultimately, to dismantle the present anti-white system of preferences and restore something of the white man's former hegemony.

By contrast, white nationalists in the strict sense (i.e., those favoring secession) have no interest in restoring the old ways, let alone regaining control of the central state, whose authority is already slipping and whose rule is increasingly dysfunctional. Indeed, the American state system, as its more astute supporters acknowledge, is now beyond reform.

Instead, white nationalists aspire to create a counter-elite to lead disaffected white youth in a movement to found a whites-only nation-state somewhere in North America, once the poorly managed enterprise known as the United States collapses in a centrifugal dispersion of its decaying and perverted powers.

Without an organizational presence in the real world and with a "public" largely of computer hobbyists, white nationalists at present have no hope of actually mobilizing the white populace in opposition to the existing anti-white regime. Rather, their immediate goal is to prepare the way for the development of a revolutionary nationalist vanguard to lead the struggle for white liberation. They aspire thus not to recapture the rotting corpse of the US government, but to free themselves from it — in order to be themselves, in their own land, in their own way.

White nationalists, as such, politically define themselves in wanting to create a sovereign state in North America. They endeavor, therefore, not to "put things back the way they were," as conservatives wish, but to rid themselves of them completely.

A National Revolution, they hold, will alone restore "the white man to his rightful place in the world."

Inspired by the birthright handed down by the blood and sacrifice of ancestors, their project, relatedly, is not about restoring the Third Reich, the Confederacy, or Jim Crow, as leftists imagine, but about creating a future white homeland in which their kind will be able "to pursue their destiny without interference from other races."[31]

i.

The embryonic White Nationalist movement has, to date, evolved quite well into that nascent and implacable child, with the drive and intelligence of an Alexander, Aristotle, and the barbarism of Leonidas. These disparate elements have taken a relatively short life-cycle to adhere, in the main, to the calling of Race, ideology, and the transvaluation of what has gone before; through the dim pubescent phases of instruction and experience, to the 'new youth' of today, what has evolved is, well, as is to be expected: No more, No less.

Through the din of personal attacks, vitriolic gossip mongering, and those few lucid and bright souls who, personally and collectively, maintain a purpose and vision for the future, it is as it should be. Or is it?

One thing that has always occurred, is the 'peer review' system, that systematic approach to those happenings and occurrences which ofttimes lend fuel to the fire of discourse and evolution but, also, lends to the obfuscation of those issues most dear to the continuum of this, our White Nationalist imperative. Those Pragmatists and Optimists, each offering their innermost desires and vision of that future which would bring the greatest happiness, independence, and sovereignty to their fellow man. All movements and theoretical experiments lead to this interplay between personalities and ego, between individualism and the collective spirit. Each are necessary, and each has a place in the Once and Future West.

As is expected, many voices have given us their input: the status quo of governmental employees, semitic jealousy, the hangers-on of traditional Christianity and its various offshoots, the revolutionaries, the rebellious, the common working class, and the ineluctable division of our intelligentsia. The written word abounds, both for and against our cause, our hope. Words, without a story, however, are like so many rivers,

---

[31] Michael O'Meara – Toward the White Republic, 2009.
http://www.toqonline.com/2009/08/toward-the-white-republic/

running together independently, never fully realizing the Source. That source, to be more precise, are those individual stories of individuals who, collectively, become the anchor-point, the harbinger of those thoughts and developmental tactics, which have brought us here, to our present presence.

White Nationalists, even today, fall into that chasm of misleading and obtuse reckoning by dividing, or letting others divide us as, 'supremacists', 'Jim Crowists', and traditional 'nativists' who, fearing for our lives and power, continue, in ways oblique, so as to misdirect our detractors and, hence, deprive our opponents of their own justice, waiting to be meted out, to those who dare remind themselves, and the world, of their sense of purpose and hard-won hegemony. As in days past, this contest of world-views remains fixed, and only real and ineluctable Power, will ever change this. This, as well, is old news.

Modern, young, and inexperienced zealots of White Nationalism have, to date, been prudently or, in more marked designations, been purposely kept from a larger nationalist view by members who, early on, were more revolutionary in scope and action. Men like Robert Miles, or Tom Metzger who, each in their own right, held views of the common man, not as dupes or potential 'membership', but saw their People first, and foremost, as being a part of an organic strata, that necessary 'work force' of the greater mass led, not strictly by devices of the word, but by action in the political realm and in the streets. Most intellectuals of the day, even as now, showed little or no commonsense in regards to the efforts and successes, by such individuals as these. In our present efforts, the same hydra lifts her tired and scaly heads.

In the final analysis, it is the common man who will make the difference, this has been Tom Metzger's policy; Robert Miles, no stranger to theoretical warfare, as well as his professional experience of marginalizing 'guerrilla' combatants knew, as do all tacticians, that it is the coalescence of mind and labor, which has always been the foundation of any movement; and while these two examples proved that this was a workable alliance, nevertheless received little support for a Nation wide campaign in this regard. Even then, the posers and sycophants were ever jealous of the trailblazers. This happened, even as now, because the conservative elements of the status quo were monied, held positions of public acclaim, were ministers and public servants, publishers and hucksters, selling wares from Classic reprints, to gold and silver. The attention of the public is always short-lived, and one cannot blame them for only seeing what this coalition mind-trust, allowed them to see. The pen, even amongst our own, is a mighty sword.

The naive and redundant proclamations of 'categories' of White Nationalist, runs through every imaginable arm-chair warrior/patriot within the White Nationalist movement; designations which, for the most part exist, and conditionally were created, by white men during extremis within the confines and, the necessity of, the times in which they found themselves, but which are now being used against us in a comprehensive and heavily subsidized attack on all White people. Titles such as, Klan, Neo-Nazi, Creator, Christian Identity, Christian patriot, Neo-Confederate, Council of Conservative Citizens, skinhead, revisionist, militia/paramilitary, underground terrorist, paleocon, race realist, and populist are, nevertheless, used interchangeably, to the *detriment* of our movement, by our detractors, as well as ourselves, continuing the disconnect of our disparate elements. This could well have been side-stepped by the intellectuals and publishers who, rather than see a changing and brighter future, closed the door to their mushroom abode, and continued to declare that the sky was falling. Even the word White Nationalist, was not utilized until relatively recently, and only grudgingly.

The longing for preemptive discourse is a reality now, as it was thirty years ago. Louis Beam, for instance, received little or no positive support for his 'revolutionary rhetoric' back in the early 80's; even so, his positions on tactics and strategy were well-grounded, and have proved successful, albeit limited because of the imperiled virtues of the mainstream conservative, unlike the Left, who *heartily* has embraced Bill Ayers, the father of the SDS, and the various sycophants of Che Guevara, Marx, and Lenin who, today, because of their unapologetic balancing between 'activism' and 'political' altruism, have gained the *preeminent* position within the political and military machine of our nation. All this, because writers, institutions, and those who represent them, did *not* fail to support financially, and to collectively support in times, both good and bad – one should not forget the example of the Chicago 7 – nor the Lawyers who defended them, unlike the cowardly response to the men of Robert J. Mathews' *die Bruder Schweigen* by those *arrogant* and *conservative* nay-sayers of the Right; both groups political and direct action oriented. One group, however, continued to grow in stature, and the other, relegated to obscurity, not by the government, they did their job, but by the erstwhile individuals who, while not being of this caliber, failed to carry these efforts to the folk-at-large, thereby making the same examples which, inevitably, leads to that *mythos* so necessary to the survival of a revolutionary movement, cease to exist before its time.

Those who subscribe to the mainstream, those milk-toast patriots, will forever be with us. It is the duty of our intelligentsia and its accompanying Press, to remember the past, and its mistakes, with a new strategy for the future, namely, to ferret out those spokesmen and writers who, while on the fringe, nevertheless make for honest copy. Until this happens, no ivory tower, or its illusion, will save them from the disconnect of their People, because of the lack of knowledge and information. Alas, where are the brave newspapermen of yesteryear, closer to the folk, and unhindered, except by their own moral code of sympathy and understanding for the downtrodden amongst them?

Where were the tellers of tales, of newsworthy reporting when discussion of the terms Territorial Imperative, or Leaderless Resistance were gaining momentum? Where was the spoken and written works regarding the acronym ZOG – *Zionist Occupational Government* – which played such a major part in the radicalization and extension of the white reaction to the dismemberment of their way of life? It must be noted, again, that these terms, not just in a rhetorical sense, were a full-bodied *casus belli*, of earlier belligerents reacting to a declaration of War individually, and collectively, by a transparent and ever-reaching agenda by interests not of our making. This history, so rich in the telling, has hardly gone noticed by serious publishers and writers; William Regnery will publish Pat Buchanan, but not Louis Beam or David Lane; Noontide Press will address historical and revisionists issues, but has always failed to address the present day activists, theoretician, and seers produced by this, shall we admit it, War, in which we all, most assuredly, are embroiled in.

Some material abounds in which the old and the new of White Nationalism could benefit by, which are works by relatively unknown persons, at least within those inbred circles of white nationalists, such as *Committee of The States (Cheri Seymour)*, *Silent Brotherhood (Flynn/Gerhardt)*, Ruby Ridge, and *The White Separatist Movement in the United States (Dobratz/Shanks-Meile)*.

Not much material, to be sure, and not even written by our own, but for one exception; nevertheless, valuable in its reach and informative tone. Information, at the time of these events, was easily obtained, either from direct sources, or second hand, with verification being more readily available, it was not taken advantage of, either for honest comparative analysis, or for the certain largess to be received from this effort. What could have been the reason? Were writers in scarce supply for the efforts of the Chicago 7? Hardly. There is the rub: one group showed courage, yes courage, in the face of overwhelming odds and social criticism, yet it was done, and done again, to the betterment of their cause.

The repetitive whining of all and sundry, about what to do, is nothing less than shameful. As any normal, or bright person could see and anticipate those things heart-felt, or publicly prudent in terms of extending our White Nationalist views, we failed, as a movement, to take *advantage* of our own sacrifice and vision. Yet, the same continues today. Mirrors, are made for reflection, and a useful tool they are. It is not the reflexion of Psyche which we seek but, rather, the reflexion of our own *persona*, our own *truthfulness*, in what and how we face the future. All it takes is knowledge and dedication, with the courage to take a risk, to stand for something, not just to belong to a club or social back-slapping orgy, that is for lesser persons – not White Nationalists.

To address 'revolutionary soldiers' in the field, as 'gangs', is the epitome of a mainstream conservative, at least an individual who, at the outset, is still fundamentally flawed in his or her outlook, within the confines of our political and intellectual activities which, as well, oftentimes brings what it does: revolution. We decide our nomenclature, not our opponents.

Revolution in thought is, perforce, a wellspring of our ideology, as the past several generations have left us, any of us, with few alternatives. Better we embrace the destiny set before us, rather than re-hashing the old and timid appraisals of the past, with the same expectations and finality expressed therein.

Who is to remind us, and inform us, as to these events, thoughts and political direction? Surely we, as intelligent and independent writers and speakers, should not give more than passing attention to those who have already published works that, at more than a casual glance ignore, or misrepresent the hard-won attempts and victories of our kind. Where, for instance, is the exhaustive Biography of Ernst Zundel, Richard Girnt Butler or Thomas Metzger, early pioneers of both thought and action? Fame of *A Dead Man's Deeds* should have been financed by our own, written by one of our own, not to discount the 'awakening' of Robert S. Griffin, author of this inspiring work.

It has been mentioned by few, very few persons, that of men like *Wilmot Robertson*, who published his own works, out of pocket, with nary a advertisement by mainstream or small town newspapers, even though we had members of Staff, editors, and reporters who saw the genius and truth of his *Dispossessed Majority*, and the seminal importance of his *The Ethnostate*. Slackers, all, who failed in their support of an idea which, at the outset, was easily digestible by mainstream America, not to mention the potential largess by these efforts for all involved.

The internet, as a viable medium has, to date, filled our expectations of the future with regard to discussion and debate. Yet, to date, the general public is still enchanted with 'published' authors, and assume that the internet is still relegated to the 'kooks' and opinions of the mob, never having had the chance to participate in the *volks geist* of a majority ethos, of which some of us were fortunate enough to have experienced. This is for the near future however, and it behooves us, all of us, to inculcate that singular presence of mind, which will only come about if we, ourselves alone, work diligently and collectively, to promote those ideals which, in their own right, play their parts in creating and establishing that Once and Future West!

The rancor and fear, of the ordinary man on the street, needs more attention than simply the yea-saying of the seer and poet, he needs the public discourse, as was the usual fare a generation ago, without the burden of 'permits', when 'free association' actually meant a clear and distinct freedom to associate with ones neighbors, in american-style public discourse; why not demand this, for instance, in print, instead of the continuing masturbatory debates about the 'colour of crime'? Demand these issues, as a matter of course, for our readers and fellow citizens. How about 'free access to our own Land'? Ownership of private property, of useful and necessary commodities like Cattle, Agriculture, Poultry and the like, with the right to sell, independent of government oversight, with nominal State interdiction regarding health procedures, being necessary to a free people. These are issues which, with only a glance, will mark us free or slave, in the coming years. Very few, indeed, will fight for truths which, although pertinent in ways the common man may not see, but who will, nevertheless, fight for rights if, and he must be exposed to this, that mark him as master of his own 'ship of state', not beholden to this pernicious world order, this plantation mentality, which even the share-croppers of old, maintained more freedom and nobility than our modern counterparts.

This was the tenor of the early White Nationalist, discounted by settled and traditional individuals, and for their lack of vision and courage, the tragic dispossessed remain engulfed by treason and empire, unworthy of their name. To the Bards of White Nationalism, you have an obligation and duty to promote, without fear or favor, those issues dearest to the long-term happiness of our people, no matter the discord, which may, for a time, ensue.

The common man believes in himself, but has little telling voice; let those who are able to speak, speak in words clear, resonating with bold truth, political foresight, and the ways and means to facilitate these visions. We have little time to waste.

Within this framework, as opposed to the modern reality of a 'multi-cultural' America, that traditional Homeland of original settlers and pioneers, those of European stock who, through blight, hunger, inevitable ethnic warfare, as well as the simple duality of human nature, carved out with their bare hands, a common presence, a common ideal, and a common people out of many, and diverse peoples, related, but characteristically independent, sovereign, arrogant, and pious in their singular and specific view of each and every opposing world-view, a legacy dominated by religion, warfare, and fear.

It was never a peaceful process, the process of carving out a Nation. Struggle never is.

Today's progeny, those children of today, increasingly, know less of these antecedents and more of a new parentage, an adoption really, of individuals who, unlike them, neither see, feel, look, respond, or spiritually comprehend what is natural, right, beautiful, and intelligent for the survival and extension of what, for now, is held by fewer and fewer individuals who see the vision of today's world through the eyes of their ancestors.

However, these children are here, they remain, living and dying, keeping both a memory and a dream alive, no matter the intrinsic evolution, and changing of the guard of yesteryear; like their ancestors, need and desire are of sterner stuff than can be quantified in cursory assessments or political careers based, not on that mystical quality of the 'dreamer', or the esoteric logic of 'freedom', but on status quo, on the absolute value of control. No longer are we one, great, connected People, designed by Providence to acquire, work, harness, and nurture the natural elements for the betterment and continuation of a particular, unique, and fragile people, a people which, at first blush, belongs to each of us.

What, then, as the dream fades, and the inherent discomfort continues unabated, do we, you and I, do?

Moreover, if resolution is possible, either in our lifetime or that of our children, what shape, contour, or specific design do we aspire? This has been the question for at least the last two generations, lost in a fog of controversy and historical persuasion, changing from one generation to the next since the "War Between The States', and the continuous maneuverings of political parricide. Is Life really so dear, that we purchase this gift with the chains of Slavery and abrogation?

Below, an article presented in the tradition of debate, and education between peers and folk which, by extension, simply accommodates the essence of the specie: The pursuit to discover what is ours to achieve. It is hoped that the pursuits in which the entire nation is being drawn, ineluctably, into the future will develop, as all new passions, into that birth which will, also, define the person in his majority.

This is an old discussion, but with new blood and bone assessing the value and inadequacies might, just might, receive a new and bolder import in the coming days.

ALL of Western man's ethos has been based, in large degree, on the supposition that the 'leader', the doer, is behind all that is good; Pericles, Caesar, Frederick Barbarossa, Gustavus Adolphus, Napoleon Bonaparte, Hermann Arminius, Vercingitorix; or, if you like, Aristotle, Goethe, Pythagoras, Archimedes, Daedalus (two of my favorites), Erastothenes, the List on both accounts, is too long to repeat.

In each and every case, it is self evident that, with time and a following, that is to say, the head and the body, they lead in their respective fields, and led well; some succeeded or were denied success in the military realms, but even in the chaos of their destruction left, in marked contrast to the jooish mind, positive instruction and example. For instance: we have the *Code Napoleon*, the legacy of *Pericles*, and many other well known 'heroes'.

Compare these efforts, in life or of the pen, with those who would have you, or force you, to restructure your past, and merge into theirs. That of the CHEKA, NKVD. Pol Pot, Marx, Lenin, Trotsky...the list goes on. Hmmm, decisions, decisions...I wonder.

No, hero worship *is* part of OUR psychology, it is a mechanism which brings both chaos and power; it is tenuous, bold, calculating; it is not always liked, nor understood at the moment, but it is behind all cultural change and restoration. It is not a ghost of the Past, but a warm-blood of today, a legacy which is granted to each generation, in vitro, sometimes needed, sometimes cast aside, but always with us.

One, particular observation, which has made itself manifest to me over the years, was when I first climbed aboard a civil war era Cannon, resting comfortably within its 'sand box' setting, open-mouthed, its spoked wheels well taken care of, steel pitted, but shiny blue, carried me well; I resonated with the inherent metal surface, its cold steel warming to my tiny grip. Scooting down the length, I fell to the soft sand below and began walking towards the large Fountain, with its gurgling, undulating stream of water, radiating a harmonic (as I understand it today) sound, relaxing one's mind and body. Atop the grand pedestal was a marker of Bronze, a Monument - a term which has, ineluctably and with malice aforethought, been taken from us, from each small village (lately, this has been the theft by mestizos, and gutter whites for money), each small town and certainly from every Major Cosmopolis in our once great Nation; for these are spiritual things; they are sacrosanct to our very selves; our psychology depends upon these subtle, intangible, yet living things, for by their very nature, their distinguishing characteristics, describe to us, their children, the Memory of, as was the case here, an Officer, a leader, sword out, pointing decidedly in that unique and, perhaps, romantic visions of the 'charge', and of victory.

I never have forgotten that experience; but after that, I never saw a new one, a new location or artistic resonance. New Parks, sure, but never again did I see another face, another ancient memory, looking back on me; psychology, to be sure, but not the jooish remonstrations of Oedipus, or Freud's perverse and simple sexual desires that he would, no doubt, foist upon the goyim. Not the beauty and memory of a time, OUR time, in which, even in 'civil war', there were lessons to be learned, of Honour and Duty, of dying and living, of extension. Yes, these things and more, have been taken from you, from all of us, but individuals who understand that to destroy ones enemies, one must firstly, deny that host the very marrow of its own body, and the mind cannot exist without the body - that is to say, a picture, a description, of that body which will, forever, look down upon its children with strength, character, and that direction of purpose which, truly, only a Hero may bestow.

Can we, any of us, anywhere, create these monuments? Try it! Perhaps, some small hamlet, some forgotten township, but anywhere else, no chance; it would be racist, forced to comply with the urban cosmopolis of Canaille, of racial hell, denying us, you and I, something to be proud of, to quietly and gracefully come, meditate, and let that sense of yesteryear, produce the strength and direction for the Future. No, this Theft is complete, and there is no restoring it; you, all of us, must never submit until we have, once again, that place, that great attempt, to lay claim to our own Land, our own Nation - only with this, will our children, and grandchildren, ever be able to share such simplistic and powerful emotions as those mentioned above - their psychology already dead upon its birth.

I digress...

Lift UP your heroes, at whatever level, the real blood and bone of your people, not the spiritualized fantasy of the 'otherworldly'...place your value, for now, with your People, your family, and your comrades, and protect the weak, work with the strong, and we shall overcome what has become, the legacy of NOT remembering where, truly, a strong psychology is begat - in the hopes and dreams of a People.

ii.

In the meanwhile, the discussions and innumerable considerations of the various political and religious camps, remains fixed, ever willing to engage in the myriad of tangential tactics and stratagems, by which they or their particular team, might do the most good, avoid negative publicity, and generally spend their time posturing to their individual groups and gatherings.

Some time ago, a friend passed me several essays by an individual, using a pseudonym, Hunter Wallace, (a young man of under thirty, as of this writing). As there is, literally, a plethora of writers and 'bloggers', with some of the greatest and marvelously produced visual and content orientated electronic pages, that it simply boggles the mind; what practical effects are to be witnessed, is another matter entire. However, this particular essay proved quite compelling as it comes, ostensibly, from a young man, from a good family in the South, and brings, also, a more detached and commonsense approach to his topics.

The electronic media, it seems, is another animal altogether.

At this point, I am *not* sure if Mr. Wallace is a White Nationalist or not, at least one I would recognize at first blush; the verbiage and associations of this individual are many, and he seems to wander along paths not yet fully developed; not a point of disaffection, but certainly something, which may indicate personal habits or a personal level of enlightenment, is worthy of reflection and careful discussion when, as we all must, face the crowd, so to speak, and *define* ourselves in a comprehensive and intelligent manner, as befits those who would instruct and lead.

As well, with many in the political realm of 'white nationalism', there is a predilection of certain people to become 'name droppers', and to instigate and create an atmosphere of conflict, at some point to merely be open to various sides of an issue but, more often than not, to excite the reader or listener with 'gossip' and drama. and even more drama.

With this said, I would also say that with Mr. Wallace, and individuals certain to follow or have already brought to bear such intellectual prose have, as yet, to finalize just what they want to do with their new-found missions in life; this, however, is simply a matter of growing, evolving into the future speakers, organizers and, perhaps, those leaders so necessary to our folk-at-large. Moreover, to the latter, I wish them the very best.

Nevertheless, as with most of my reading and analysis, it is appropriate, at his juncture, to introduce the reader to a common thread amongst old and new members of the White Nationalist struggle, bearing in mind, at least for this work, the numerous articles and essays, brilliant though many are, I felt it more practical to share with the reader the 'up and coming' views and talents from which to draw our more immediate interest:

Vanguardists vs. Mainstreamers[32]

Hunter Wallace

A reasonable "mainstreamer" movement is needed.

[...] has asked me to address one of the thorniest issues in White Nationalism: the quarrel between the older, "vanguardist" wing of the movement and the newer, "mainstreamer" wing. In recent weeks, Arthur Kemp has thrown gasoline on the fire and a debate has raged here and at other sites. Leonard Zeskind and Carol Swain have published books about White Nationalism that revolve around this division.

Origins and Beliefs

The lineage of the "vanguardists" can be traced back to a number of twentieth century neo-fascist fringe groups. The most prominent are William Dudley Pelley's Silver Shirts, Gerald L.K. Smith's Christian Nationalist Crusade, George Lincoln Rockwell's American Nazi Party, William Pierce's National Alliance, Glenn Miller's White Patriot Party, Richard Butler's Aryan Nations, Ben Klassen's World Church of the Creator and Cliff Herrington's National Soc-ialist Movement. Let's be

---

[32] *Hunter Wallace* is a nom de plume. http://www.occidentaldissent.com/

sure not to forget the oldest, most storied vanguardist group of them all, the Ku Klux Klan. A constellation of pro-White vanguardist organizations has existed on the far right since the Roaring Twenties.

The vanguardist wing has a few distinguishing characteristics: a willingness to advocate or resort to physical violence, esoteric rituals, symbols and dress, a strong or exclusive emphasis on the Jewish Question, a skeptical or hostile attitude towards democratic politics, a rigid attitude on doctrinal purity, a total rejection of incrementalism, and above all else, a belief that only a minority of Whites can be swayed to our political views, always combined with a focus on creating small organizations of the elect few. Insofar as they have a strategy, vanguardists dream of seizing power in the aftermath of their long anticipated "collapse" of the federal government.

In a certain sense, the "mainstreamers" have always existed. America was explicitly founded as a "white man's country." Racialists dominated American politics from the ratification of the U.S. Constitution until the Civil Rights Act of 1964. Usually Southerners, these people were ordinary, respectable middle class businessmen, doctors, and lawyers, the traditional elites of the small towns, who found their racial beliefs under attack by a hostile liberal elite and the black underclass. They are not the sort of people who naturally gravitate towards the political fringe. The mainstreamers were pushed to the margins after America's WASP ruling class was overthrown by monied, urban Jews in the mid-twentieth century.

The split between the "mainstreamers" and "vanguardists" can be traced back to the aftermath of the Brown decision. Whereas the Klan resorted to violence and intimidation, the traditional Southern elite, the incipient "mainstreamers," created the White Citizens' Council. They litigated integration, protested in the streets, created sovereignty commissions, hoisted the banner of states' rights, invoked interposition, engaged in economic boycotts, outright refused to comply with federal court orders, defunded or closed the integrated public schools, created private academies, and voted for George Wallace in his presidential campaigns. They promised and delivered "massive resistance" to integration.

In the final days of Jim Crow, the "mainstreamers" kept the "vanguardists" at arm's length. They generally wanted nothing to do with them. Outside of the liberal imagination, there was no cognizance of belonging to a shared political movement. The mainstreamers were not the type of people who went around firebombing churches and lynching negroes. Typically, they hated fascism and took pride in America's role in the Second World War. Many of them had actually fought in Europe. These people were FDR's voters and the base of the Democratic Party. In every way, they considered themselves normal, decent, patriotic Americans who combined their rac-ialism with a strong belief in liberty, federalism and Protestant Christianity.

Unlike the "vanguardists," the "mainstreamers" are defined by their belief in engaging in democratic politics. They believe a majority of White Americans can be persuaded to share our views. They advocate an electoral path to victory. The "mainstreamers" reject violence, strongly disapprove of vanguardist esoterica, reject or downplay the Jewish Question, advocate moderation, incrementalism, and mass membership organizations. They reject the vanguardist myth of social collapse and attack fringe groups for their lack of a practical strategy.

Since the late 1980's, the "mainstreamer" wing has enjoyed a resurgence in the pro-White movement. According to Leonard Zeskind, Willis Carto was the trailblazer with Liberty Lobby and the Populist Party. David Duke is the most notable racialist to make the transition from vanguardist to mainstreamer. He took off the Klan robes, moderated his message, and successfully ran for elected office in Louisiana. The White Citizens'

Council evolved into the Council of Conservative Citizens. Jared Taylor, the most prominent mainstreamer, launched American Renaissance. Peter Brimelow launched VDARE. There are a number of other websites and bloggers pushing the "mainstreamer" point of view.

In the 1990's and 2000's, largely due to the spread of the internet and the death of "vanguardist" leaders, the "mainstreamers" wrestled back control of the pro-White movement from the "vanguardists," who had dominated the scene in the 1970's and 1980's. The typical White Nationalist is now a middle class, White male professional unaffiliated with any organization. These people are usually non-violent, college educated and internet savvy. The majority of them have been recruited online and participate in the movement exclusively in cyberspace.

The Mainstreamer Catastrophe, I

Ever since the resurgence of the "mainstreamers," a destructive myth has begun to circulate and gain traction, namely, that the "vanguardists" are responsible for the marginalization of racialists. If only the costume clowns would disappear, the Kluxers and the Nutzis, media access and respectability will follow, or so the theory goes. Hence, the triumphant mainstreamers can often be found advocating a massive purge of the vanguardists from the White Nationalist movement.

This theory rests on a severe case of historical amnesia. The "mainstreamers" once dominated the entire American nation, but they progressively lost control of it over two centuries and ruled only in the Jim Crow South by 1964. This historical process had been going on for over a century before the Civil Rights Act of 1964, before the crusade against fascism in the Second World War, and long before the emergence of any of the vanguardist organizations.

The Northeast was the first region of the country to succumb to anti-racism. The American Revolution was quickly followed by the abolition of slavery in the area. Vermont, New Hampshire, New York, and New Jersey never passed anti-miscegenation laws. Pennsylvania repealed its anti-miscegenation law before joining the Union. In Massachusetts, the state anti-miscegenation law succumbed to abolitionist pressure in the 1830's. In the name of "liberty" and "equality," the remaining anti-miscegenation laws and the few segregation statutes in the region were repealed in the wake of the Civil War.

The Midwest was strongly racialist in the Antebellum Era. Several Midwestern states imposed stiff fines on black settlers. Jim Crow was pioneered in the region. In the Midwest, anti-slavery was often synonymous with anti-black sentiment. As in the Northeast, racial attitudes weakened in the aftermath of the Civil War, and most of the anti-miscegenation laws and segregation statutes came tumbling down in the late nineteenth century.

The West held out the longest. This is undoubtedly due to the fact that it was sparsely settled. In this region, the Indian Wars were still fresh in the historical memory. Chinese and Japanese immigration represented a potent threat to White labor. A weaker version of Jim Crow prevailed in the West until the aftermath of the Second World War. From 1945 to 1964, the Western states voluntarily repealed their anti-miscegenation laws and segregation statutes.

In the South, racial attitudes hardened after the Second World War. White liberals like Claude "Red" Pepper and Franklin Graham were thrown out of office. Southerners dug in their heels and defiantly resisted the national consensus on race. Jim Crow was overthrown by force: Northern

Democrats and Northern Republicans united in Congress to defeat Southern filibusters and ratify the Civil Rights Act of 1964 and the Voting Rights Act of 1965. The latter piece of legislation revolutionized Southern politics and destroyed White voting power in the socially conservative Black Belt counties.

In 1945, White racialists controlled the Jim Crow South. We controlled parts of the Jim Crow West. There were explicit laws that mandated segregation and outlawed miscegenation in these regions. An informal system of segregation existed in the Northeast and Midwest, but White racial attitudes had dramatically weakened there. By 1964, they had collapsed in the Northeast, Midwest, and West.

In 1964, Jim Crow was overthrown in the South. The Southern anti-miscegenation laws were struck down a few years later in Loving v. Virginia. From 1964 to 1991, White racial attitudes collapsed in the South and steadily began to approach the national norm. Simply put, the South was Americanized as the national television, radio, and print media penetrated the region and changed its culture. Hitherto, the South had remained an outlier because Southerners had always gotten their news from local newspapers controlled by segregationist editors.

The Mainstreamer Catastrophe, II

At this critical juncture, the "mainstreamers" suffered a catastrophe from which they never recovered, one that had nothing to do with the "vanguardists." The bulk of racially conscious Southern Whites responded to the defeat of Jim Crow by getting involved in conservative politics. They bought into the moderate argument that the way forward was to fight the Civil Rights Movement through non-racial arguments against "big government." Instead of fighting the racial battle, they would focus instead on defending their culture. They would engage in "practical politics," strategically retreat, and extract revenge on the hated liberals who had usurped control over the Democratic Party.

The first tentative steps in this direction were taken in the 1964 presidential election when Barry Goldwater carried several of the Deep South states. In 1968, the liberal integrationist Hubert Humphrey was defeated by Richard Nixon, Wallace carried the Deep South, and the Democrats lost every Southern state but Texas. In 1972, Nixon defeated McGovern in a landslide and Wallace won several Democratic primaries. In 1976, the South was lured back into the fold by Jimmy Carter, a Southern candidate. In 1980, Reagan wiped the floor with Carter, who had been discredited as an enfeebled liberal, and again with Mondale in 1986.

In the 1990's, the Bush/Clinton years, American politics settled into its familiar pattern. A socially liberal New England and West Coast became the base of the Democratic Party. A socially conservative South became the base of the Republican Party. The sectionalism of the two parties hardened under George W. Bush into the famous "Red State" vs. "Blue State" divide. The Obama/McCain electoral map masks the fact that Obama barely won Florida, North Carolina, and Virginia.

To cut a long story short, the ex-segregationists became conservatives, got into the habit of voting for the Republicans, focused on "practical politics," and became steadily deracialized over the next forty years. This is where their descendants are still at today: checking the box for every fraud with an (R) beside his name.

Vanguardists Triumphant

The "vanguardists" who gained hegemony over the pro-White movement in the late 1960's, 1970's, and early 1980's didn't win through superior arguments. They inherited the mantle of White leadership by default. The "mainstreamers" suffered a catastrophic loss of their base and most of them quit the field to get involved in conservative politics. The fringe groups left behind moved into the vacuum and recreated the pro-White scene in their own image. The media happily played along.

In the late 1980's, the "mainstreamers" began to stir again, but found themselves up against the backdrop of the previous twenty years, when the pro-White scene had sunk to an all time low in the United States. They found themselves branded Neo-Nazis and Klansmen in the press. The fringe group image stuck and lots of "mainstreamers" began to draw the erroneous conclusion that it was the cause of their predicament … which brings us to where we are today.

Vanguardists vs. Mainstreamers

There is a lot of merit to both sides of this argument. In the "mainstreamers" favor, the "vanguardists" have attracted the dysfunctional, kooky, sociopathic types that are always found in fringe politics. They have been unable to create viable or stable organizations. The "vanguardists" have no strategy aside from waiting on a mythic social collapse. The costume scene is ridiculous, stagnant and brings White Nationalism into disrepute.

In the "vanguardists" favor, it is easy to talk about winning elections, but in reality it is a near impossible mountain to climb. The racial situation is so far gone that victory at present looks like a pipe dream. The "mainstreamers" might be able to achieve some political success, say, a few city councilmen or state legislators, but will never possess the majority required to enact necessary constitutional changes. The "mainstreamers" are following in the footsteps of the conservatives, but will never be as successful, and with all their electoral success, the conservatives have nothing to show for it. They retort by pointing out that mass membership organizations are flypaper for the dregs of society. If that were not enough, the "mainstreamers" are accused of dishonesty and dishonorable conduct on the Jewish Question.

Synthesis

In my view, the critiques of both sides are more impressive than either of their platforms. I come down somewhere in the center of this debate. I can see a need for "practical politics," but I am convinced that it shouldn't be our primary emphasis. We should spend roughly 80% of our time and resources trying to change the culture; 20% on building momentum and attracting new recruits through political campaigns. Without a stable cultural foundation, which I define as pulling the national discourse on race in our direction, political victories will only prove costly and temporary.

There is a residual level of racial consciousness in the Deep South. We should take advantage of that and try to build a real world base in the area. If we can't win in Mississippi and Alabama (winning is changing attitudes), we are doomed. It is conceivable that we could win a few state legislature seats and get on some city councils in this region. That will require a moderate platform: pro-identity, pro-immigration restriction, anti-affirmative action, anti-multiculturalism, anti-political correctness. For good measure, throw in some economic nationalism and cultural conservatism. This is not unlike what Kemp suggests.

The Jewish Question and White Nationalism are too radical for voters to digest. However, I don't think they should be ignored. Along with racial differences, they should be the focus of educational campaigns. There will always be websites that focus on these matters and we could use more of them. These issues will have to be introduced incrementally into the national mainstream. Once again, "incrementalism" is forcing the mainstream right to become more like us, not the other way around.

The esoterica/costumes are weird, unnecessary, and off putting. Neo-Nazism and Third Reich fetishism are losers. Holocaust revisionism is an irrelevant waste of time. Better quality control is a no-brainer. A private, invitation only "vanguardist" organization could work; every social movement needs a capable leadership. I'm not opposed to creating pro-White political action committees. As Kemp says, it is too late to create a third party. It just won't work in the American context.

After ten years, I have given up on waiting for "the collapse." It could happen, but I wouldn't bet on it. The recent economic crisis has shown that White Nationalists are unable to capitalize on fortuitous current events. We should hope for the best; prepare for the worst. If nothing else, that means keeping the pro-White flame alive like St. Benedict in the Dark Ages.

The Fringe

In dealing with the fringe, we should follow the example of the Left with the anarchists. We should keep a respectful distance and ignore them in public. Instead of slamming Neo-Nazis, we dismiss them as mostly harmless kooks and patiently explain why pro-Whites are driven to such extremes. Whenever possible, I think we should try to romanticize and rehabilitate our extremists. There should be an element of prestige to being uncompromising. The Left has done this with any number of figures: Malcolm X, Che Guevera, Stokely Carmichael, Rosa Luxemburg, etc.

Look at it this way: If a gangster like Omar from The Wire can be a sympathetic figure, President Obama's favorite television character, why not Bob Matthews or David Lane? Murderers like Jesse James and Billy the Kid have been folk heroes before. The Klan was rescued from disrepute by a single film and went on to dominate Northern states like Oregon, Colorado, and Indiana. The Birth of a Nation was wildly successful. Unfortunately, it is one of the few examples of the Right successfully using film to change the culture.

Via the Overton Window, extremists can play a useful role in pushing the margins of our national discourse. Next to a William Pierce or Alex Linder, who are unthinkable, a Jared Taylor can appear merely radical, next to a Jared Taylor, a Pat Buchanan can look "acceptable," next to a Pat Buchanan, a Lou Dobbs can appear sensible. The Left has mastered the Overton Window and has steadily pushed the cultural envelope in their direction by staking out ever more extreme positions and then running a "moderates" that appease them.

The best example of this is gay marriage. It runs completely against the grain of traditional Christian mores. It is a political albatross for the Left. It has gone down in flames in over thirty states. A few decades ago, gay marriage was unthinkable. Now the debate is over whether it is radical or acceptable. The same was once true of abortion, feminism, and civil rights. Gay marriage is starting to garner the momentum of inevitability.

Next to Malcolm X and Stokely Carmichael, Martin Luther King, Jr. was seen as an acceptable moderate. FDR was seen as "moderate" compared to Huey Long nipping at his heels. The argument was successfully made that we had to enact civil rights reform, affirmative action, or the minimum wage/social security to stop radicals from swooping in and taking over. The fringe has been exploited and put to good use by more capable men in the past.

Final Thoughts

I will let this stand as my decisive statement on the issue. A reasonable "mainstreamer" movement is needed: one that incorporates "vanguardist" insights, one that doesn't scapegoat the "vanguardists" for every setback, one that recognizes the fringe will always be around and has a role to play, and finally one that doesn't slip into fanaticism at our chances of political success.

Vanguardists vs. Mainstreamers:

A Response

The recent Essay by Hunter Wallace, a voice which, to date, has resonated with many White Nationalists, in the ofttimes vitriolic arena of conservative and nationalist rhetoric; in many essays, unlike the vast and temperate mainstream (to coin a phrase) of the American political abyss I, as well, have found this voice a stable, level, and consistent voice hammering out, as it were, a balance between elements who which, each in turn, have tried and are trying, to vie for the hearts and minds of the White ethnic sons and daughters of the far-flung West.

As voices can be, and ofttimes are, those 'crying in the wilderness', seemingly, heard by few, and relegated to general obscurity have, nevertheless, gained tremendous foot-holds within the communities and politicos of both a National and conservative mindset. Hence, as Mr. Wallace has so cogently and eloquently delivered his "Vanguardists vs. Mainstreamers" reminds me, as well, of all those years previous, the conflicts, the chicanery, the betrayals of those who, many years ago, debated and obfuscated over the same inferences, issues and, ultimately, the fate of those Western stock which resided, lived and died in this, our northern continent.

The elemental structure was the same, although the nomenclature varied from the present, yet struck at the very same inward strategic mindset of the day, as well as the tactical imperatives in which, for the most and varied part, was felt by individual groups and individuals, namely, the Organizational leaders and social constructs of Fraternities, religious groups, and racial nationalists; all, each in turn, felt a god-given imperative in which to conduct a defensive war against the enemies of our People. Alas, then as now, what should be a working duality has, for the most part, been a ever-battling dichotomy between generations, not necessarily between working strategy and tactics, rather, between those who would 'do' and those who would 'study' those who do.

A brief passage, beginning this essay, begins thus:

"A reasonable "mainstreamer" movement is needed."

This, for myself, set the tenor and tone, of the essay, and left me, not uneasy, but with a sense of *deja vu*. I have addressed this issue before and, for the most part, have seen this act play out again, and again. Be that as it may, as Mr. Wallace's points are worthy of repetition, however; let me add too, if I may, another voice on the matter, with the intent, as before, to encourage and educate, the embryonic yet powerful forces of White nationalists, everywhere.

I do not wish to address the usage of nomenclature, as utilized by many in the White Nationalists community, however, I will use my own, and point out that "vanguardists' and 'mainstreamers', by any other name, is still the age-old nemesis between 'conservatives' and 'revolutionaries'. No other comparison could be made which adequately compels the student of history and racial politics to attend to both study and reality. In short, this story is, ultimately, between those men of *action*, and those men of *thought*. Any true and heart-felt nationalist will know, as should we all, that *both*, of course, are *requisite* to any permanent and socially imperative design to establish those two elements necessary to the survival of the West, both in its corporate self, and marked by its individual components, namely, its racial citizens, and this is: *Territory* and *Political sovereignty*. No other attempt at a reunification of those elements as in days past is any longer a working reality; on the contrary, this has proved suicidal.

As well, with all discussions which affect us as a People, as a corporate racial imperative, should always be afforded a fair and balanced hearing in matters destined to affect all of us collectively. I reject, setting up 'two camps', *opposed* and *divided* against itself; it matters not who, or how long individuals have remained in the spotlight, or have engaged, either effectively or ineffectively in the political arena to date, for in either case, it is only a starting point, a fledgling 'yea saying' which is attempted, and not a visceral and deliberate accommodation of racial and political dogma. It should be, it could have been, many times, if not for the *canard* of opposing 'views'.

Such a view, is encapsulated thusly:

> The lineage of the "vanguardists" can be traced back to a number
> of twentieth century neo-fascist fringe groups. The most prominent

are William Dudley Pelley's *Silver Shirts*, Gerald L.K. Smith's *Christian Nationalist Crusade*, George Lincoln Rockwell's *American Nazi Party*, William Pierce's *National Alliance*, Glenn Miller's *White Patriot Party*, Richard Butler's *Aryan Nations*, Ben Klassen's *World Church of the Creator* and Cliff Herrington's *National Socialist Movement*. Let's be sure not to forget the oldest, most storied vanguardist group of them all, the Ku Klux Klan. A constellation of pro-White vanguardist organizations has existed on the far right since the Roaring Twenties.

Not a unworthy summary, yet it encapsulates, perhaps arbitrarily, an over-broad and disparate conglomerate; a conglomerate which, if reviewed by anyone who has played an active and parallel role, would know that many of these groups represented, not White Nationalism, but traditional *nativist* evolutionary politics, even Ben Klassen's WCCC, but a simple western religious construct, adding a simple *exclusive* racial component. To compare, as well, the more recent NSM with, let's say, Richard Butler's Aryan Nations, a Theo-political *pan-racialism* was, truly, a large step away from traditional native-regionalism, and diametrically opposed to the traditional 'thinkers' of the racialist movement; yet, if one is honest, even this embryonic pan-racialism, was simply the natural evolution of our European antecedents. Religion, as a tactical imperative, is always a bait and switch precisely, why, today, most white americans, have discarded, or severely modified, the religious technics of their fathers and mothers, as most of the present generation, rightly or wrongly, see the traditional conservatism as blindly short-sighted, and cowardly, for having allowed this state of affairs to have continued, gaining momentum to this present outrage.

Those individuals and groups who, for the most part, continued the struggle of their fathers, and hence, designated 'vanguardists' were, in effect, simply the 'true-believers' of a long line of true-believers fighting a rear-guard action, highlighted by the European attempt of a pro-active terminus; a goal which, today, still maintains, or should maintain, the absolute direction and impetus of all White Nationalists, that is, the very blood and bone, of our People. Victory, at any cost, is the watch-word for these persons.

The inevitable split of political aspirations, as in all human psychology, is a duality, which is lucidly described by Mr. Wallace:

> The split between the "mainstreamers" and "vanguardists" can be traced back to the aftermath of the Brown decision. Whereas the

Klan resorted to violence and intimidation, the traditional Southern elite, the incipient "mainstreamers," created the White Citizens' Council. They litigated integration, protested in the streets, created sovereignty commissions, hoisted the banner of states' rights, invoked interposition, engaged in economic boycotts, outright refused to comply with federal court orders, defunded or closed the integrated public schools, created private academies, and voted for George Wallace in his presidential campaigns. They promised and delivered "massive resistance" to integration.

In addition:

In a certain sense, the "mainstreamers" have always existed. America was explicitly founded as a "white man's country." Racialists dominated American politics from the ratification of the U.S. Constitution until the Civil Rights Act of 1964. Usually Southerners, these people were ordinary, respectable middle class businessmen, doctors, and lawyers, the traditional elites of the small towns, who found their racial beliefs under attack by a hostile liberal elite and the black underclass. They are not the sort of people who naturally gravitate towards the political fringe. The mainstreamers were pushed to the margins after America's WASP ruling class was overthrown by monied, urban Jews, who enlisted the burgeoning ranks of the 'new' white middle class, who were experimenting with their new-found 'white man's burden', and the expectations which this new 'faith' demanded, in the mid-twentieth century.[33]

A view, of which, I wholeheartedly subscribe.

It has been known to Nationalists for many years, having been deceived, damned, and defiant to the end, rather than compromise those necessary

---

[33] The insidious ramifications of the falsity of Brown v. Board of Education, became the clarion call of all 'civic minded' whites, and ushered in the reckless and traitorous social experiment which has disrupted, not only those of Western stock, but the black race as well, with the exception of a few [black] race-cultural spokesmen. Thomas Sowell comes to mind. FLS.

and vital moral imperatives which will see them to the final truth sought by all Nationalists, that one must consciously promote, and achieve, a *government* and definable *territory* for the future of our People, if we are to survive.

There are literally dozens of places, countries, and States which have seen tremendous upheavals and burgeoning Parties and leaders throughout the Western world; indeed, the entire planet. From these individual and unique areas, we find various levels of Nationalist participation and success; many of these individuals and nations go under the 'radar' here, in this country, for to carry the clarion call of 'nationalism' is a dangerous and implacable term; it advances the 'extremist' against the 'conservative' elements, making the status quo arbitrary and potentially useless.

Since, in certain quarters of our fair land, it is becoming unacceptable to speak of individuals and leaders of the Nationalist variety, at least those not accepted by the novice, the weak, and the jealous, I thought it appropriate to spotlight another country, and an individual which is not known by many; indeed, I came across this material just days ago.

A little background:

In the early 70's, the aggression of the old Communist empire, Tito being the best example, had marred the eastern European cohesiveness, disrupted any chance of those Ethno-states finding common ground by which to become stronger thereby; one such State, Croatia, has a history which both divides and harmonizes its political and racial awareness; this is the Folkish, or National Identity which was denied many in the East, until the last thirty years or so.

Bruno Busic, a Croatian Patriot, dedicated to the independence of his homeland, standing tall against the 'system' which spoke for his countrymen, yet would betray their inner most desires. He was part of a fledgling 'independence/nationalist' movement; soon, he became their leader. A reader and warrior, he gave his life for his cause.

His younger brother, Boris Busic, believing the same ideas as his brother, continued in like fashion. In the early 70's, Bruno was assassinated by communist provocateurs, some say mossad, since Franjo Tudjman was consider by many to be a National Socialist/Ustasha member. Boris, upon learning of his brother's death, vowed to continue where Bruno had left off, and demanded independence for his countrymen.

Both these men were extremists in the pure sense; they vowed to *create* a viable Homeland for their People.

There were many who felt that these types of individuals were 'harmful' to the 'movement', these were the people who, as is always the case, purported to work for the future their way, and 'no matter how long it takes' would stick to their guns. However, Life moves at its own pace, and history is replete with those characters and 'souls' who dare to go beyond the norm. If these characters fail in their attempts, the conservative elements can pronounce, for all to hear, that these individuals were 'extreme' and received their just deserts; a smaller portion, perhaps, continue to support their 'heroes', and keep a candle burning. If these characters 'succeed' in their attempts then, one and all (including the conservatives) proclaim them Victorious, thereby achieving the status they, themselves, seek.

Boris Busic, served 32 years in american prisons for hijacking a plane, in which he, apparently, utilized to command world attention regarding both the assassination of his brother, but also the Croatian Independence movement still in its infancy. He was branded a 'criminal' by the world-press, the conservative national leaders found a rock to hide under, and this left but few individuals to keep a candle burning for one of their few, but very high-profile spokesmen on their behalf.

Mr. Busic was Released from american custody, after lengthy and delicate negotiations; the release of this man was the Croatian President's (Franjo Tudjman) obsession, a man who had fought from the ground up to achieve his political status. When this 'criminal' was returned to his homeland, he was greeted by thousands, and hailed as the returning Son and keeper of a Free Croatia. He faces a future which will, most assuredly, task him, but with the true believers of his Nation's potential future, and having flushed out those conservative elements, perhaps, in the next ten to fifteen years, will see a new nation, independent, and sovereign, like his brother, and all true patriots, dreamed.

Nevertheless, those who believe in an *idea*, in a *hope*, must acknowledge those few and unusual individuals who crystalize the hopes and dreams of those lesser men and women, who are called in a different way; the only difference I see clearly here, is that in this case, the people and nation of Croatia, did not leave their failed, wounded or killed, on the Field, but remained true for the most part, and were finally brought together, after 32 years, to pay their respects.

The lessons to be learned from Conservatives are many; we see it on a daily basis. Rather than fearlessly proposing the truth, come what may, they would die a thousand deaths, and claim they 'withstood' the test of time.

Many of these persons follow their own ambitions, and natural callings, and a person can only do what seems right to themselves, providing their ego is consistent and selfless, a rare commodity, indeed. Below are a few aphorisms, coined by *David Eden Lane*, a stalwart, humble and recalcitrant Nationalist, disowned, and left to die in the field, by the 'conservatives' of his day, which may help to define what many White Nationalists struggle and, in certain cases, have died for:

> *In the final analysis, a race or specie is not judged superior or inferior by its accomplishments, but by its will and ability to survive.*

> *Political, economic, and religious systems may be destroyed and resurrected by men, but the death of a race is eternal.*

> *No race of People can indefinitely continue their existence without territorial imperatives in which to propagate, protect, and promote their own kind.*

> *A People without a culture exclusively their own will perish.*

And:

> *In a sick and dying nation, culture, race or civilization, political dissent and traditional values will be labeled and persecuted as heinous crimes by inquisitors clothing themselves in jingoistic patriotism.*

> *A People who are ignorant of their past will defile the present and destroy the future.*

> *A race must honor above all earthly things, those who have given their lives or freedom for the preservation of the folk.*

> *The folk, namely the members of the race, are the Nation. Racial loyalties must always supersede geographical and national*

boundaries. If this is taught and understood, it will end fratricidal wars. Wars must not be fought for the benefit of another race.

And finally:

The latter stages of a democracy are filled with foreign wars, because the bankrupt system attempts to preserve itself by plundering other nations.

In a democracy that which is legal is seldom moral, and that which is moral is often illegal;

The difference between a terrorist and a patriot is control of the press.

Since the 70's, and into the early 80's, there were many influences, of which Mr. Wallace does not mention; here are five individuals who, while being of a different 'political' manifestation, nevertheless, motivated some very prominent and politically savvy persons: *Wesley Swift, Bertrand Comparet, Richard Girnt Butler, William Potter Gale, and Robert E. Miles*. These five individuals collectively, became the heart-beat of the theological/militant wing of the soon-to-be, White Nationalist collective, a term loosely contrived to describe the embryonic evolution of American racial politics.

This brand of nascent racial-theology, was contravened by one of the only true conservative intellectuals of the day, *Revilo P. Oliver*, a truly magnificent mind who, as the years accumulated, turned his back on traditional chrisitanity, and embraced the full faculties of his passion for intellect, Culture, history, and personal experience and, in consequence, parted ways with some of the countries most dynamic and revolutionary dogmatists. The end result was, once again, the preliminary evolution into 'white nationalism' at the expense of both political and ideologically inept 'traditionalists' and 'revolutionary' dogma – the "vanguardists" and "mainstreamers" of Mr. Wallace's lexicon.

As was said before, this duality has been seen many times, and it will be seen again; the question for today's White Nationalists is: Do we repeat the Past, or do we, for the first time in ten generations, follow a different path than that of our Fathers?

One of these points of direction, if I may, is one of that singular value of Propaganda, and the borrowing of implicit valuation, such as the utilization of commentary by opposition forces; a value, which, to some, have a viable and proper use.

When elements of the White Nationalist Press, which truly does exist, as any cursory viewing of the primarily electronic and printed media available to us will attest, collectively attempt a thing in unison, namely, to promote an idea, or political construct with the usage of verbiage coined by the forces of opposition, to buttress a position or idea we seek to maintain is, without equivocation, a parlance of suicide.

Since the late 1980's, the "mainstreamer" wing has enjoyed a *resurgence* in the pro-White movement. According to Leonard Zeskind, Willis Carto was the trailblazer with Liberty Lobby and the Populist Party. David Duke is the most notable racialist to make the transition from vanguardist to mainstreamer. He took off the Klan robes, moderated his message, and successfully ran for elected office in Louisiana. The White Citizens' Council evolved into the Council of Conservative Citizens. Jared Taylor, the most prominent mainstreamer, launched American Renaissance. Peter Brimelow launched VDARE. There are a number of other websites and bloggers pushing the "mainstreamer" point of view.

We have our own credible and definitive sources on these accounts, which belong to us. As White Nationalists of long duration, we should ever seek to inform our brethren from our own lips, not fearing the timid hearts who might not wish to address personal and professional issues, at the expense of one's reputation or largess; those days of 'anonymity' are long past. Using members of the opposition to 'prove a point' is not a liberal one, rather, it is a misguided and fruitless gesture, as these opponents care little for 'fair and balanced', and have always seen this weakness as fortune delivered, and as a sword thrust to the heart.

A conservative, or more succinctly, an individual person, has always had much to lose, but when compared to what our People face, I ask: where is your sense of Honour, courage, and dedication in the face of the enemy?

Be that as it may, it is too those individuals who, like Mr. Wallace, that the obligation exists to serve their Folk-at-large, and answer and define the historical implications and maneuvers of members of our own, rather than 'snakes in sheeps clothing' like Mr. Zeskind, and his serpentine ilk. The veracity of information, even if received by the opposition, if applicable, should never be discounted, but to insert these individuals does not, as I'm sure was the intention, to give legitimacy to the point expressed, gives undue air-time to those who, like Joe McCarthy's side-kick, will forever wait, until the time is right to sink, deeply, the fangs of opportunity and fame.

The conservative and nationalist ideological position can also be broken down into the sub-genre of 'youth and age'.

Nationalist are always young.

This 'spirit' of youth may be mental, physical, or ideological. This youth is the way-sign of the nationalist, insofar as the impetus for nationalism comes from a sense of romance, idealism, and the vagaries, which accompany youth; in short, the technics of the nationalist consist of a burgeoning sense of experimentation – of one's coming of age. The modern conservative sees this as juvenile behavior, and resents the political manifestations of this type of romance, for he feels it will supplant him. It is very true that in most cases, the nationalist seeks to reaffirm what is traditional, what he [the nationalist] sees as the better part of the past – the golden age of his experience – but knows that he cannot salvage all of it. The modern conservative sees this as fanaticism.

Like all young people, there is a certain shock value associated with the 'doing' of youth, and the intellectualizing of the elder. The nationalist shocks the complacent conservative (truly, a "mainstreamer") out of his cultural stupor by bringing to light, by reaffirming, the *original* idea, the primal origins of their shared beginnings, to the forefront. These manifestations may be recognized as ideological, racial, cultural, or civil discontent. It may very well bring out emotions long suppressed: hate, fear, survival, love, and sympathy.

Hate, because those who are supposed to be looking out for them, those who have been entrusted with the power to protect and serve, have abrogated this duty, have given the halls of justice and leadership over to the enemies of their kind. Fear, because the nationalist can see clearly the underlying betrayal of his national borders, the abuse and rape of his economic system, and finally through the cowardice of the body-politic, of the timid conservative, in allowing the disgraceful dissection of his ancient traditions, either through the written word of his forefathers, or the direct interpretation of the nations laws and precepts. Survival becomes his highest priority, and the feelings of love and sympathy for his fellow man becomes ever the benchmark of his aspirations. The Nationalist, in almost every case, sees a betrayal, by those in power, in whatever the Age who, as guardians, who decided to change or redirect those things, which had gone before; in other words, to make a change against what was seen as right for generations. As seen by the Nationalist, these changes had not come from any continuity of interests, or over a slow evolutionary period [seen in hundreds of years, not in dozens], but rather through the impetus and social construct of the personal wishes of individuals, rather than the needs of the People at large, devoid of contact with the real world of the living, outside his marble halls, and insulated by his money and sycophants. Such breaches of longstanding Tradition were the elements of France in 1789 – which brought about a victory in revolution by its adherents – at least the victory of 'mass' over 'quality'. The conservative, alas, has not understood this past so apparent for he continues to rationalize his position.

While the Modern rationalizes his position, the Nationalist reacts to his. It is instinct.

Granted, his emotions tend to place him outside the accepted sphere of influence of modern society. Indifferent though they [the mass] may be, being of the same race-soul, nevertheless, is drawn to it as well. They share the same instinct. Yet, as if it were deaf and dumb, the mass feels indifference to what they 'feel' intuitively as evil to their way of Life – they react in the same fashion to those that would act against those things felt, even if seen unclearly, that affects all in its path. To the mass, the conservative elements within certain white nationalist circles, still attaches such 'code words' as patriot, constitutionalist, legitimate power, etc., to instill a sense of continuity with the past. The mass will not see just how far they have been controlled for they are kept busy with work, worship, and raising families; after all, they seek nothing of the truth of the matter, they remain simply content with things the way they *are*. The mass, generally, are oblivious to the sequence of birth, life, and senility of their waking consciousness. The mass rarely will accept the fact that their legacy is dead, they too, are afraid of the rising tide, a new West, unaffected by the traditional closed door agreements of the past, for this new nationalism belongs to the ancient, unspoken attendance of a new generation of Nationalists, wrapped in guises that have long gone untaught by the powers of the State, in whom, the traditional con-servative, remains attached.

The Nationalist of Western racial stock faces the same consistent elements of *status quo* – on either Continent. The 'american' flag, the *symbolic* representative of that long and honorable tradition of nationalism, *as* a symbol of America, is no longer the symbol of the original *presence* of the Western race-culture. Let us be clear on this point: The 'symbol' of America no longer functions, in any *real* sense, as it did in its inception. This symbol, this flag, was a symbol of War – of that hostile act of belligerence and warfare against kindred, related by blood – Western blood. It was *between* white brothers. The fact that non-white elements played various parts in this conflict, on one side or the other, is of relative significance. The symbols, political technics, and the like, were founded by, and for, one people – alone.

The symbol of the flag represented an *intrinsic* stability inherent in a *unified* effort. This effort was War – an act of *betrayal* against a body politic which had led the Western experience for five hundred years or more in relative unbroken succession. But it was more; it was 'order' without law, it was law based on consent – not of the people, this a common fallacy – but in *harmony* with them.

The common ground between the nationalist and conservative of the past, has been, and is, for the most part, the issue of 'bearing arms', but for different reasons, and generally belittled; at least publicly, the standard acceptance of Race, and race-culture. The Conservative elements, then as now, believes in the documents of the past to maintain this 'right'; the Nationalist believes that there is no 'right', other than the right to choose for himself the 'right' to self-determine his role in relation to his surroundings. If the reader will take, good naturedly, another reminder, let it be this, and ever this: If there is anything such as a 'god-given right', it is up to man to *enforce* it (!). Man has made his political State what it is, not god. The Conservative awakens from his slumber – his attacks against the positions of his erstwhile political brethren, multiply daily.

Within the 'white nationalist community', these refrains are coming to fruition again, as in days past; from England and Europe there are those, as Mr. Wallace would affirm, are "mainstreamers", proposing the same old rhetoric of inclusion and immersion within the established order securing, it is hoped, a few scraps from the table of LongShanks, in the hopes of a few hard-won days in the sun, fighting themselves, as well as their cousins, for who should share the kudos of the day; unity, of course, no matter the cost, being relegated, once again, to those 'fringe' elements, maintaining a safe distance, compromising in speech and deed – hence, compromising the very life-blood of their People.

It is that 'alien' mentality with which the nationalist is very much at odds - that of the modern 'wannabe' white nationalist. The Nationalist is, by far, more vociferous in his attack against the play-acting nationalist, than he does the conservative – but without the larger media aid of the conservative it is apparent who still holds the upper hand. While the childish argument continues, the nefarious State of today, closes its grips upon both; this monstrous governmental technic continues to reserve for itself the right to maintain weapons in the hands of its militancy, its police force, its national security services. This, above and beyond, the majority of those Western people's who demand the same right, also, but who, as of this writing, have not the power to enforce their will.

The issue is not, nor ever has been, over 'gun ownership', this was simply the clarion call of the Conservative, the 'sound-bite' for the masses. The issue is Freedom, pure and simple. Freedom to maintain a race-cultural imperative; to protect Family; one's Home, self, and ultimately, the freedom to defend oneself from the tyranny of a technic, individually or collectively, of any infringement of one's Liberty by a foreign or domestic power. Period.

The Nationalist realizes that defense against *all* predators is a *law* cognizant with nature. The nationalist knew, and has always known, that the issue of gun ownership was his first line of defense - that the issue of 'sporting arms' was the pleading of the conservative to the traditional governmental technic, like a son pleading with his father for favor, for his 'inalienable rights' when, actually, the basis of his pleadings were based upon documents of the past which, at the outset, granted *no* rights, it simply *verified*, as a device of communication, recognized and battle-won, yes, those hard won rights decided in *struggle* and *contest*; decided by blood and sacrifice. Through Blood and Iron; through the contest, of culture and civilization.

This was made abundantly clear when, in the early 80's, White Nationalism (even the phrase, with some contested debate, originated in the early part of that decade, by a member of Robert J. Mathews' *die Bruder Schweigen*) took to the field in a blaze of glory, sending all the conservative elements into, a mainstream position; a position, to this day, which affords the most dubious of spokesmen and leaders, a continued safe haven to 'fight' the system.

The canard of 'extremism', used by these timid souls calling themselves 'white nationalist', never admitting the source or the power of this definition, pushed a few souls into the arena of political mandate, without the logical impetus of the very populous they claimed to advance! Hence, the proverbial merry-go-round between these two camps, continued unabated. Alas, for our own *Gordion Knot*, and the hand which would undo its complexities! It is not the fault of Nationalists, if the conservative elements lack the 'leadership princip' necessary to draw and control all comers for, of necessity, revolutionary change will not come from men and women who, albeit a purely idealistic world-view, look for a kinder and gentler evolution rather, than a more realistic understanding of revolutionary tactics and the necessity which fosters it. Kooks and sociopaths to some, are the disenfranchised, humiliated, and beaten common folk of our everyday lives – restraint, after all, is a gift given sparingly in these sundered times. In essence, as before, Mr. Wallace is more than up to the task of putting this distinction, as relates to White Nationalism, in sharp clarity:

There is a residual level of racial consciousness in the Deep South. We should take advantage of that and try to build a real world base in the area. If we can't win in Mississippi and Alabama (winning is changing attitudes), we are doomed. It is conceivable that we could win a few state legislature seats and get on some city councils in this region. That will require a moderate platform: pro-identity, pro-immigration restriction, anti-affirmative action, anti-multiculturalism, anti-political correctness. For good measure, throw in some economic nationalism and cultural conservatism. This is not unlike what Kemp suggests.

The Jewish Question and White Nationalism are too radical for voters to digest. However, I don't think they should be ignored. Along with racial differences, they should be the focus of educational campaigns. There will always be websites that focus on these matters and we could use more of them. These issues will have to be introduced incrementally into the national mainstream. Once again, "incrementalism" is forcing the mainstream right to become more like us, not the other way around.

The esoterica/costumes are weird, unnecessary, and off putting. Neo-Nazism and Third Reich fetishism are losers. Holocaust revisionism is an irrelevant waste of time. Better quality control is a no-brainer. A private, invitation only "vanguardist" organization could work; every social movement needs a capable leadership. I'm not opposed to creating pro-White political action committees. As Kemp says, it is too late to create a third party. It just won't work in the American context.

After ten years, I have given up on waiting for "the collapse." It could happen, but I wouldn't bet on it. The recent economic crisis has shown that White Nationalists are unable to capitalize on fortuitous current events. We should hope for the best; prepare for the worst. If nothing else, that means keeping the pro-White flame alive like St. Benedict in the Dark Ages.

And more:

In dealing with the fringe, we should follow the example of the Left with the anarchists. We should keep a respectful distance and ignore them in public. Instead of slamming Neo-Nazis, we dismiss them as mostly harmless kooks and patiently explain why pro-Whites are driven to such extremes. Whenever possible, I think we should try to romanticize and rehabilitate our extremists. There should be an element of prestige to being uncompromising. The Left has done this with any number of figures: Malcolm X, Che Guevera, Stokely Carmichael, Rosa Luxemburg, etc.

Look at it this way: If a gangster like Omar from The Wire can be a sympathetic figure, President Obama's favorite television character, why not *Bob Matthews* or *David Lane*? Murderers like Jesse James and Billy the Kid have been folk heroes before. The Klan was rescued from disrepute by a single film and went on to dominate Northern states like Oregon, Colorado, and Indiana. The Birth of a Nation was wildly successful. Unfortunately, it is one of the few examples of the Right successfully using film to change the culture. [emph. added]

The latter statements, the marks of true tactical appreciation, will serve our community in ways unrealized in generations before, but not by those who seek to wear the mantle of statesmanship in the present hierarchy.

I take issue with the "…esoterica/costumes are weird, unnecessary, and off putting. Neo-Nazism and Third Reich fetishism are losers," as I, personally, unabashedly embrace the practical implications and fraternal logistics, if not discounting, as well, these modern manifestations – our job is to 'take control' of these orphans, not abort them. A position, I might add, in which the "mainstreamers' wholeheartedly endorse. But these issues aside, there is much truth in Mr. Wallace's assertions and heartfelt observations. I take issue with certain points as a Comrade might, and not as an opponent, a lesson lost on most and sundry who claim the mantle of White Nationalism.

Moderation, however, is a practical aside, and should not be eschewed nor actively opposed by members of the White Nationalist community; as has been said before, this duality is a natural one, and should always look to the other for support. The traditional financiers and publishers of traditional and non-traditional material and corporate units should, at all costs, refrain from the fear of networking and inter-personal relationships, being aware to either have the savvy in this regard, as the world is fraught with danger, and broaden their horizon, as the goal is worthy, and the righteous deserve these benefactors, or should simply admit their inadequacy

The appeal to publishers and financiers has been made before and, soon, their time will have come to an end; those new spirits, willing and able to take their place, are becoming more numerous as time moves ever onwards. The experience of these elders, however, is valuable – the hands of camaraderie are outstretched, waiting for a respectful contact. Fate is a strange mistress, and he who dares, wins!

Chapter V

On the Natural Rights of Nationalism:

The Foundations of the
White Nationalist Struggle

Natural law is a *controversial* and *misunderstood* concept.

First of all, there is the unfortunate habit of using 'law' as an all-purpose word for referring indiscriminately to, among other things, an imposed rule (*'lex'*), a rule validated by immemorial custom or practice and not invalidated by reason, a deduction from a description of some 'ideal society', an agreement among rational beings (*'ius'*), and a condition of order. As a result, many people fail to distinguish between 'law' in the sense of a rule that ought to be obeyed or followed (as one would obey or follow a commander or a teacher) and 'law' in the sense of something that ought to be respected (as one would respect another person or, say, a thing of beauty). Understandable misgivings about 'natural laws'—assuming these to be rules that we ought to follow because they supposedly are 'given by' or 'found in' nature—are then easily, but without warrant, extended to the notion of a natural order of things that we ought to respect.

But, is this the whole story?

Part of the controversy surrounding the concept of natural law stems from the difficulty many have, in taking the word 'natural' seriously. Indeed, natural law *theory* often is derided for being 'metaphysical' or even wedded to a particular theology. However, the fact that some theories of natural law are metaphysical or theological does not mean that natural law *is* something metaphysical or theological. A theory of *mice* and *men* can be metaphysical but the metaphysics is in the theory, not in the mice and not in the men. Natural law theories are, but natural law is not, a product of the human mind, although human minds are essential elements of the natural law. While natural law theorists may learn from their predecessors, their *object* of study is the natural law, not 'the literature'.

The possibility that, despite such philosophical debate, the observable signs of Natural Law is *passe'* or, in the obverse, does not exist within both a racial construct nor, as well, within the racial-political construct of what many decendents of European forebears would ascribe to themselves, as adherents to White Nationalism, as defined by its tribal nomenclature and *ethno*-nationalist manifestation of a significant and manifestly *organic* body of persons which make up, as some have stated, a White tribe, replete with uniform codes of conduct (such as mores and financial institutions), modes of mechanization and governmental infrastructures which, if one cares to compare, differ very little, in the main, from one another. The abstract conclusions of difference and conflict come, perhaps, from a dis-jointed, or *conflicted* view, of the concept of 'natural law'.

The philosophical debate, or simple disagreements of observational *form*, such as comparing Plato and Aristotle to St. Augustine or St. Thomas as opposing motifs in the grand panoply of Western man's evolution, continues to this day; there was a time, not too far distant, that this rhetorical debate had, at least for a moment, become quieted, the debate and secular political posturing was coming to grips with a larger, greater vision: That the *existence of our People and a future for White children* was, in fact, a natural, self-expression of, as *Nietzsche* put it, "a will to Power," which can be ascribed to an individual or, manifestly, in an organic *body* of persons, inhabiting a local valley or a modern Nation State. The natural recurring elements exist in both, that is, Life and Death, not necessarily in that order.

Those of us, today, who call ourselves White Nationalists, as well as those of yesteryear, already had conceived, or were *ineluctably* drawn, by an instinct, a desire or inner knowledge, as may be the case, to an organic similitude of the truism of *ethnic-nationalism*, that rudimentary and biological underpinning of Family, Nation and Culture. This momentum, this irascible and sometimes benign duality, which makes men, all men, subject to its laws and predispositions, as well as the creation of Slaves and, to others, Conquerors seems, nevertheless, to exist only in the receding gray-matter of shared experience, of hostile and warlike peoples who, at the outset, followed laws of their own, of their specie; the intractable and willful belief of their antecedents that, as *a priori*, their existence was *unique*, embryonic as it were, of something larger and less festooned with *obligation* and *servitude* to those whose foresight was dimming, as was their waking sight. Blind, blind to the ever-present discourse of freedom, land, group-governance and the notion that, in the main, a natural *force* within each man, declares his humanity.

This was his by *right* of natural law.

First, natural law presupposes an *account* of nature that makes human freedom possible. The conflict, however, is that the mechanistic tendencies of modern natural science appear to call into question human freedom. Secondly, natural law presupposes a moral law rooted in nature. A duality, in this case, creates its own conflict. Nature can be, and usually is, *distinguishable* from what is the product of human deliberation and design. How, then, can we reconcile human freedom with obedience to a moral law? The solution to this difficulty lies in the distinction between the ultimate end, which is fixed by nature, and the means to the end, which is *subject* to human deliberation and choice. The natural desire for the ultimate end, which is encapsulated in the first principle of the natural law (e.g., do good and avoid evil), is the starting point of all [Western] moral reasoning. However, this raises a second difficulty, at least for Christian thinkers such as St. Thomas: If natural law is based upon our natural *end*, how can natural law be reconciled with a *supernatural* goal? If our ultimate end is eternal beatitude, is not the natural law vitiated by *grace*? The solution to this problem, at least for St. Thomas, seems to rest upon a distinction between a *formal* account of man's ultimate end—one that is founded upon our natural desire for the good—and the concrete *realization* of this end which, as it turns out, is supernatural in *character*.

For *Aquinas*, the natural law includes, first, a concrete understanding of the supreme goal [of human life] and the subordinate goals that we must seek to be happy, and, second, a true understanding of the various means to this supreme goal and its integrated subordinate goals, that is, the means we need to adopt if happiness is to be truly realized.

It has been argued, that the fundamental structure of St. Thomas's moral thinking and his understanding of the first principles of the natural law are based upon the philosophy of *Aristotle*.

While there are those opposed to those Thomists who seek to equate Thomism with Aristotelian philosophy, some see it as kind of anti-Aristotelianism that can be found among many Thomists. In the area of moral philosophy, this anti-Aristotelianism is exemplified by *Jacques*

Maritain, who posits a *split* between Aristotle and St.Thomas regarding the nature of the human good. According to Maritain, since moral philosophy can only be practical if it *guides* us to our ultimate end, and since our ultimate end in the present order of divine providence is eternal beatitude, Aristotelian moral philosophy cannot serve as an adequate guide to the moral order. The problem here arises from Aristotle's account of man's ultimate end as a comprehensive good, one that leaves nothing to be desired. Since St. Thomas, guided by his Christian faith, gives an account of the comprehensive good that differs from Aristotle as, secular humanism (in its true form, as Logic), it seems that we must choose between two rival accounts of the human good. It is noted that, St. Thomas, based upon his reading of the *Nicomachean Ethics*, concluded that Aristotle did not believe that human happiness—the comprehensive human good that Aristotle articulates in his formal account— could be perfectly realized in this life. This paves the way for St. Thomas to subsume Aristotle's account of the ultimate end into the Christian vision of the ultimate end, one that overcomes the vicissitudes of this life.

White Nationalists, however, do not base their reasoning upon the *similtudes* or *differences* of theology while, at the same time, acknowledging the vicissitudes of life as, perhaps, theology describes best. White Nationalism, after all, is the study and implementation of these laws as can be best ascertained and, therefore, to reasonably strengthen and uplift our fellows for a brighter and more certain future.

Natural law, as Aristotle saw it, harkens to a more, shall we say, ethno-nationalist point of view, presupposing *a priori* of racial existence, a natural law which, of itself, belongs to the natural product of the specie.

Aristotle observes:

> He who thus considers things in their first growth and origin, whether a state or anything else, will obtain the clearest view of them. In the first place, there must be a union of those who cannot exist without each other; namely, of male and female, that the *race* may continue (and this is a union which is formed, not of deliberate purpose, but because, in common with other animals and with plants, mankind have a natural desire to leave behind them an

image of themselves), and of natural ruler and subject, that both may be preserved. [emphasis added][34]

In the view of White Nationalism, as both a social and political construct, Natural Law defines the corporate body as organism. David Eden Lane, a true White Nationalist who, by all accounts, gave his life in the service of our people, and whose legacy and acumen in the nuances of racial discourse led the vanguard of today's ethno-nationalism; yet, today, redacted from the eyes and ears of the common folk, yes, those very, seemingly, inimportant and sturdy folk whom are depended upon by those who foster their ideas and political agendas upon these very same folk, to extend in the real world, those very same aspirations and political realities, as if they were found, but yesterday, leaving them to fend for themselves without benefit of proper instruction or example. Unlike the Left, *conservatives* always leave their wounded in the field.

On natural law, as it embraces White Nationalism, Mr. Lane[35] has this to say:

Until the white race realizes that there is only one source from which we can ascertain lasting truths, there will never be peace or stability on this earth. In the immutable Laws of Nature are the keys to life, order, and understanding. The words of men, even those which some consider "inspired" are subject to the translations, vocabulary, additions, subtractions, and distortions of fallible mortals. Therefore, every writing or influence, ancient or modern, must be strained through the test of conformity to Natural Law. The White Peoples of the earth must collectively understand that they are equally subject to the iron-hard Laws of Nature with every other creature of the Universe, or they will not secure peace, safety nor, even their existence. The world is in flames because Races, Sub-races, Nations, and Cultures are being forced to violate their own Nature-ordained instincts for self-preservation. Many men of good will, but little understanding, are struggling against symptoms which, are the result of disobedience to Natural Law. As is the Nature of Man, most take narrow, provincial stances predicated on views formed by immediate environment, current circumstances, and conditioned dogma. This is encouraged by that powerful and ruthless Tribe which has controlled the affairs of the world for untold centuries by exploiting Man's most base instincts. Conflict

---

[34] *The Republic*

[35] Lane, David – *The 88 Precepts*

among and between the unenlightened serves as their mask and shield. A deeper understanding of the Fundamental Laws that govern the affairs of Men is necessary if we are to save civilization from its usurious executioners…

1. Any religion or teaching which denies the Natural Laws of the Universe is false.

2. Whatever People's perception of God, or [the] Gods, or the motive Force of the Universe might be, they can hardly deny that Nature's Law is the work of, and therefore the intent of, that Force.

3. God and religion are distinct, separate and often conflicting concepts. Nature evidences the divine plan, for the natural world is the work of the force or the intelligence men call God. Religion is the creation of mortals, therefore predestined to fallibility. Religion may preserve or destroy a People, depending on the structure given by its progenitors, the motives of its agents and the vagaries of historical circumstances.

4. The truest form of prayer is communion with Nature. It is not vocal. Go to a lonely spot, if possible a mountaintop, on a clear, star-lit night, ponder the majesty and order of the infinite macrocosm. Then consider the intricacies of the equally infinite microcosm. Understand that you are on the one hand inconsequential beyond comprehension in the size of things, and on the other hand, you are potentially valuable beyond comprehension as a link in destiny's chain. There you begin to understand how pride and self can coexist with respect and reverence. There we find harmony with Nature and with harmony comes strength, peace and certainty.

In a more practical, if not commonsensical way, this aphorism should contextualize the meaning of a 'natural' law, as law itself provides for both instruction and indoctrination of what is observable, Mr. Lane continues:

9. A proliferation of laws with the resultant loss of freedom is a sign of, and directly proportional to, spiritual sickness in a Nation.

Moreover, to every facet of this discussion, be those 'property rights', 'marriage' , (as such in a contractual sense), or 'economics', as well as 'art' and 'literature', as the original "do good and avoid evil" reminds us, as both the latter elements define and refine the elemental persona of what will extend us, as a people, and remind us what will destroy and exterminate us, if we pass by the obvious good nature of experience.[36]

The above, as noted, by David Lane, are not necessarily new or monumental discoveries; but they are part of the discourse and path of the modern White Nationalist as stated in his *88 Precepts*. Unlike many a pontificating critic of brief and sublime observation and analysis, such succinct appraisals were all that was needed to establish a cursory discussion of what 'natural law' meant to men and women of the West, those who call themselves White Nationalists, in the not too distant past.

The challenges of quantifying the elements of 'natural law' are numerous, as is the wont of a specie which adores words and images; it will continue long after we are all gone. Moreover, to ascribe a definitive ledger of fixed laws is, itself, problematic, and constraints of this nature are arbitrary and capricious, if done without the acceptance or acknowledgment that time, that hoary mistress, will have something to say in the matter. But if one continues his search for what we, as a People, must needs be concerned with, that which would define ourselves as unique and quantifiable, the natural law of instinct, of reason, of civility, should be paramount in our minds.

In Rise of the West, a work which discusses many such issues as listed above, and more, has this to say:

Since the beginning of time, our morality has not changed; it is the technics by which our various epochs have molded themselves, which have molded us, changed us, as a people in the process... The division between dogma and morality changed the face of Western man for the unforeseeable future – whether for good or ill, it remains with us. The 'consciousness' of man was, forever, given back to him. He was to reform himself, and mold a new reality from the old; he saw it as the inevitable outcome of 'infancy' to 'adulthood'. Constraints, as seen by the child are always bonds, chains which keep him in check, bound to his parents and authority which ever seeks to limit his aspirations. Children almost always

---

[36] *Rise of The West – pg. 88.*

hate, and are jealous of their parents – this is *natural law*. It is part and parcel of the very stages of maturity.

As with all ruling authority, however, power and control, are factors that must, at all cost be maintained. This is natural law.

For instance, if a unitarian system existed, without the basic tenets of 'natural law', what would be its boundaries? What glue, so to speak, would bind a system, such as envisioned by passionate men everywhere, that wish the best for their own people? If, natural law is an absurdity, what then? To see what might happen, what did happen, when discounting the material as well as existential realities of what White Nationalists refer to as "natural law", we might see an eternal opposition, as supplied by *Marx* or *Hegel*.

Pointing to the existence of natural law, drawing the reader into the paradigm of opposites, or *tensions*, one can not mistake this interdiction of 'methods and operations' within our own movement, let alone these manifestations of the real world around us:

> There is some merit to the allegations by some, that modern democracy has become the 'new' communism of the present age. The 'egalitarianism' of Karl Marx, for instance, or Lenin's political dictums concerning 'aristocracy' and 'monarchy' included the 'democratic' ideal of the 'masses' which, taken to the extreme, ushered in the enslavement of the very mass the communists claimed to speak for. Laws of an extremely excessive nature 'forced' the mass to accept the 'leveling' of their society in the name of 'progress'. No Hereditary or Traditional institutions, were allowed to remain, since it was 'through these selfsame institutions' that the 'people' had been denied 'choices' of their own; to be sure, the decadence of the existing leadership was obvious, and cannot be discounted as reasons for such wide-spread discontent, but to replace the old with democracies of the mob, is to say that the only prescription necessary for an ailment is poison.

The Dialectics of Hegel, [George Wilhelm Frederich Hegel, born 1770, Germany], itself a system of natural law, was essentially in opposition to the 'marxist/lenninist' doctrine but, nevertheless, was studied by the revolutionist of both the Menshevik party and the Bolsheviks in Russia were not the logical dynamics of 'negation' and 'knowledge'. Hegel was fascinated by the works of Spinoza, Rousseau, Kant, and Goethe and by the revolution of France. Modern philosophy, culture, and society seemed to Hegel fraught with contradictions and tensions [the 'struggle' in 'natural law'], such as those between the 'subject' and 'object' of knowledge, mind and nature, 'self' and 'other' [inner and outer man], freedom and authority, knowledge and faith, the Enlightenment and Romanticism. Hegel's main philosophical project was to take these contradictions and tensions and interpret them as part of a comprehensive, evolving, rational unity that, in different contexts, he called "the absolute idea" or "absolute knowledge".

According to Hegel, the main characteristic of this unity was that it evolved through and manifested itself in contradiction and negation. Contradiction and negation have a dynamic quality that at every point in each domain of reality – consciousness, history, philosophy, art, nature, society - leads to further development until a rational unity is reached that preserves the contradictions as phases and sub-parts of a larger, evolutionary whole. This whole is mental because it is the mind, which is able to comprehend all of these phases and sub-parts as steps in its own process of comprehension. It is rational because the same, underlying, logical, developmental order underlies every domain of reality and is ultimately the order of self-conscious rational thought, although only in the later stages of development does it come to full self-consciousness. The rational, self-conscious whole is not a thing or being that lies outside of other existing things or minds. Rather, it comes to completion only in the philosophical comprehension of individual existing human minds which, through their own understanding, bring this developmental process to an understanding of itself. [37]

Natural Law, as defined by Locke and Hobbs is, *theological* in nature, as the sublime manifestations of 'god' transcend the mundane, finishing up with a convenient 'end', that cause which all else succumbs, unable to bear its light. These debates, in my mind, have little bearing upon that which White Nationalist thinkers and strategists predicate their rational approach to the tenets and consequences of natural law. What has bearing upon us, now, in the present? What rules, be they metaphysical or physical, do we follow?

---

[37] *Ibid*, - See Note, pg. 53.

Natural Law first, and foremost, remains rhetorical within White Nationalist circles, precisely because pro-active and militant reactions remain *isolated* and *disparate*, both in cause and effect. Militancy is in harmony with the needs and desires of fledging race-cultures; it is also consonant with the natural law of organism, that it acknowledges a cycle of birth, life, and senility. This is observable, and continues in an ever-revolving cycle which, by Western experimentation, becomes quantitative and empirical. Natural law is the obvious; it is what is good for our people, it is what makes us, not united necessarily, but is that commonsense which allows us to mark each individual as belonging, each in turn, to that larger state of being, to that tribe and family, which survives or dies with each of us.

Do we have a 'natural right' to life, liberty, and the pursuit of happiness? In the abstract, no. However, as sentient beings, living now, today, yes, we do. We have natural rights, common to each of us as White Nationalists, as the prism of Race and solidarity are unfamiliar to the majority of deracinated individuals who share, however unpleasant or cumbersome at times this, affinity. Still, the natural law of toleration and acceptance reminds us more of our similarities than our dissimilarities, and manifests itself time and time again, a law which is natural to our specie – it is called, *Loyalty*. It is a law, for to break it, brings many emotional and intellectual challenges, which may, or may not, have consequences unforeseen by either party; it is unseen, yet felt implicitly and demonstrably, time and time again.

Natural Law, in large part, is a matter of *influence*.

What designs an individual or group embodies, is a matter for the Fates to decide; outside of this, it is the interdiction of an idea, a motive, which empowers the agent of change. Dialectically, it is a matter of vision, of that capacity of a Seer, which sees the elements of Natural Law, and follows a rigid set of extensions, or laws, by which to achieve certain ends. Thomas Edward Lawrence was such an individual.

In the *Seven Pillars of Wisdom*, T.E. Lawrence seemed to embody the natural law of the specie, insofar as he visualized an outcome, influenced its particular parts, and sat astride a Revolutionary and historical phenomenon which, by all accounts, resonates to this day.

Is natural law a law of the specie? Does racial instinct define the parameters of this natural law? And what of Politics; does it measure itself by the confines of natural law, or any law?

Influence, by its very nature seems, at the outset, to be intangible, marginal, and less than attainable in most of our lives. By its very nature, however, influence is governed by laws, just as any other dynamic, and must needs be quantified for our present discussion, as well as for future implementation. Below, you will find a set of 'laws', as seen by T.E. Lawrence which, by extension, are 'natural laws', whereby influence may become tangible:

Lawrence's Pillars of Wisdom

1. You do not need to be in a position of power. You need only be in a position to influence those in power. Few are in the prior and fewer are those who are not in the latter.

2. Find the Prophet. This is the person whom you will influence to make your vision a reality.

3. Keep your agenda a secret from those who would undermine it.

4. Share your agenda with those whom you trust. This will allow you to drum up support when the time is right.

5. Focus your vision by giving it a goal. Give your vision a "Damascus."

6. Do not seek permission to influence those in power.

7. Seize the opportunities to influence events as they come your way.[38]

To the modern White Nationalist, the existential debates of a *continuum* of debates, lessens with time, as the element of time itself, becomes ever more a distraction in the real-time actions of the present. The status of god-given rights, or the rights of man, that which is carved out and maintained by force, that primitive law of survival, are good fodder for armchair discussions and late-night dissertations, but does not disclose the 'end' of the matter; only the man of vision, with the ability to harness that natural

---

[38] *Seven Pillars of Wisdom*, T.E. Lawrence, emph. added.

law which, with time, may happen to manifest itself in that end most worthy for our people, will matter.

The issue of natural law, as far as White Nationalism is concerned, is not about economics, but about *blood*; the affirmation of those instinctual constructs which constitute an organic body, itself part of a natural law relying, almost entirely, upon the unseen, upon those natural and inevitable 'natural laws' which define our Struggle. We must, in any event, 'do good and avoid evil' which tolerates no compromise in this Life or Death struggle.

The preceding considerations, questions, analogies, propositions, and possibilities have been presented in the hope that the people of the West, including this America, will realize, and become aware of this rising, this ascendancy of Culture over that of civilization, the macrocosm of the institutionalized common man. For, in all reality, this rising has happened already. The waking ascendancy of real politics, its essence, is manifest in our daily happenings, in our hustle and bustle, these little, but so essential, human elements, of our very lives. This is the same essence of ages past. It is the essence of need, desire, and will-to-power of all citizens of humanity – it is organic – its Life animates in all our outward forms; it ignites our imagination and stirs deep waters in the memories of our past. It belongs to struggle, that which all organisms are formed in the crucible of contest and survival. This essence will be, is being marked, by the very struggle between the race-cultures of the World. It truly has brought the compulsion to great politics.

Politics is the great technic of Nature. Nature divides the mediocre from those with merit; from those that are skilled and unskilled. It establishes supremacy of the one, over the other – this can be the individual or institution – this natural law ever is, and will be: the one will survive, and one will die. This is Nature's Law. Politics is, or should be, the greatest of compulsions to emulate, where possible, the rhythms and currents by which nature seeks ever to instruct and guide. The examples are myriad; as students, in this great experiment, we have the ability to seek instruction through the records of the past; we can receive instruction from the various individuals who have had many years bestowed upon them; and finally we have the instruction of common sense, which we utilize on a daily basis. Nature is a part of us, and if we but listen, and recognize that low soft whisper of intelligent reasoning, we shall see our path, clear, and undeniable.

Nature, herself, is not lineal but, rather, rhythmic, flowing as a tree in the wind, bending with the changes in the continuing evolution of the cycle of life. The presentation of this work is in keeping with this cycle. This concept alludes to times and places; to happenings we see passing in the twinkling of an eye – the lineal lacks the subtle rhythm and continuity of the organic growth inherent in the real world that surrounds us; this, the orderly cycle of nature.

The cycle of birth, life, and senility accompany each and every great civilization, not the least of which has been ours – that great family of Indo-Europeans which founded and, still maintains, the greatest living history and working Culture yet experienced on this planet terra. Modern historians however, over the past seventy-five years, have concerned themselves only with this traditional 'school room' variety of lineal history, circumscribing the root cause and effect of actions and events that affect civilizations as it affects the individual. Distortion is the inevitable result of failing to address history as a living, breathing, manifestation of life: Culture itself, becomes ambiguous.

The lineal portrayal of history leaves our vision of the past distorted, ambiguous. These many, and diverse pictures, delivered in sequence, numbered, dated, and clouded by time, leaves us confused; the simple enormity of historical data simply boggles the mind. These clouded perceptions have been handed down to us by well intentioned authors of history but, limited by design and the seemingly chaotic, unpredictable value of chance, have delivered to us only half the product. For the most part, these authors have failed to recreate, for the most part, such events and situations that would take into account the very essence of the Age and Civilization of which they study. With the few exceptions of *Spengler*, *Yockey*, *Adams*, and *Gibbons* there has been little or no attempts at this recreation of history that would define our Western Culture, that is, the Race, if we say this a million times over, that is the creative force behind all that we know; it is the organism which pumps the blood into the body to continue life. Without this understanding, History, and all its various forms of philosophy, ethics, and the ancient value placed upon the present, and its reporting, would be a dead thing, it becomes, as with all dead sciences, simply a 'specialization of content'.

Visions and perceptions of our life seen, albeit dimly, have surpassed our wildest imaginations while confounding, at times, our most able scholars. These men search, they study, they become redundant with historical fact, dates, and actions mimicked by those before them. The living organism of the race-culture defies their assaults, precisely because they fail to acknowledge the very nature of organic life: a root, a purpose, a people. Too what do we owe the living reminder of the past – to the monuments, the living literary achievements, the art? This, all this, was left to us by a People. Our People! To the Fathers and Mothers who created us, we, you and I, are but their extension; we represent their lives, their presence, in our own destiny. In the coming and going, each of us tell of that small, yet significant story; the seed for our children. This people have their manifestations of God, of Life, of Religion, and a definite vision of the world – it is our distinctive volksgeist – that was made manifest by, and for the race-culture. This was their creation. It was intended, as a matter of course, to be seen and utilized by their children, their Posterity; it was to prepare and perpetuate their kind in a progressive setting – both in the present and the future. It was to carry on the life cycle of the Original birth. This, a living history that will outlast time itself. The visions of our ancient life survive as history to us – it is the continuation of the present presence of our past. Only through an understanding of Life, and its organic application, can history have any true significance to us who, at this moment, are but the living history of our tomorrow.

Chapter VI

A Future for White Children

What must we do to secure a fairer existence

For ourselves and our Posterity?

A people is lost as a people and is dead, if, in surveying its history and in testing its will to the future, it cannot discover unity. No matter what forms the past may have taken in its course, when a nation arrives at the point of truly denying the allegorical images which stem from its first awakening, then it has denied the roots of its being and of its becoming and it has condemned itself to unfruitfulness. For history is not a development from nothing to something, nor from something insignificant to something great. It is not even the transformation of an essence into something completely different. Rather, the first racial folkish awakening brought about by heroes, gods and poets is the ultimate achievement for all times. This first great supreme *Mythic* achievement cannot, in essence, be perfected. It can merely take on other new forms. The value breathed into a god or hero is what is eternal in good and evil. *Homeros* represented the highest enhancement of what was Greek and guarded this even in decline.

What *unity*, then, do we teach our own children, what method of traditional or proven methods of strength do we instruct the young minds of our own issue? Our children learn by example, by the observation and personal interaction of social intercourse at school, church, or on the visual mediums of 'games', or in the myriad channels of news, erotica, and 'opinion' journalism; all this, and more, *without* parental supervision. The conversations amongst adults, witnessed by innocent psyches, sporadic and irregular, seems to lack a certain grace, or sustained intelligent direction, when seeking to explain how 'world affairs' affect their future, and that of their own offspring.

Take a modern experience, for instance, which millions of children, specifically those of the West, are to rationalize, to come to grips, and thereby predicate these lessons on a larger 'world view' which will carry them, and the rest of us, down the road of experience and a better life…or will it?

i.

The cacophony of musings and gnashing of teeth recently, regarding the rebuilding of 'ground zero', has become palatable, gaining momentum within the national consciousness created, in part, by mainstream media outlets (MSM) outlets, and their incumbent agendas, driving the focus of the latest (and greatest) calamity to befall the 'survivors', both nationally and personally.

Over the last several years, a mantra has begun: No invasion of the National psyche by outsiders, seen here in a Religious context, which would compromise the new status of Sacred Ground, as ascribed to the remnants of a once vibrant, economic citadel; the banner, if you will, of everything modern, up-to-date, and extending that persona around the world.

To prove this point, the staging of a new, re-designed center, is to be named, appropriately enough, the *One World Trade Center* building, seemingly, to assuage the wounds and scars left by the most tragic political/cultural affront in American history. This has led to an interesting development, which, as happens in all evolutionary struggles, morphing into something different, unique, and continues to whatever end in which nature has in store.

The cacophony of interests, as well, has prompted an almost angelic appreciation of struggle and overcoming, a thing unique to natural disasters and War. The latter, indeed, is the clarion call of today's adherents of a new world-view, a *new* America, in which the disparate elements, both racially and religiously, will forge a new *will*, a new *direction* for the betterment of all concerned. Sacred Ground, after all, *establishes* a parlance of sincerity, of oneness.

I have often found historical parallels potent stuff, when dealing in the hear-and-now; this case affords us the same clarity. What lessons, then, have the children of the West learned since the era of Clinton and Bush the Elder, two individuals who had the best interest of the 'mob' at heart, yet encouraged the relinquishment of Western youth's primary source of survival, that of Tradition and race-culture. Since our youth must learn by experience, let us, then, look at the most cogent of similar experiences. *Kosovo.*

In the eastern fields of American history, there can be no doubting the evolution of culture and spirituality; of violence, loyalty, and simply the will-to-exist of our antecedents, those Mothers and Fathers who bore us. Indeed, that ever-long struggle with the environment, disease, conquest and that richness of identity, of tribal inclusiveness, those mechanisms of science and industry which, working harmoniously together, defines that victory of man's interdiction into Life itself. All these parts, grinding together, gears contacting each other, turning that greatest of machines, that of the human organism, makes itself that much more personal, robust and important, when faced with extinction.

The human element of *survival,* cannot be considered in its proper perspective, unless one realizes the implication of *finality*, and of human *passing.* Such is the marker of Death, personal loss and family tribulations which, as may be the case, effects the *entire* familial setting, the extended family as it were, and promotes the various manifestations of the Irish Wake, the Catholic dirges, as well as the various manifestations of *memory*, those snap-shots of Life, as we remember them, thereby extending the life of that person, or persons, into the next state of being, held by us, individually, to continue for the future.

When we inter those memories, that practical and substantive quality of life, we claim this 'portion of soil', and declare it, *sacred ground.* This is shared, in one way or another, by all race-cultures, and remains a sustaining part of the mechanism of survival.

ii.

Such is the memory of Kosovo and 'ground zero'. Both have a resonance, clear to each party to its birth, life, and death. This comparison is two-fold:

1. Each center comprised the nexus of its own unique ethos;

2. Each seeks to establish a memory of that Life which had gone before.

The american public, in the modern world seems, at the outset, to be shy on both respect and memory, for they appear to want one value, yet have fostered and enabled this very value to be torn from those who would live and fight in other fashions, but for the very same *essence* as is promoted in the tragic destruction of parts of our native soil. Moreover, this dichotomy was enacted, using the name of the 'american people', as the sole *raison d'etre* of american foreign policy in saving the American 'way of life', and to continue the expansion of 'equality' for all peoples.

A little reflection on both instances is in order:

Kosovo Field:

Kosovo Field (or Kosovo Polje) is the site of a famous battle in 1389 that the Serbs regard as the tragic demise of their mediæval flowering. If all this seems a little remote to today's conflict, remember that the symbolism of Kosovo and the battle here is at the heart of Serbian nationalism not just in this region, but across the whole of the former Yugoslavia. The Ottoman Turks were the new super power of the fourteenth century. Originally horsemen from the central Asian steppes, they settled in Anatolia and in the twelfth and thirteenth centuries took over almost all of modern-day Turkey. In 1357, they burst across the Bosphorus into Europe and conquered Macedonia, Serbia and Bulgaria and continued to threaten Western Europe for the next 200 years.

The heroism of Prince Lazar, the Serb ruler, at the *Field of Blackbirds* has now become the founding legend of Serbian nationalism. Six hundred years later, pilgrims were still visiting his bones at Gracanica monastery, nearby. According to the legend, at the start of the battle, the Ottomans offered Lazar the choice between fighting to the death and surrendering.

Elijah appeared to him with a message from the Virgin Mary:

What kingdom shall I choose? Shall I choose a heavenly kingdom? Shall I choose an earthly kingdom? If I choose an earthly kingdom, An earthly kingdom lasts only a little time. But a heavenly kingdom will last for eternity and its centuries.

Prince Lazar chose death.

The Ottomans, of course, were non-western, and Muslim.

iii.

As a Spiritual value, Kosovo represented the last 'resting place' of those who had given their lives in *extending* the cultural and racial history of this people. It had become, indeed, Sacred Ground.

The religious *entanglements* between Islam and Christianity, as used by opposing forces is well documented, and the Christian West of that time, faced incredible forces, as the Europeans of that day and region, were outnumbered and out gunned. The incredible courage and stalwart defense of the West, not to mention its *faith*, must have been a marvelous thing to live through, rough though it was, for it saw the minority regional population stop, for some six-hundred years, the inroads of both racial and religious *aliens*.

After the Kosovo War, and the 1999 NATO bombing of Yugoslavia, the territory came under the interim administration of the United Nations Mission in Kosovo, spearheaded by the US, and in the name of *equality* of religion and personal dignity, gave this territory to those same invaders, albeit under the banner of Islam, and received kudos for doing so, garnering enough momentum that the commanding general of this mission, Wesley Clark, could utilize this conquest to run for President of the United States as a 'war hero'.

Was *sacred ground* enough of a deterrent to keep our bombs from destroying not only buildings, but of the very 'spiritual center' of this kindred nation? Hardly.

Now, of a sudden, we are all to remember the 'war dead' of our own soil, to declare a portion of our territory as sacred ground, and refuse the very interests which we willingly and with aforethought, demanded of the Serbian people. The American Ox has been gored, and we demand justice for the wrongs inflicted upon us; how then, in retrospect, can we not expect the same treatment, indeed, the same result as Kosovo for our valiant efforts of the past?

The vicious circle of 'international affairs', fostered and led by those who know 'what is best for us', have left a hollow, sinking feeling, in the hearts and minds of our countrymen. What is, really, in the best interests of our Nation and those children of the West who, as has been noted before, know very little, if anything, of the connection between ourselves and these far-flung *colonies* of our antecedents? This disconnect is overwhelming, considering that what affects one does, indeed, affect the other. Thus, it is the understanding of Race-Culture, which should provide the answers, if not limited by State sanctioned 'public policy' and its revolutionary attendants.

The destruction of edifices, of material goods, is nothing like the destruction and dismantling of the spiritual edifices of our traditional past. The coming compromises will dwarf, in many instances, what our forefathers suffered after much greater loss of life and liberty. Will we, then, allow this destruction to both ourselves and our distant kinsmen? Only time will tell, but in the passing of time comes a place, a line, which if crossed, will prove once again, that once a people is conquered, the road back is ever a winding one.

So, with this in mind, as with all experiences, with what do we encourage the youth of today and tomorrow, to become better, more noble, and respecting themselves and the nation which bore them?

iv.

For three years in a row, between 2006 and 2008, a North American secessionist convention was held where delegates from actual secessionist organizations and interested observers gathered to discuss the possibility of decentralizing the United States into smaller political units. Thus far, it does not appear there will be another convention for 2009. I suspect this is for the better. I only attended the third such convention, but to my knowledge there was no growth in attendance or media coverage of these events over the three years they took place.

In spite of the fact that the secessionist movement in North America seems to have peaked for the time being, there has been a subsequent growth in so-called "state sovereignty" resolutions, i.e, legislation passed or at least introduced in state governmental bodies upholding the federalist principles of the Tenth Amendment to the U.S. Constitution. A majority of the fifty

154

states have either considered or enacted such resolutions. The highlight of this movement was Texas Governor Rick Perry's no doubt insincere comments expressing sympathy for secession.

For the most part, these state sovereignty resolutions are simply matters of partisan political grandstanding initiated by members of the opposition Republican Party in order to embarrass or antagonize the Obama regime. I used to hear a lot about the Tenth Amendment the last time the Republicans were out of power, during the Clinton era, and it was often said in those days that Republican politicians carry copies of the Tenth Amendment in their back pockets but carry capitalist whore money in their front pockets.

During the era of the Bush the Younger, the roles reversed a bit, and it was not uncommon to see individual localities and a few states with liberal leanings issue resolutions denouncing the Iraq War or the Patriot Act. About 300 local governmental bodies did so. Now that the Democrats are back, the tides have turned once again. Only a handful of these recently issued state sovereignty resolutions include any genuinely radical provisions or even hint at secession.

Nevertheless, these resolutions may provide a rhetorical tool that genuine radicals can exploit. But a change in tactics will be necessary for the decentralist movement. Thus far, efforts to promote such actions as secession have involved holding continent-wide conferences attended by only a few dozen people, who in turn represent very small organizations or movements. However, these self-appointed secessionist organizations often claim to speak for entire regions containing millions, tens of millions, or even hundreds of millions of people. This would seem to be a case of putting the cart ahead of the horse.

Of course, this is not to say that the secessionist movement thus far has achieved nothing. Past efforts have brought a certain amount of publicity, and the Zogby poll commissioned by the Middlebury Institute indicates the raw materials do indeed exist for the development of a large scale secessionist effort at some point in the future. Yet, to continue to move such efforts along, it needs to be understood that before we can run, we have to crawl.

It is highly unlikely that secession by individual states or regions of any size will be viable for the forseeable future. For instance, the League of the South is the largest single secessionist organization with membership in the thousands. The southern nationalists do indeed raise legitimate and serious issues concerning the hysterical prejudice often displayed by liberal elites against white working class Southerners, and their history, culture, religion, language, and so forth. Yet, it is also true that sympathy for what used to be known as the "Lost Cause" (i.e., the Confederate secession) is at an all time low among Southerners. This is because quite a few people can be found in the South today who have no historical connections to the Confederate era, e.g., transplanted Northerners and their offspring, European immigrants and their offspring, more recent immigrants from Latin America, and, of course, a large African-American population that is alienated from Confederate heritage for obvious reasons, and many liberal, cosmopolitan, urban whites who resent the South's conservative image. In other words, the prospect for a unified secession by the former Confederate states under the Stars and Bars is just about zero.

This is not to say that instances of a full-blown, secessionist fervor by certain states are not possible. It is imaginable that Texas and Vermont, both of which were once independent nations, could actually secede at some point. The same could be said concerning Alaska and Hawaii, neither of which are connected to the American mainland and both of which have their own indigenous cultures that have been subject to colonial subjugation by the United States. The indigenous people of the American mainland itself are another possibility for secession.

For the most part, however, it is far too soon in the game to begin thinking of secession by entire regions, such as Cascadia, New England, Novocadia, the former Confederate States, or California. Instead, it is better to begin with something a little less grandiose, and start agitating for secession by towns, cities, neighborhoods, counties or communities.

This is not to say that we should not have a long-term vision. In my view, the only way we will win in the long run is if we have numbers on our side. For instance, the majority of the population of the United States will need to either recognize the right of secession or not actively oppose it. Right now, the numbers are only at about twenty percent. Also, it is likely we will need for there to be a secession by at least a majority of the territory of the United States, and at least the majority of the residents of the seceded territories will need to hold pro-secessionist sympathies. This does not mean that an individual secessionist tendency cannot be very small. For instance, a single county or small town. But such a secession will need to be part of a much larger pan-secessionist alliance, or at least under the umbrella of such an alliance. Otherwise, the secessionists will end up like the Branch Davidians.

It would seem that the best course of action at present would be to begin promoting the decentralist idea in local communities. This gives us a great deal of leeway in terms of how to proceed. For instance, we can simply stick with the idea of secession or independence as an end unto itself and do so in a non-ideological manner, or we can advocate secession for a broader ideological purpose. If one wishes to pursue the former approach, then our local propaganda should simply emphasize the common benefits of independence: "Wouldn't it be better if our tax dollars stayed in our community without going to the parasites in Washington?"; "Did you know that our locality gets less in services than what we pay in taxes?"; "Wouldn't it be better if we could simply make our own laws here in our community rather than suffer the dictates of the feds or the state capital?"; "Look at Liechtenstein! If they can do it, why can't we?"

The other approach would be to agitate for a more specific ideological program, the way that the Free Staters are doing in New Hampshire, or the Christian Exodus has attempted in South Carolina and elsewhere. If this approach is what one prefers, then it is essential to pick an actual locality where the local culture is conducive to one's wider agenda. There are also options as to how radical one wants to make one's secessionist platform. In certain communities, it may at present be a bit of an overload to advocate full-blown secession from the United States itself, even if that is the overall goal. Instead, it might be better to advocate secession by regions (for instance, turning northern California into a separate state within the U.S.), or by cities (turning New York City into the 51st state), or by municipality (turning Long Island into an independent city from NYC). This more moderate approach does not mean that we cannot maintain the dissolution of the present state-capitalist regime as an ultimate goal, and there may be at present certain regions or localities where agitation for full-blown secession from the U.S. is the proper route.

At this point in the game, the cultivation of effective propaganda is obviously a primary task. Hans Hermann Hoppe has remarked that answering the question of "How to Win?" means asking the question of "How to win the sympathy of the youth?" The reasons for this should be obvious enough. If and when the pan-secessionist movement becomes a mass movement, those who are currently older will most likely be deceased. Youth are the future. So our propaganda should primarily be directed at younger audiences. Also, it is the younger people who have demonstrated the greatest proclivity towards secessionist sympathies, and who have the weakest degree of sympathy for the present regime. For instance, the writer Tom Wolfe once remarked that the incidents of September 11, 2001 did little to inspire long-term patriotic sentiments among young Americans, as much as it was just another event they saw on television. Likewise, it has been said that while the older members of the current "post-paleo" movement who came out of the Ron Paul campaign adhere to older paleoconservative ideas, many of the younger members adhere to more radical libertarian, anarchist or anarcho-capitalist positions. And we have seen the rapid growth of national-anarchism in North America in recent times as well.

v.

Our propaganda campaigns should include three indispensable elements.

First, the principle of "peace through separatism" should be upheld to the letter. It makes little sense to advocate secession only by those sharing a uniform ideological stance if one of our objectives to maintain and respect genuine cultural diversity and if achieving civil and political peace is one of the reasons for separatism.

Second, the "good riddance" argument must be emphasized. We should say to conservatives: "Don't you want to be rid of all those godless atheists, ungrateful minorities, bitchy feminists, perverted homosexual deviants, tree-hugging eco-freaks, gun-grabbers and smelly, drug-addled, tofu-munching, lice-infested hippies?" Likewise, we should say to liberals: "Don't you want to be rid of all those Bible-banging, flag-waving, share-cropping, inbred, gun nut, gay-bashing, fetus-hugging, cross-burning, goose-stepping, trailer trash?" In other words, we should exploit and capitalize on the hatred that the dominant factions of the mainstream "culture wars" have for one another.

Lastly, we should ignore the forces of political correctness when they attack, as they inevitably will. There should be no capitulation, accommodation, apology, rebuttal, attempted clarification, recognition or respect given to the forces of PC. To give an inch of ground is to play into the hands of the enemy. PC is not only the ideological superstructure of the ruling class, but its primary rhetorical and propaganda weapon. We should disarm our enemies by openly defying them.

I have, in the past, mentioned the possibility of infiltration into larger organizations by those holding pan-secessionist and related sympathies. For instance, the minor political parties, local units of the major parties, and single-issue pressure groups. Mr. Larry Kilgore, a conservative Christian activist, ran for the Senate in the Republican primary for Texas on an explicitly secessionist platform and won 225, 000 votes. That's quite an achievement. I would suggest the use of local symbolic electoral campaigns as a propaganda tool. The goal would not so much be to win as much as to publicize the separatist cause. Let's say that in a few years a wide network emerges of young people running for mayor, city council, or state representative positions in local elections, and doing so explicitly as anarchists, national-anarchists, pluralists, tribalists, decentralists, and avowed secessionists. The uniqueness of such an action, e.g., a large number of such campaigns occurring simultaneously and the radical nature of the ideas of the campaigners, will likely be enough by itself to generate a fair amount of media attention. Likewise, a wider participation in ordinary, mainstream community activities and community activism by those holding such views, for example, "adopt-a-highway" campaigns, volunteering for shelters and homeless feeding programs, setting up neighborhood watch and cop-watch programs, will naturally enhance our credibility. In the process of building up the classical Spanish anarchist movement, prior to the Civil War, it was not uncommon for some villages and towns to have anarchist mayors, and anarchists were among the ranks of prominent community leaders, and not just fringe figures as they are today. So, we have a historical model to draw on. It need only to be adapted to contemporary circumstances.

A future for white children depends on understanding and action.

Understanding the obvious relationship of our present life, with that of the attacks and agendas of our opposition should, with all said and done, provide the necessary impetus for we, as a culture and people, to get off our collective duffs, and combine our energies in supporting those issues and individuals who will actively participate in the process. Staying at home, watching tv, or spending time at 'church' will have little effect on the future life of our children.

Get serious, Western man and woman...your children deserve your attention.

Chapter VII

A Matter of Foreign Policy:

White Nationalism World Wide

Over the past several years, perhaps ten to fifteen years, White Nationalism has made an impact upon millions of white men and women around the world. Initially, the rhetoric and political manifestations remained fixed, limited to certain 'true believers' who, in turn, made inroads into various organizations and tribal enclaves which, also in turn, began to write, do radio, and presented printed media to their various adherents. Following the initial planting, these seedlings began to sprout and then began to graft themselves to other, more traditional groups and organization.

The growth of 'white nationalism' then, began the natural and expected morphology of all organisms: with the addition of 'new' adherents, removed from the original intent and motivations by time and circumstance, then developing, in stages, a more personal and appropriate direction, started that slow, but inevitable change in *direction*. Not meaning to deviate from the original intent, the recent recruits into the ranks of national and inter-national race-cultural politics have separated from the 'main trunk' in ways which seem to be growing and creating a path which, if left unchecked, will cause untold conflict and unnecessary debate.

One of the most divisive and contentious debates, has been the 'islamic peril' perceived by many of these 'new recruits' as the singular most pivotal aspect of their newfound political direction; seemingly, almost a badge of honor within the newer circles and peer groups which are participating in activities, written positions, and personal conversations around the country.

Before we get any deeper into this conversation, let me be clear on several points:

- White Nationalism is a unique and race-specific philosophy;

- White Nationalism understands that a race-specific philosophy does, in fact, embrace *any* Race which recognizes the inherent 'natural law' which nurtures and extends that specific race-culture;

- White Nationalism *increases* racial understanding, of *all* racial groups and mechanisms – it does not seek to deprive any race-culture of their inherent natural state, nor to dictate to other race-cultures how they must view their history or religious imperatives – excepting an obvious national threat here, at home;

- White Nationalism embraces *empirical* science;

- White Nationalism embraces Spirituality – the seemingly conflicting aspirations of religious and secular adherents is a disagreement in form and function *only* – and white nationalists are passionate in their appreciation of the value of 'faith' as well as a studious inculcation of traditional tenets of 'spirituality' as past to us by our ancestors;

- White Nationalism is the *vehicle* by which the voice of our people can be felt within the context of our political aspirations – it is not a Political Party, as such, but a root, a water-mark, for others to gauge their direction, its codes of conduct enumerated by many of those who have spoken, written or lead by example, for others to emulate;

- White Nationalism is *based* on Race, Family, and National extension;

- White Nationalism is summed up in this phrase: *We must secure the existence of our People and a Future for White children.*

****

Pretty simple, really, the tenets of White Nationalism.

So, how then, can the many adherents of this essential rhythm, this movement, are we separating from each other on points of the most important aspects of this philosophy regarding the International and national aspects of our present day rhetoric and outlook?

Let us, then, get to the quick of the matter.

A dialogue, testy and rude in many cases goes thus:

"I hate Islamic fundamentalism."

"As a woman, how can any [male] white nationalist support Arabs who support 'sharia law'?"

"Arabs/Islam bombed us, anyone who speaks up for these people are anti-white."

In conjunction with this type of dialogue, is the follow-up discussion of the 'military' involvement in the 'war on terror':

" Why is there so much antagonism for those fighting in foreign wars?"

"Why are white nationalists on the wrong side of the 'fighting men and women' of the military?"

"America, to be strong, must support the military in its various wars to 'protect our rights' here, in America."

And the most recent attack from this 'new wing' of so-called white nationalists is":

"If you do not support existing 'foreign policy', you are not american or a 'white nationalist."

There are many such debates, but fall outside of this 'foreign policy' assessment.

There is as well, a *gender* issue, which, heretofore, has not been seen with such vitriol and mean-spirited accusations in the past. We will address this gender issue later.

To the issue of foreign policy, a subject which all white nationalists should acquaint themselves for, on the horizon, is a white nationalist government waiting in the wings for its chance at mobilization, and all members of this political reality should have their questions and answers ready for political dialogue.

Since White Nationalism is a racial imperative first, and foremost, the average white nationalist may, in general, be wrapped too tightly, when looking at non-white foreigners here, at home, seeing directly the *damage* and *anarchy* they have brought to our lives and country; and therefore, fail to see the foreigner proper, as a unique and sovereign entity in *their own nations*. This is the pivotal difference between White Nationalists and those who have been dismantling and rearranging our tradition founding principles.

The Arabian situation, as a matter of 'foreign policy' should not effect us, but as anyone with eyes can plainly see, is affecting us on a daily basis. This, however, existed when I was a child, and that of my parents. It is how large empires control the flow of information, giving here, taking there, all to that end which serves their own 'world view', rather than that of the nation-at-large – that is, the *racial* nation.

The 'middle east' is a cornucopia of lies, deceit, and ruthless international crossroads which allow for the many and myriad agendas worldwide, to converge.

These 'conflicts' are staged, phony, and kept alive with the meddling and financial encouragements of 'anglo-american interests'; this situation will continue, until a true government of the Western peoples begins, firstly, in America, and extends world-wide into the lives of our European brethren. Judeo-christianity, as well, plays an epic part in this conundrum, and is hard for the average white-american to fully fathom – and this has become a continuing problem for white nationalists who are, in the main, secular in nature and political persuasions.

Arabia since the time of T.E. Lawrence, most commonly known as 'Lawrence of Arabia', seems to be most relevant to white nationalism today. This man, a member of the English military establishment, was *embedded* and lived with the arabic peoples at the behest of English and European interests (America at this time, was still in its infancy regarding foreign political intrigues, as most Americans were 'nationalistic' in outlook, and cared mostly for the future of their own interests). The lesson to be learned from this example, and can be followed-up in Lawrence's tome, *The Seven Pillars of Wisdom*, are classic studies in the way white nationalist politics has been shaped over the years.

The opposing camps *within* White Nationalism come from a different source: Theology and the media.

The developing 'americanism' of our early beginnings, that *ethos* which has shaped most of our national outlook was based, in large part, on our 'christian' upbringing; but this upbringing has been largely a *mythos*, a perception of these beliefs, rather than an educated understanding of the 'word' itself. The new generation of 'white nationalists' who are flooding the ranks of traditional racial politics, bring with them the baggage of what they were told by their parents or grandparents of the relationship of the 'jews', 'jesus', and the *holy writ*. This *perception*, rightly or wrongly, colours not only the national dialogue, but also white nationalist political endeavors.

Moreover, the international dialogue becomes confused with that of theological 'historicity' and race reality, making the traditional and smooth synchronicity of White Nationalism conflicting realities.

This must not be tolerated.

Arabia, and its environs, wherever this is in traditional arabic lands, *belongs* to Arabia, *not* to the West.

Pan-Arabianism is a threat to Israel, such as the House of Hapsburg was to certain families of the West two-hundred years ago in Europe. It is a family affair between the two analogies above, and must be left to the individual parties to resolve; interdiction politically, financially, or morally is to the *detriment* of the 'outside party' who becomes involved. These tribal threats are increased, rather than being decreased, by american involvement. Period.

Pan-Aryanism, as well, or the concept of a *direct* relationship between members of the West, is a phrase which has been used interchangeably for various nativist platforms in the white nationalist movement; conservatives, on the other hand, have eschewed this type of description, afraid that it would take away from 'american' descriptions, but utilized by american politicians as late as the 1920's as well as writers and the common folk.

All peoples have a right, a *natural* right to be *who* they are – this is real diversity – not the diversity of the modern liberalism of the Twentieth and early Twenty-first centuries. Interdiction amongst these nations and peoples is, without question, *anti*-American, that is to say, *anti*-Western interests. Therefore, military interdiction in these foreign lands is un-American by its very nature, as these foreign involvements serve the Western race-culture very little. This is why we have a 'diplomatic corps', *diplomacy* which should speak for American legitimate interests, at a fair return for our efforts – not in the interests of our so-called *allies* in the region. This is gamesmanship, and is fraught with foreign 'entanglements' discouraged by true American patriots like George Washington, and Thomas Jefferson, to name but a few.

The wailing and gnashing of teeth can be heard even now.

These sounds of distress, however, come from the modern neo-con, israel-firsters, and the like – such are the divisions in white nationalism.

Take away the *theological* implications, and the *subversion* of traditional Americanism, and what do you have left, but a logical and un-biased perception of american and Western interests. This is White Nationalism.

To spend the life-blood of Western men and women for some ethereal 'political reality' is of the most base, and pernicious frauds perpetrated against the American people, its future generations. Those who sell you this programme are liars and cowards.

i.

Islamic Fundamentalism is another matter.

When white nationalists become embroiled in these discussions with fellow patriots, it exists as a *false* dichotomy only, as Islam belongs to the semetic branch of the peoples of the world. As a religious construct, it parallels Christianity only in the respect that it belongs to a 'faith' held dear by a particular Race-Culture: Christianity for the West, and Islam for greater Arabia. If there is a contest of cultures, as seen by White Nationalists, it is only one of race and race-culture, not of theological contests – conservatives and religious persons, on the other hand, make it much more.

The *spread* of Islam is, however, another matter.

White Nationalists *opposed* the war against Serbia, and were vilified by mainstream media sources, as well as public political figures who knew, as White Nationalists knew, that this 'war' was a war against Western values, namely Christianity, as the Serbians and the surrounding Balkan environs maintained both a devout and nominal Orthodox Christianity for many generations before, and had fought the 'spread' of Islam when faced with Turkish aggression in our eastern quadrant, and maintained their relative identities, even through communistic aggression and Western betrayal after the second war of fratricide; that is, until the cold hammer of 'american' interests smashed these stalwart peoples over the inherent instability brought with religious (i.e. racial imperatives) toleration, and political expediency.

America, once again, on the wrong side, but championed by those in power who care nothing for our people, but who care most robustly for their own rears. Who is then left holding the international onus for these maneuverings – the *people* of the West, and Americans in particular within the international community.

Who was worried about 'islamic fundamentalism' then? Not the politicians, nor the military commanders in the field. No, it was White Nationalists and common people here, in America, that generally were appalled. By inculcating 'islam' in our eastern quadrant, of necessity, encouraged political/religious 'islamists' to gain more of a foothold, thereby encouraging the *entire* Islamic world. These events are special to white nationalism, as they create a phenomenon, which requires political and physical responses – but only because these events were *allowed* to happen – these became the transparent betrayals against the interests of the West.

No amount of conservative rhetoric will assuage the White Nationalist in this regard. Those who fall for this type of 'action vs. reaction' are confused, or simply ignorant, and must be educated – debate should be limited to attempts at *reconstruction* of our fellows – but should not be allowed to enter into positions of White Nationalist leadership in either regional or national debates.

ii.

On the matter of Sharia Law, or the so-called 'gender issues' with which our traditional enemies have developed for the 'west', and has now made itself known within certain white nationalist circles, must now be addressed.

Historically, up until the last three generations here, in America, has been the role of Parochialism, or Patriarchy, and was developed over time with the male element of Western society being predominant; this had many causual implications, but hunter-gatherers, warfare, genetic predispositions being the main causes. Moreover, our legal systems and political outlooks were based, in part, on these constructs.

In America, the history of 'sufferage' is well known; what is not as well known is the tradition-destroyer's role in *convincing* Western women that they were being shorted, not just in the 'vote', but in *all* aspects of society. This pernicious and hateful lie, was disseminated to the point of *revolution*, making men and women of the West mistrusting and incapable of peaceful interaction in those days.

Family 'values', at that time, began to change, perhaps because of the disconnect which, for a time, marked the genders as 'competitors' rather than helpmates – in actuality it was the burgeoning sentiment that women should take charge of their lives, as *singular* and *independent* 'units', rather than being a part of a working mechanism, or tribe, which could only be extended through the *natural* interaction of men and women – through Births.

As soon as Western females began to become *empowered*, the natural response was the *acceptance* of birth 'control', not contraception, but in *control* of life's destiny; abortion and certain types of 'planned parenthood' became part of the national debate, which has not stopped to this date.

White Nationalist men are, in the main, very traditional, and this is often seen in the male-inspired white nationalist imperative of *protecting* and *extending* their families, by creating larger and larger families to instill, yet again, a larger family *ethos* nationally. This was not done with the intention of denying their mates any say in the future; the contrary was true. Motherhood is valued as the *preeminent* value of White Nationalism – a romantic view perhaps – but one in which fills the largest part of white nationalist politics. This can, however, be used *for* and *against* us.

The *canard* of 'sharia', as it relates to White Nationalism, disrupts only those who, truly, are not well versed in white nationalist philosophy; as the well-spring of this philosophy stems from the understanding that each unique and independent 'race-culture' has evolved independently of the West. Therefore, to align one's [western] *moral* imperatives in viewing other cultures, and then proceed to attack or malign those cultures based, in part, on non-western ideals of 'morality', is to put oneself in a rather blatant, and untenable position.

Sharia law, incidentally, is summed up thusly:

> Sharia law based on the Qur'an and the Sunnah were seen as laws passed down by Allah that should be applied to all parts of life, including the organization of the government and the handling of everyday problems.

At first blush, one thinks of many historical 'western' applications of theological determinism, not the least of which filled pages of historical documentation of our own early 'american' experience;

the latter, let it be added, that while not all 'Christian' in nature, the spiritual and political indoctrination of our forefathers is pronounced and, with time, as this *symbiotic* 'religious' relationship, was *replaced* with more and mote non-western ideas and agendas, and is seen by most observers as playing a pivotal role in the *downward* direction of western, as well as 'american' moral supremacy. Even the term 'religious right' is framed within the same dictum as 'sharia law'.

Fundamentalists exist in every culture where there was an original concept or institution of long-standing, involving religious 'faith'. Such are the 'traditional' values of this country based, and has walked a fine-line with secular political debate from our very inception. However, the balancing act between 'christianity and islam' is being lost, while money and political intrigue, have taken center stage. This is the *trap* in which white nationalists must guard against.

In any event, as White Nationalists, *what* direction a particular race-culture takes, as it basis of theological or moral imperatives, is *not* the purview, or the interdiction of, members of the west who seek to 'do good' in the name of their fellows based, in part, on their own perceptions and disciplines of 'theological' and 'moral' directives; and in direct contravention of the concept of 'liberty and freedom' which wells up from the hearts of any particular people.

The only time that we, as members of the West, and as White Nationalists in particular, should fear, or mobilize a moral or military response is when, and only then, when faced with military *incursion* here, on our own soil; 'territories', as adjuncts to western spheres of influence, if directly affecting our national state, would fall under a National 'white nationalist' governmental response – this is only common sense.

If those elements of female 'white nationalists' who, individually or collectively, feel that this foreign 'patriarchy' stands in opposition to the patriarchal inclinations and predispositions of white nationalism in general then, it would be proposed that the more vocal of these individuals not fall into the trap of 'crying wolf' when feeling attacked by passionate and traditional white nationalists, and then utilizing the 'pack', and 'shaming' tactics, when addressing their *brothers* in public or in discussion venues.

I have noticed, as well, that there seem to be more and more 'commissars', of certain PC tactics, roaming around and 'isolating' those who are perceived to be archaic Neanderthals, or misogynistic – these individuals should be *rooted* out, and presented to the public at large for the provocateurs that they really are – as to not hound these people out of the white nationalist mainstream, would be to continue promoting a wedge directly between the natural poles existing between men and women which has served well the white nationalist movement, and encouraged marriage and births which, in part, is the heart-beat of white nationalism.

Sharia law, then, is a false-flag within the ranks of white nationalism, and will be *seen* as such.

iii.

In War, there truly *are* combatants and non-combatants. Moreover, human passions are wellsprings of emotion, and revenge and justice are high on this list.

In the 'attacks' on 9/11 the 'physical body' of America was damaged, of this there is no doubt; the extent and causal relationship of this attack has still not been addressed by an honest national government. White Nationalist have begun to split along these same lines, such as the relationships with which we burden ourselves with and, in consequence, embroil us in an ever spiraling involvement in foreign affairs, which does nothing but employ more 'civil servants' who, in the main, have been educated in the same agendas as those who benefit directly from this involvement – the american people, in turn, are simply along for the ride.

The insertion of thousands, if not millions of 'new' nationalists who lack a broader appreciation of White Nationalist politics, bring with them an untold amount of conservative baggage which has been perpetuated for generations when it comes to this relationship with our 'friends' in the middle-east. It is a long process, and their reeducation must continue unabated.

170

As to the relationship of our military involvement, it must be clear that the position of White Nationalists is the *support* of our individual men and women who *serve*; with that said, it is also imperative that white nationalists commit themselves and their interactions with the public or their own families who, as is often the case, have members serving actively in these 'wars', to know that their patriotism is honorable, and essential to a free republic yet, at the same time, to know *unequivocally* that White Nationalists see these 'wars' as serving interests which are not sympathetic to either the republic nor to the members of the West. The points of interest should be subjective to each and every case, as long as this political and moral imperative is driven home.

White Nationalist men and women weep, with great and unbridled tears, for those men and women who have been maimed, psychologically destroyed, who lost lovers and spouses, and who live with those actions which deprived their counterparts in 'the field' of those very same things; and in doing so, left no real mark of national honor – only the 'art of war', with no pragmatic end in sight. White Nationalists would see these members home, displaying their courage and indomitable will, in support of their own hamlets, townships, and states – a real American tradition.

When our fighting men and women of western stock are seen in the ranks of the White Nationalist common cause, in active and supporting roles, then the image of 'imperial war machine' might be taken from them. In the days ahead they will, indeed, face their rubicon – their positions and beliefs, at this time, will be for all to see.

iv.

Supporting the *existing* 'foreign policy' machine, is to take leave of the sense with which you were born with. Every night, the news and its various pundits, are replete with the 'give and take' of rhetorical nonsense which, by the end of each and every hour leaves one with the absolute feeling of defeat and uselessness. This will continue as long as there is a non-policy in place, a policy of ignorance and personal aggrandizement, leaving the Nation vulnerable to the slings and arrows of international intrigue.

The mass numbers of existing and new rank and file white nationalists members should continue to develop, and disseminate programmes and platforms by which to introduce and extend the organism which is white nationalist political life, based on the aforementioned considerations.

Supporting candidates, in fact encouraging fellow peers to run for office, is a matter of course for a positive white nationalism, and the development of a coherent foreign policy in simply one of many aspects with which one needs to become acquainted, if we are to succeed in developing and implementing a strategy, which will usher in an existence for our people and a future for white children.

****

With these collective efforts comes a new harmony, and the voices of all begin to be heard in a new song, that song of *albion*, which is a song of the West, at once both a sonnet and a drama of epic proportions.

Remember, do not be *afraid* of the Lightning.

Appendice I

The Final Address of David Lane:

To the Jury at 1988 Ft Smith "Sedition" Trial

From the era of Plato, Socrates, and Cato to that of DaVinci and Michelangelo, to Locke and Shakespeare, to Jefferson and Franklin, Western civilization has sprung from the creative genius of one kindred people. In the vast panorama of time, this period was but a fleeting moment and a glorious dream. The near future will show what manner of civilization will follow the passing of the White man. How sad and ironic that the American republic, which was formed exclusively for the preservation and promotion of Western man, became the vehicle through which he was destroyed both here and in his European homeland.

For many years I have struggled in whatever ways were available to a single powerless person to crack the iron media curtain and show my people that those very things which are protected, promoted, and forced upon us by those who today control the affairs of the Western world have destroyed every civilization we have ever built. I refer to such things as infanticide through abortion, a practice which has led to the murder of fifteen million babies of my kith and kin, and which is protected by the government and the Federal courts; homosexuality, whose adherents are forced upon us as role models and even teachers of our children by the government and Federal courts; and worst of all, the deliberate destruction of our very racial existence.

Those who have set out to mix and destroy the last remnant of Western man know full well that no people can continue in existence without a nation of their own in which to propagate, protect, and promote their own kind. They also know that a people who are not convinced of their own uniqueness and value will perish, and that is why I am slandered and destroyed when I show that nearly every improvement in the human condition has come from the fertile mind of Western man.

The White man is now a tiny minority in the world, yet he is denied not only a nation of his own, but the integrity of the territorial imperative necessary to his survival. The guilt of those who partake in the destruction of this Race of men cannot be adequately described in the vocabulary of mortals. Regarding the prosecutors in this case, I say only that if the perpetuation of power is predicated on perjury, then the U. S. Attorneys are as solid as the Rock of Gibraltar. But, if nature's laws allow for the concepts of justice or karmic debt, then they walk on quicksand.

That this trial even occurred is a violation of every Constitutional protection against double jeopardy. The legalistic machinations and chicanery involved in jeopardizing a man for potentially unlimited times for the same offense, by changing the legal description of that offense, by changing jurisdictions and so on are utterly repugnant to the sense of Anglo-Saxon justice as well as totally contrary both to the spirit and the intent of the Constitution. The mad frenzy of those who now control the Federal government of the United States to punish and destroy any White man who resists the deliberate admixture and murder of his rapidly disappearing Race is evident.

History predicts unspeakable horror for the last generation of White children, if I, and others who shall come after me, are not more successful in awakening our people from their sleep of death. Our task is as simple as it is overwhelmingly important: WE MUST SECURE THE EXISTENCE OF OUR PEOPLE AND A FUTURE FOR WHITE CHILDREN! In the face of that overriding historical imperative, what you do to me does not matter. I am not a brave man; I die the thousand deaths of the philosopher instead of the single death of the soldier. But I willingly sought this destiny, and I will not shrink from it.

Soon you will hear from another who will undoubtedly speak of his religious beliefs. Perhaps even at this late date, the power of a religious creed can save Western man, or perhaps Divine Providence will indeed lend a hand. If not, then those who rebel against tyranny must still accept the consequences with a shrug, or they are neither patriots nor men.

I say no more....

Appendice II

The Last Statement of:

<u>Gordon Kahl</u>

[Gordon Kahl was killed in a massive assault on Ginter's farmhouse in Lawrence County, Arkansas, on June 4, 1983. The events described below are from a typed statement by Kahl, probably written on the day of the described events, February 14, 1983.]

I, GORDON KAHL, a Christian Patriot, and in consideration of the events which have taken place within the last few hours, and knowing to what-lengths the enemies of Christ, (whom I consider my enemies) will go to separate my spirit from it's body, wish to put down on paper a record of the events which have just taken place, so that the world will know what happened.

I feel that the awesome power which will be unleashed, to silence forever, my testimony, will, if not checked by the power of my God, who is the God of Abraham, and Isaac and Jacob, will cut short my time to leave to the world, these happenings. Therefore, I'm going to make this record, and leave it in the hands of those who I know will bring it to light, even though I may in the meantime be extinguished.

While urgency, or human weakness, tells me to run, my spirit says write, so this I am going to do. And if my God continues to protect me, I shall write first, and flee from the hands of my enemies later.

We had just finished our meeting in Medina, concerning how we could best implement the proceedings of the Third Continental Congress, which was to restore the power and prestige of the U.S. Constitution up to and including the 10 Articles of the Bill of Rights, and put our nation back under Christian Common Law, which is another way of saying God's Law, as laid down by the inspiration of God, thru His prophets and preserved for

176

us in the Scriptures, when word was received from someone whose identity I am not able to give, that we were to be ambushed on our return to our homes.

I realize now that we did not take this warning as seriously as we should have. The reason for this was because it has happened so many times before, when nothing happened. I see now that the many false alarms were to cause us to lower our guard.

As we pondered what to do, someone suggested that we take two cars instead of one. Consequently, I went with Dave Brewer, and my son Yorie, Scotty Paul, my wife Jean, and Vernon Wagner, went in our station wagon. At this time none of us really expected any trouble, but just to be on the safe side, my son Yorie, myself, and Scotty prepared to defend ourselves, in the event that an attack upon us, should take place.

As we came over one of the hills just north of Medina, I saw on the top of the next hill what looked like two cars parked on it. About this time they turned on their red lights, and I knew the attack was under way.

We were just coming to an approach and I told Dave to pull in on it and stop. Our other car pulled in just beyond us and stopped, also. I looked back in time to see another vehicle coming from behind with it's red light on. I picked up my Mini-14, and I got out and got myself and my weapon ready as the vehicle coming from behind skidded to a stop about 20 feet away. The doors flew open on it and the two men who were in the front seat aimed their guns at us. My son Yorie had jumped out of the other car and had ran over to a high-line pole. The two cars which we had seen ahead of us, pulled up and stopped behind us.

A man got out of the vehicle which had come from behind us, and ran out into the ditch on the east side of the road. During this time there was a lot of screaming and hollering going on but nothing else, so it appeared to be an impasse.

About this time a shot rang out and the driver of the car who I believe at this time must have been supposedly in command, turned around and stood up so he was looking at his man in the east ditch, and toward the cars which had come from the north and yelled "Who fired, who fired?" The other man who was with him, echoed his question.

At the time the shot rang out I heard Yorie cry out "I'm hit, I'm hit" I took my eyes off the two men who were yelling "Who fired", and looked over at Yorie. He was still standing, but I could tell he was in pain from the way he stood. About this time, another shot rang out, and I heard Yorie cry out again. I looked over and saw that he was hit again and laying on the ground. I looked back toward the two men and saw the one in the passenger side aim at me and I was sure then that they felt the situation was no longer under their control, and the only thing to do was kill us all.

Before he was able to fire, I loosed a round at the door behind which he was standing, and while I don't think I hit him, I caused him to duck down behind the door.

I looked around again toward Yorie, and saw Scotty Paul running over toward him. I turned my head again in time to see the driver of the vehicle which had followed us raise up from behind the door and aim his gun at Scotty. I moved my gun over and fired at him before he could shoot. I didn't hit him either, the bullet striking somewhere near the lower left hand corner of the windshield. He ducked down behind the dash so I could only see his head. About this time the other man raised up and aimed at me again. I shot again striking the door and causing him to duck. This happened several times, with the two men alternating and my shots causing them to duck each time before they could aim and fire. I don't know how many times I fired, until the man on the passenger side fell, and I was able to tell he was out of the fight. The driver must have seen this as he moved his gun from Scotty's direction toward me.

I fired several more shots at him each time he raised up to shoot at me. I finally realized this could keep up 'til my 30 round clip was empty. My bullets appeared to be ricocheting off the windshield and door post. I ran around toward the side of the vehicle, firing at the door as I went to keep him down until I got around far enough to get a clear shot at him, at which time I know he was out of the fight also.

I ran back where I could see the third man from this north-bound vehicle just in time to see him raise up to shoot at Scotty, who had ran over to Yorie. Before he was able to pull the trigger I fired and he fell to the ground. At this time I saw the man who was behind. the front end of the green Mercury, raise up and aim at, Scotty. He saw me swing my gun in his direction, and he ducked down behind his car. I could see his feet or legs beneath the car, and I fired, striking him and putting him out of the fight.

I ran over to the man in the east ditch, thinking he might still be in fighting condition. When I got nearly to him, he raised up his head and said "Don't shoot me again, I'm all done". He had his hand on his shotgun so I took that and his pistol which was in his holster and threw them in the back seat of the green Mercury. I didn't see the man who had been behind the Mercury, and who I thought I'd hit in the leg, so I don't know where he'd gone to.

A pickup had pulled up behind the north-bound vehicle, but I didn't notice anyone in it or around it and I assume it was the pickup we saw on the top of the first hill as we came out of Medina, and which I believe belonged to the city, but as to who was driving it, I have no knowledge.

Scotty tells me he saw one and possibly two men run out into the trees and hide, but I have no way of knowing who they were.

I think from the reports I've heard on the radio which was in the Mercury, that the car which came from behind, was the one the Marshals were in. If this is so, they weren't the ones who fired the first shots. The two men who were in the front seat were both looking in the direction of the green Mercury when they were shouting, "Who fired?"

Yorie's .45 auto which he had in his shoulder holster had either a rifle or pistol bullet imbedded in the clip, shattering the grips on both sides. Had he not been wearing it he would have been killed instantly.

Whether this was the first or the second shot that was fired at him I don't know, One was buckshot and the other was either a rifle or a high-powered pistol from the way the bullet looks.

I didn't see it, but it sounded as though Yorie's gun fired after he was hit. I think probably his finger tightened on the trigger when he was hit, but I know neither he nor Scotty fired before this, and whether either of them fired afterwards, I don't know. I know that if they did, they didn't hit anyone, as I knew when I hit each one of them, myself.

I saw a man in the clinic when we took Yorie in, who I think must have been the man in the pickup, who pulled up behind what I think was the marshals' vehicle. He had blood on his face and I think he was probably hit either by a bullet or bullets which glanced off the marshals' vehicle when I was firing at them. I didn't see him, and I know I didn't shoot at him, and I know neither Yorie nor Scotty shot at him.

179

Vernon Wagner was unarmed, so I know he didn't shoot at anyone and Dave Brower didn't shoot at anyone either. My wife had nothing to do with it, other than the fact that she had rode along with us, so she could visit with a couple of the other ladies who were coming to the meeting.

I want the world to know that I take no pleasure in the death or injury of any of these people, anymore than I felt when I was forced to bring to an end, the fighter pilots lives who forced the issue during WW II. When you come under attack by anyone, it becomes a matter of survival. I was forced. to kill an American P-51 pilot one day over Burma, when he mistook us for Japs. I let him shoot first, but he missed and I didn't. I felt bad, but I knew I had no choice.

I would have liked nothing other to be left alone, so I could enjoy life, liberty and the pursuit of happiness, which our Forefathers willed to us, this was not to be, after I discovered that our nation had fallen into the hands of an alien people, who are referred to us as a nation within the other nations. As one of our Founding Fathers stated, "They are vampires, and vampires cannot live on vampires, they must live on Christians". He tried to get a provision written into the U.S. Constitution that. would have prevented Jews living inside the U.S. He warned his brethren that if this was not done their children would curse them in their graves, and that within 200 years, their people (the Jews) would be setting in their counting houses rubbing their hands, while our people would be slaving in the fields to support them. This has happened exactly as was predicted.

These enemies of Christ have taken their Jewish Communist Manifesto, and incorporated it into the Statutory laws of our country, and threw our Constitution and our Christian Common Law (which is nothing other than the Laws of God as set forth in the Scriptures), into the garbage can.

We are a conquered and occupied nation; conquered and occupied by the Jews, and their hundreds or maybe thousands of front organizations doing their un-Godly work. They have two objectives in their goal of ruling the world. Destroy Christianity and the White race. Neither can be accomplished by itself, they stand or fall together.

We are engaged in a struggle to the death between the people of the Kingdom of God, and the Kingdom of Satan. It started long ago, and is now best described as a struggle between Jacob & Esau.

I would like to write more but the Spirit says this must suffice for now. Should the hand of Elijah's God continue over me, and protect me, I shall someday see this once great nation swept clean of Christ's enemies, and restored to its former greatness. If it should be the will of our Father, and the Father of our Lord Jesus Christ, that it is to be, there will be no way Ahab's god and his people can stand before us. Mystery Babylon with all its greatness, will be destroyed. Take heart, my fellow Christian Americans, God has said that there will be a great shaking in the land of Israel. That started this evening. Let each of you who says that the Lord Jesus Christ, is your personal Savior, sell his garment and buy a sword, if you don't already have one, and bring his enemies before Him and slay them.

If you've been paying tithes to the Synagogue of Satan, under the 2nd plank of the Communist Manifesto to finance your own destruction, stop right now, and tell Satan's tithing collectors, as I did many years ago, "Never again will I give aid and comfort to the enemies of Christ". To those of you who were engaged in the ambush and attack on us and were spared, thank God you have a chance to remove your support for the Anti-Christs who rule our nation.

To those of you who have been supporting the Edicts and Commands of the Great Whore — Stop now and come out of her, as her time is getting short and when the hour of her judgment comes, that you be not judged with her.

I must cease now, and move on. If it should be the will of the Father that I have more to do for him, He will protect me, and no devise whatever that is used against me will succeed. To my wife Joan, who has been with me for so long, I know this will be a hard and painful experience; however, remember the prophecy will be fulfilled, and you have now been a witness to some of it. Remember I love you as much today as I did when I first saw you more than 50 years ago. Put your trust in God, and whether I live or die, He will be with you to end of your days.

To my son Yorie and my dear friend Scotty -- you both displayed the qualities of first rate Soldiers of Jesus Christ. May God bless all of you.

I must now depart -- I have no idea where I'm going, but after some more prayer, I will go where the Lord leads me, and either live to carry on the fight, or die if that be the case, and for the present at least, I bid you all good-bye.

Gordon Kahl, Christian Patriot

14 words

Appendice III

A Nation of Men

by

Yorie Kahl

Fiat justitia,

Yorie Von Kahl #04565-059

C-1 Box 1000

Leavenworth, KS 66048-1000

October 23, 1996

Federal District Court Judge John Bailey Jones

U.S. Federal Courthouse

Sioux Falls, SD 57102

Dear Judge Jones,

As you know, I have a Habeas Corpus sitting in your Court collecting dust, while I suffer daily under a manifestly clear miscarriage of justice. In fact, I think that is a rather mild expression in terms of the events which destroyed my family and catapulted me into this ugly and painful abyss. I mean not to appear disrespectful toward yourself, nor the Court wherein you sit. However, I have a right to be no less than bitter and feel confident you do appreciate my frustrations. I am not, through this letter, attempting to amend the Motion and Brief awaiting your astute attentions. Rather, please consider this letter an attempt to "redress grievances" and possibly cause you to appreciate the urgency justice has long demanded in this most important matter. "GOVERNMENT LAWLESSNESS IS A GROWING MENACE." Sound familiar? This was the heading of an article from the St. Petersburg Times, Sept. 1, 1993, originally published in the Los Angeles Times. The first two paragraphs speak truthfully of the contemporary status of our Government. "What will become of 'law and order conservatism' now that we know that our law-enforcement agencies - from the Justice Department to local police forces- can be as criminal as the miscreants that they are supposed to pursue? " Unspeakable acts of cold-blooded murder and fabricated evidence now routinely characterize every day acts of law enforcement in the United States." The author? Paul Craig Roberts, former Assistant Treasury Secretary; now chairman of the Institute for Political Economy. Is it true, murder and fabricated evidence are "routine" acts of our Justice Department and other agencies? Of course it is. You know this as well as I. But, we are not alone. Millions of Americans are gradually coming to see the truth of this as well. Such articles and commentaries are becoming as "routine" as the heinous and criminal acts of our Government. I'm sure you've heard the Government has finally admitted it (or "they") is indeed one of the largest illegal drug distributors in our fine land. Of course, I've known this for almost twenty years. It was no surprise to me, in the least. I rather chuckled when I heard the story break. Khun Sha, military drug-lord of the Golden Triangle, [had] said years ago the U.S. State Department was his primary customer. Federal agents have so stated this for years, generally suffering serious retribution. And, of course, the Federal Government itself has always lied and attempted to cover-up the leaks.

It's true, crack babies are a product of our Government; teenage prostitutes and drive-by shootings; prisons bursting at the seams and our nation's elementary schools are drug-infested war zones. The Government's justification? (They always have one, don't "they?") They need the money to finance a war. Covert operations, etc.... I wonder... Do you suppose one day we'll hear the U.S. Supreme Court "find" the Government's power to do such criminal acts against the people under the "necessary and proper clause" of the Constitution? Or maybe on the far extremes of the Penumbra Doctrine? Yes, I am being cynical. Yet, I am none the less quite serious. I bring this to your attention to illustrate that the Government has in fact and in deed become exactly what the Anti-Federalists feared most. The security of the Bill of Rights turned out to be no security at all. Who is safe? Everyone fears the Federal Government. Certainly not without reason. The Federal Government is exactly what my father taught me it was. He tried to tell others. The Feds murdered him, as you know, and... sure enough, fabricated evidence to cover it up. It's "routine," you see. My father told me "they" were going to kill him. That was many years ago, and who would've believed it. I did. Recall a few short years ago... Randy Weaver? A strange case. BATF wanted an informant to infiltrate the Aryan Nations in Northern Idaho. Crime-free Northern Idaho...strange place for their interests to rest. Our cities are raging with crime. (Products, no doubt, of our Government's drug enterprises.) Randy was setup. The BATF created a crime to use to extort Randy into infiltrating the Aryan Nations. No doubt, had he done so, they would have demanded he in turn "setup" others. (After all, it's "routine.") Randy said, "no." For this lawful act of refusal, his wife and young son were murdered by U.S. Marshals. Randy, already victimized once, was "tried" for murder. The creators of the crime were trying the victims. To do so, of course, required (can you guess?), fabricating of evidence. Of course, as the entire country knows, the prosecution got caught hiding evidence, fabricating evidence and suborning perjury. All of these things are crimes, but since America is obviously a "nation of men" and "not of laws," the prosecutors and the officers who committed perjury and attempted to obstruct justice and put the innocent victims in prison... are still out there following the routine. I don't understand it, but an investigation by the Justice Dept. concluded with the recommendation that the officers who caused the crimes be tried for their crimes. This is not routine. But, being a "nation of men,"... well, you know,... instead, the criminals received commendations from the U.S. Marshals Service. Back to the "routine"... One last quote from Mr. Roberts' article, before we move on..."Noted defense attorney Gerry Spence told the Montana Trial Lawyers Association in July that he had never been involved in a case with the Federal Government in which the government had not lied and manufactured evidence to gain a conviction. 'These are not the good guys,' he said. 'These are people who do what they believe is necessary to bring about a conviction.' The law gets hung with the victim." As I said, we are a nation of "men," not "law." All those virtuous-sounding slogans we read from the courts so often, notwithstanding. There are many people who feel justice can no longer be obtained through the courts of this nation. For the most part, I certainly agree. There are, nonetheless, many people waiting with high hopes resting upon you that justice will be done in this case; and soon. I, of course, am at the forefront of such hopes. You have undoubtedly read the Motion, briefs in support and affidavits, and certainly reviewed the documentary on the case, Death and Taxes, long ago. There is, as I'm sure you've surmised, much more evidence anxiously awaiting exposure.

I have had a number of lawyers review the issues and evidence, and all agree - "if the court follows the law" it will be overturned and dismissed. Thus far, every single lawyer has used this phrase. "If?" Well, I understand. This is a nation of "men." Nevertheless,... I hope. To some degree, you are now aware of the criminal efforts of Government agents to prevent us from having a fair trial. To say it is obvious we did not receive a fair trial is a gross understatement. I think it is fair for me to further expose this long trail of tragedy for you to see why immediate action should be taken, not for the simple sake of "justice," for I realize what would constitute "justice" in this case is simply beyond our means; but rather to stop the constant and continuing injustice I, and what remains of my family, continue to daily endure. The Government claimed - as did the media – that my father was "wanted" for violating probation (most reports stated "parole") - i.e., he allegedly wouldn't sign a form, or depending upon which article one reads, he didn't file a tax return. This, as is "routine," was merely a fabrication of evidence. The real reason was at least in part due to him giving an interview to a local newspaper. This is documented and is part of the U.S. Marshals' file on my father. This was available at trial, and I insisted my attorney introduce it during Deputy Marshal Wigglesworth's testimony, but my attorney refused. The government wasn't bold enough to admit the truth- i.e., they were trying to shut my father up - because it is a clear violation of the First Amendment. Consequently, they instead lied. At the time of the "shoot-out," no one in our party was aware there was a pending warrant for my father's arrest. To this day, I have some doubts about that. I do know that the warrant that was offered into evidence at trial by the Government was stamped "received, U.S. Marshals Office, Fargo, N.D., Feb 14, 1983;" the day following the "shootout." If it was true (as Wigglesworth testified), that he had the warrant with him at the scene of the "shoot-out," why did they offer one into evidence he couldn't have had at that time? This, too, was something my attorney, Mr. Sogard, refused to pursue. At any rate, there was no obvious attempt to arrest anyone that day. The thugs, who I only later (after surgery) found out were Federal thugs, made clear attempts to both terrorize and murder us. By "us," I mean my father, mother, co-defendants Scott Faul, Dave Broer, Vernon Wagner and myself. I was, as you know, shot almost fatally. I lost a kidney, gallbladder, part of my intestines, (which sustained thirteen perforations), two major wounds to my liver, one to my right lung, a round through my left shoulder, one through my right hand, a graze across my lower abdomen and one that split my chin. Upon hitting the frozen ground, my teeth shattered from end to end. (Since I've been in these Federal hellholes, I have yet to receive any medical or dental attention, although I've tried. They refuse to repair my chipped teeth and consequently I have to sand them with sandpaper, as they continually chip away.) When I awoke in the hospital at Jamestown, N.D., I was told I was being charged with murder. I didn't even know who had been shot, besides myself. I tried to get a phone call, as I obviously needed lawyers badly, but was allowed no contact with anyone. Immediately upon my becoming conscious, I was told by an officer, "they're saying you shot first." When the FBI came to see me, I told them I knew they thought I shot first. They denied it and wanted to know which officer told me this. They asked me if I did shoot first and I told them, "I may have shot first, I really don't remember." They then went straight to the media and told them I "admitted" I may have fired first. The media played this up with bold headlines, unknown to me, as I wasn't allowed to know anything that was going on with the case. At my initial hearing with Magistrate Hill, I asked him to turn the TV on as he was leaving. He asked me why had I requested that. I told him the Marshals weren't allowing me to know anything that was happening in my own case. They refused to allow me to read newspapers, magazines or watch TV. He ordered the Marshal present to get newspapers for me and to let me watch the news. As soon as the Magistrate left, I asked the Marshal to turn on the TV. He replied, "you're not watching TV, and you're not reading any newspapers." Consequently, until I was in the county jail for four days, I knew virtually nothing, and was completely unaware of the massive and inflammatory propaganda campaign that was ensuing via the media. While I was in the hospital, the doctor had to perform some operations on me he stated should be done in the operating room, but the Marshals were making it very difficult for him to work with me.

The night-shift Marshals would put shackles on my legs and chain my feet to the end of the bed. I ended-up with knots the size of golfballs in my tendons in the lower back of my legs. I had difficulty sleeping at night- or what I presumed was night- because they kept the light on all the time. When the nurse would turn it off, they'd yell at her. She insisted I had to have rest. They insisted with belligerence and vulgarity- intimidating the poor nurse – that I didn't, and would go back to reading their pornographic magazines, which they carried with them. That night-shift was the most unprofessional and despicable examples of law enforcement officers I had ever seen; until arriving at the Bureau of Prisons. At least the day shift was very self-disciplined and professional. At my initial hearing, held in the hospital, my attorney failed to show up. In his stead came an assistant, who, although I liked him, I, nevertheless, represented myself, after he assured me he wasn't qualified to represent me at trial. My attorney of record, Sogard, finally came to see me for approximately five minutes the last day I was in the hospital. He was unable to answer any of my questions and seemed to know virtually nothing of what was going on. Finally, the doctor told me he felt, because of the Marshal's behavior, that I was only going to get worse, as I needed to be up and around. Consequently, he was going to release me so I could get to a jail cell-block and get some exercise.

I had an abscess on my right lung from a bullet wound and, although I was stable, it was still a potential problem. He insisted I needed to be up and walking, which I was, for the most part, unable to do at the hospital. I was taken to Moorhead, Minnesota, to the county jail. Instead of going to the cell-block, as the doctor had insisted, I was put in the "hole." I could barely get around as I had become very weak. Within three days, I was no longer able to get out of bed; I had grown even weaker. I laid on the bunk for so long that the still-healing bullet wounds through my back had grown to the bed. On the third day the cell-door was opened, and the guard told me I had a phone call. I tried to get up, but couldn't. I finally rolled off the bed, tearing the wounds loose from the bed, and fell on the floor on my hands and knees. When I did this, I felt a tear on the in side of my abdomen where I had recently been split open for the various operations. Finally, I was able, after several attempts, to get up. Although it was probably no more than sixty or seventy feet to the phone, I had to stop three times before getting there to rest against the wall. When I tried to say "hello," I found my vocal chords no longer worked. I don't know if it was due to my extremely weak condition or because I hadn't used them for so long. I whispered during that call. It was my sister, Lorna, calling. She said her and my other family members had been calling every day I had been there, but the jail officials had kept telling them I didn't want to talk to anyone. The truth is, the jail personnel never so much as told me anyone had called. In fact, other than when they processed me into the jail, they had not talked to me. During this time I was indicted by the Grand Jury. The Grand Jury was no doubt as biased by the media as was the petit jury whom later tried me. In fact, if possible, this may be more true of the Grand Jury, as I had no means to challenge them, and as evinced by Chief Judge Lay's dissenting opinion in our appeal (see 748 F2d 1205, 1223), at least fifty percent of the pool of talesmen were admittedly biased. (Most of the remainder were biased as well, but lied during voir dire to be seated on the jury.) All of the witnesses and evidence that went before the Grand Jury had to pass through a friend and fraternal brother of the dead Chief Marshal Muir. None of the victims (the defendants) were called by the Grand Jury to testify, although all but my father were available. That alone smacks highly of an obvious intent of the friends and fraternal brothers of Muir to prevent an independent investigation by the Grand Jury. The witnesses, of whom I am aware, which testified at the Grand Jury were questioned by a friend and fraternal brother of Muir. The Grand Jury, as contemplated by our forefathers, had obviously been "abolished." Kenneth Aldridge, a self-admitted friend of Muir and fraternal brother, was the chief investigator in charge of the case. Later at trial, every single witness he interviewed and took statements from denied making statements tha the had recorded in his written statements. I do not know when that particular Grand Jury began to sit, but if it had been sitting for more than a month, which is likely, the chances are members thereof probably had a personal contact with Muir or Wigglesworth and possibly other Marshals involved in the "shoot-out." But, regardless, clearly friends of Muir directing the investigation, asking the questions, censoring the evidence and picking the witnesses removes all doubt there absolutely was not, and could not have been, an independent Grand Jury, and, thus, no safe guard to protect myself or the other victims of this Federal Tyranny. Ausa Crooks admitted in his interviews with Jeff Jackson that Washington was so concerned special overseers were sent to Fargo to "assist" the case.

I had asked my attorney, Sogard, how long it would be before the trial would be held. He estimated at least two years. I knew for certain right then he had no comprehension, whatsoever, what we were up against. I asked him what was the soonest- the absolute soonest- it could be. He replied a year, possibly nine months, but couldn't fathom it. I guaranteed him it would be a matter of weeks. This was about mid-March, and the Court scheduled the trial to begin on May 2nd. Sogard was incredulous, and had not done a single thing I had asked him, of which I demanded through research into the legality of the warrant the Government was alleging they had, full research into the jurisdiction of the U.S. Marshals operating within the territory of the State, and personally visiting all of the witnesses and traveling to Medina before the Government had an opportunity to frighten possible witnesses into silence. Sogard, later, during the course of the trial refused to ask witnesses critical questions, which I had written down for him; refused to offer documents into evidence, which I had obtained from a co-defendant, as Sogard never shared any of the discovery materials with me (except the statements of Lanenge's); and refused to subpoena witnesses or even contact them for me. I specifically instructed Sogard to demand Judge Benson recuse himself due to his fraternal ties to Muir. Sogard was literally terrified of the Masonic issue, refusing in any way to raise it. He insisted that if he so much as mentioned it Benson would cite him for contempt, throw both of us in jail, and try me in absentia. The trial was postponed for one week, although the attorneys insisted they needed at least an additional thirty days. Sogard was totally unprepared. Allowing only such a brief delay was astonishing when you consider this was, and remains, the most notorious case in North Dakota history. Trial began on May 9th. Jury selection lasted almost four days. Judge Benson refused to allow the attorneys to examine the jurors, and questioned all the prospective jurors in the presence of those yet to be queried. Those who were biased, that wanted to sit on the jury, thus learned how to conceal their bias and avoid being removed for cause. At this point your Honor, I wish to impress upon you that I am, by no means, exaggerating. To proceed, allow me to demonstrate I do so within the terms of the law. In the Motion my attorney has filed in this case, along with the Supporting Brief and affidavits, exists proof beyond any doubt that a juror, namely August Pankow, knew Ausa Crooks much better than he indicated during voir dire. Pankow admitted only that he knew who Crooks was. Which, if true, is nothing. The actual truth, however, is something quite different. Pankow went to school with Crooks, knew him personally, and knew his family (something else he denied during voir dire). Furthermore, as soon as Pankow was alone with the jurors, he admitted he knew Crooks personally, went to school with him, etc.... The following statements are on tape and have been transcribed. They are available, as are the interviewers. (August Pankow's examination during voir dire concerning the matter is found in Vol. I, pp. 42-43, may 9th and Vol. III, pp. 174-175, May 11th of the trial transcripts.) Juror Marlys Klimek was asked about Pankow's relationship with Crooks, and she commented, "Well, I was surprised at that too because August did say that he was a friend, or that he, I don't know if they were close friends, but they went to school together, you know... And I thought you weren't supposed to know anybody involved in the case." Klimek also said, "...I just felt like I would never lie to get out of serving on a jury, but I wouldn't lie to get on

one either, and there are a lot of people who would. I found that out."
Pankow, in an interview, said, "...Yes, it did. That was one of the first
things I thought of after I got picked to be a juror – that I knew him
(Crooks). I was in high school and they were in the grades at that time."
"...Oh yeah, I know him (Crooks) from small on up til he went to college."
Even Crooks, unable to suppress his arrogance, stated, regarding Pankow,
"And I don't know if he was telling me that just to stroke me a little bit
because he (Pankow) happened to be a guy I had known and probably most
of my life... and to this day I don't understand why they left (him) on the
jury. A guy named Pankow... who had known my family, and I guess had
known me when I was just a little shaver."

Pankow talked to Crooks after the trial"...He (Crooks) came home here and
I did talk to 'um. And we talked a little bit about it (the farce of a trial), and
how I'd liked to have been on that jury." Pankow's answers on voir dire
clearly revealed he had no intention of letting either the Court or
defendants know the information they were seeking with the questions.
Yet, he was uninhibited in bragging to the other jurors that he knew Crooks
personally and went to school with him. His intention to hide his bias
knowingly is clearly evident. Crooks is at least as liable. He sat in the court
room and allowed Pankow to lie about their personal connections. The
Constitutional "right" to a "fair trial," "impartial jury" and "due process"
was completely divested of the defendants in this case through Pankow's
willful and deliberate lying to conceal his bias and his desire to sit on the
jury. This is as clear a case of Fraud on the Court by both Pankow and
Crooks as can be demonstrated. It is obstruction of justice. It is contempt.

14 words

A Note on the Author of *"Remember Tomorrow"*

The author of many articles, books, essays, and poems detailing his life-long work to secure the existence of his people, those numerous and diverse individuals belonging to that greater family of Western stock and, without whom, this author would never exist; it is sincerely hoped that this debt will be paid in kind through the works and words of this author, and may be found in numerous forms and venues for consideration.

Other Works

Rise of The West
Song of Albion

14 words

Made in the USA
Middletown, DE
26 October 2022

13530948R00135